P9-DEO-320

Light Shining in a Dark Place

Light Shining
in a Dark Place

Discovering Theology through Film

EDITED BY
Jeff Sellars

PICKWICK *Publications* · Eugene, Oregon

LIGHT SHINING IN A DARK PLACE
Discovering Theology through Film

Pickwick Publications
An Imprint of Wipf and Stock Publishers
199 W. 8th Ave., Suite 3
Eugene, OR 97401

www.wipfandstock.com

ISBN 13: 978-1-61097-309-0

Cataloging-in-Publication data:

Light shining in a dark place : discovering theology through film / edited by Jeff Sellars.

xx + 232 p. ; 23 cm. Includes bibliographical references and index.

ISBN 13: 978-1-61097-309-0

1. Motion pictures—Religious aspects—Christianity. I. Sellars, Jeff. II. Title.

PN1995.9 S345 2012

Manufactured in the U.S.A.

Contents

131181

Contents

Notes on the Contributors

Bruce L. Edwards is Professor of English and Africana Studies, and Associate Vice President for Academic Technology and E-learning at Bowling Green State University in Bowling Green, Ohio. He has been a faculty member and administrator at BGSU since 1981. He has served as Fulbright Fellow in Nairobi, Kenya (1999–2000), a Bradley Research Fellow at the Heritage Foundation in Washington, DC (1989–90), and as the S. W. Brooks Memorial Professor of Literature at The University of Queensland, Brisbane, Australia (1988). His publications include: *C. S. Lewis: Life, Works, and Legacy* (4 volumes); *Not a Tame Lion*; *Further Up and Further In: Understanding C. S. Lewis's The Lion, the Witch and the Wardrobe*; *A Rhetoric of Reading: C. S. Lewis's Defense of Western Literacy*; *The Taste of the Pineapple: Essays on C. S. Lewis as Reader, Critic, and Imaginative Writer*. He is also a contributor to *The C. S. Lewis Bible*, and many other collections of essays about Lewis and the Inklings.

J. Sage Elwell is Assistant Professor of Religion, Art, and Visual Culture at Texas Christian University. He is the author of *Crisis of Transcendence: A Theology of Digital Art and Culture* and the forthcoming artist's book *Viscera*. Dr. Elwell holds an MA in Philosophy of Religion from the University of Kansas, an M.Litt in Philosophical Theology from the University of St. Andrews in Scotland, and a PhD in Religion and the Arts from the University of Iowa. He has published and presented on religion and suffering in modern art, theology in the digital age, and contemporary digital art. He also works as an artist in digital media, photography, and book arts.

Michael Leary teaches courses in religious studies and biblical studies at Fontbonne University and Emmaus Bible College/Sydney College of Divinity.

Fr Peter Malone, MSC, was the inaugural president of SIGNIS, the World Catholic Association for Communication, and is currently serving on its cinema desk. He is also Associate of the Australian Catholic Office in Film and Broadcasting. He is the author of *Lights, Camera . . . Faith! A Movie Lover's Guide to Scripture* and the editor of *Through a Catholic Lens: Religious Perspectives of 19 Film Directors from Around the World.*

Kevin C. Neece is a writer and speaker in Fort Worth, Texas. He is currently a media and pop culture columnist for *New Identity Magazine*, a blogger for Art House Dallas and a contributing editor for *Imaginatio et Ratio: A Journal of Theology and the Arts*. An expert on Jesus films, he writes and speaks on the genre at www.jesusfilms101.com. He also writes and speaks on Star Trek at www.undiscoveredcountryproject.com. More information on his other work is available at www.kevincneece.com.

Simon Oliver is Associate Professor of Theology at the University of Nottingham. He is the author of *Philosophy, God and Motion, Radical Orthodoxy: An Introduction* and the editor (along with John Milbank) of *The Radical Orthodoxy Reader*. Simon Oliver's forthcoming book is titled *Creation's Ends: Teleology, Ethics, and the Natural.*

Kim Paffenroth is Professor of Religious Studies at Iona College. Kim earned his BA from St. John's College, his MTS from Harvard Divinity School, and his PhD from the University of Notre Dame. He is the author of numerous books on the Bible and theology. His book *Gospel of the Living Dead: George Romero's Visions of Hell on Earth* won the Bram Stoker Award in the non-fiction category. Kim is also an author of horror fiction, including the novels *Dying to Live: A Novel of Life among the Undead* and *Dying to Live: Life Sentence.*

J. Ryan Parker is the founder and editor of and main contributor to Pop Theology (www.poptheology.com), a website that explores the intersections of religion and popular culture. He received his PhD in Religion and the Arts at the Graduate Theological Union in Berkeley, CA, where he focused on film and religion. His dissertation, "Ministers of Movies: Sherwood Pictures and the Church Film Movement," chronicles the re-emergence of church-based, independent theatrical film production. Ryan received an MDiv from the Divinity School at Wake Forest University. His research interests include the history of Hollywood, the history of religious film, contemporary religious cinema, and filmmaking as spiritual/religious practice.

Travis Prinzi is a popular author and speaker on the intersection of fantasy and politics, myth and culture in J. K. Rowling's Harry Potter novels. He is the author of *Harry Potter and Imagination: The Way Between Two Worlds* and editor of two essay collections on the Harry Potter series. Prinzi appears on The Leaky Cauldron's PotterCast as a "Potter Pundit." He has been a featured speaker and led panel discussions at five Harry Potter conferences and has lectured on everything from *Harry Potter* to religion to education to hit TV shows like *The Office* at university campuses and libraries in the United States and Canada.

Megan J. Robinson's academic interests integrate the disciplines of anthropology, sociology, philosophy, religion, and literature. Her undergraduate thesis explored the practice of creative writing at the intersection of ancient faith and contemporary culture. Megan's developing interest in the use of digital media for spiritual discipleship and teaching inspired her recent move from the DC-Metro area of northern Virginia to Dallas, Texas to study theology and media arts at Dallas Theological Seminary. Megan is also the Associate Editor of *The C. S. Lewis Review*, an online journal reflecting on the life, work, and influence of Clive Staples Lewis and other Christian writers and thinkers in a similar tradition. She is somewhat obsessed with the color green, Pepsi, and C. S. Lewis—not necessarily in that order.

Jeff Sellars, PhD, teaches philosophy and humanities in Northern California and Southern Oregon. His creative endeavors include art, film, fiction, and music. His current academic research centers mainly on theological aesthetics and the study of music, literature, and film. He is the founder and senior editor of *Imaginatio et Ratio: A Journal of Theology and the Arts*.

Scott Shiffer is the leader of Pop-Culture and Faith Ministries, a group dedicated to helping believers engage culture through the lens of faith and ministering to those who create culture through prayer and support. Scott is currently completing a PhD in Systematic Theology at the B. H. Carroll Theological Institute and he teaches as an adjunct at Dallas Baptist University and Cedar Valley Community College.

James H. Thrall teaches religious studies at Knox College in Illinois, where he is the Knight Distinguished Assistant Professor for the Study of Religion and Culture. He earned his doctorate in Religion and Culture at Duke University, and holds a master's degree in theology from Yale Divinity School. He studies religion primarily as a social phenomenon, especially as communicated through cultural products of literature, film, and other media. Most recently he has been studying representations of religion in postcolonial science fiction.

Alissa Wilkinson teaches writing and humanities at The King's College in New York City and is co-editor of *Comment*, a journal of public theology. She earned her M.A. in humanities and social thought from NYU and is currently completing an M.F.A. in creative nonfiction at Seattle Pacific University. Her essays and criticism appear in a variety of publications, including *Books & Culture*, *Paste*, *Christianity Today*, *The Gospel Coalition*, and *The Other Journal*.

Acknowledgements

I WOULD LIKE TO thank all of the contributors in this volume for their creativity, time and help. It has been a pleasure working with all of you. I especially want to single out Kevin C. Neece for his help and dedication to the project. I would like to thank Dr. Simon Oliver for his help in forming the scope of this project, and I would also like to give a special thanks to Austin Roberts for his help and his conversations regarding this project. Finding the contributors for this project was certainly not done alone, and I would like to thank several people for helping me in this regard: to Dr. Bruce L. Edwards for helping me locate contributors; to Dr. Courtney Campbell for his help in locating possible contributors; to Dr. Rachel Wagner for leading me to Dr. Elwell and Dr. Thrall; to Dr. Mark J. Boone for leading me to Kevin C. Neece; to Allison Backous for leading me to Alissa Wilkinson; to John Granger for leading me to Travis Prinzi; and to Matt Cardin for leading me to Dr. Kim Paffenroth. Kim Paffenroth's "Apocalyptic Images and Prophetic Function in Zombie Films" is reprinted from *Reel Revelations: Apocalypse and Film*, Eds. John Walliss and Lee Quinby, Sheffield Phoenix Press, October, 2010. Reprinted with permission from Sheffield Phoenix Press and Kim Paffenroth.

Introduction

JEFF SELLARS

WHAT IS IT ABOUT film that so attracts us? What is it about the moving image, the flicker of light dancing on a screen, that so entices us? How does film relate to theology? And why should we care about film and its relationship to, or with, theology? Hopefully, the essays in this volume begin to give an implicit response to these questions (and ones like it). I, however, certainly would not dare to presume to speak for all of the wonderfully diverse contributors in this volume. I can only speak for myself. The most I might venture in this direction is to say that film has gripped us (the contributors) in some way, at least enough to make us write about it.

Broadly, the argument could be made that film is the *lingua franca* of the modern West (with television and some iterations of the internet being the obvious media rivals). Where else does one find the vast amounts of people, across divides of all kinds, who can "gather" around a shared narrative, who can experience and share the same story (either individually or with an audience)? There is also the sheer power of film to be taken into account: it is an embodied experience of mind, eyes, and ears; it is a combination of image, sound, and narrative. Film is affective, emotional, and rational on a level that creeps under the skin—that reaches us at a "gut" level (or, to paraphrase Pascal, it has reasons which reason does not understand). Film works on us in ways we cannot always quite explain; the argument runs deeper, subterraneously, so to speak.

Of course, there are dangers to this as well. There is the inherent danger of images of which Plato wrote. Plato warned us in the *Republic* that art and poetry are not to be admitted in the perfect city. For one, poetry is merely mimesis, and is thus far removed from the truth.[1] When someone crafts something (such as a bed) we see that it is an "imitation" bed (from the Form). When the artist, however, makes a painting (e.g., of a bed), we see that this is a copy of a copy. It is thus further removed from the truth. A second problem with poetry is the "soul" impact: an artist is making a work that is inferior to the truth and is thus appealing to the inferior part of the soul of the receiver of the work.[2] But Plato does allow some forms of poetry to remain.[3] Why is this? Art that terminates on itself (the merely "pleasure giving" poetry) is not allowed to remain, but art that can retain its "liturgical" quality is allowed to remain. The proper function of art then becomes to revert back to its source, to point one back to the truth. If the art participates in the divine, it can be saved. Additionally, as Catherine Pickstock notes,

> As well as demonstrating that Plato did *not* wish to drive a wedge between form and appearance, the strongly positive view of *methexis* (participation) in *Phaedrus* frees him from the charge of otherworldliness and total withdrawal from physicality, for the philosophic ascent does not result in a "loss" of love for particular beautiful things, since the particular participates in beauty itself. Thus the philosopher is synonymous with the lover of beauty, as also with one of a musical or loving nature (248d). Although, as Socrates acknowledges, the philosopher separates himself from human interests, turning his attention toward the divine, and is often thought to be insane, it is precisely within the physical world that he recognizes a likeness to the realities, and then is "stricken with amazement and cannot control himself" (241a).[4]

One recognizes that the likenesses are not just "mechanistic mimesis," but are a "*constitutive* representation of that in which" the likenesses participate.[5] The likenesses to be found in the so-called mundane world are not

---

1. Plato, *Complete Works*, 1202.

2. Ibid., 1202–3.

3. "But you should also know that hymns to the gods and eulogies to good people are the only poetry we can admit into our city" (ibid., 1211).

4. Pickstock, *After Writing*, 14.

5. Ibid., 14.

just empty representations—nor are they neglect of "lower" things. We are to reject "a *mundane apprehension* of physicality as merely immanent or crudely separated from the whole . . ."[6] We recognize the Forms, Truth, by and through the "mundane" world.

Coupled with the above is the general idea that film could lead us dangerously astray or, perhaps worse, to idolatry. Beware: *hic sunt dracones*. Yes, like any human creative act or faculty this too might mislead, or be corrupted—this also lives in a post-lapsarian world. So, of course, these things must be carefully, cautiously observed and analyzed. We must not slip into passivity or intellectual hebetudinous-ness (and, hopefully, the essays in this collection make an implicit case against this type of viewing). But certainly there is a case to be made for the storied arts: Christ's own use of parables comes immediately to mind (and the penchant for using the "ordinary" to explicate the "extraordinary").[7] Of course, James 1:17 also springs readily to mind—that every good gift and every perfect gift is from above, coming down from the God of lights—and, of course, its echo and following exegesis in Saint Bonaventure's *De Reductione Artium ad Theologiam*. There are obviously many avenues along this line of reasoning. This is not to mention, of course, the other numerous stories contained in Scripture. Hans Urs von Balthasar keyed in on the significance of this. Specifically, he noted the importance of the "whole phenomenon of theatre."[8] His stated aim in his *Theo-Drama* was to demonstrate how "theology underlies it all and how all the elements of the drama can be rendered fruitful for theology."[9] Theology is thus not to be recast

> into a new shape previously foreign to it. Theology itself must call for this shape; it must be something implicit within it, manifested explicitly too in many places. For theology could never be anything other than an explication of the revelation of the Old and New Covenants, their presuppositions (the created world) and purposes (its infusion with divine life) . . . If theology, therefore, is full of dramatic tension, both in form and content, it is appropriate to turn our attention to this aspect . . . a natural dramatic dimension is presupposed by, and prefaced to, the supernatural drama,

6. Ibid., 15.

7. For example, the use, in quick succession, of ordinary things to explain the great mystery of the kingdom of heaven in Matt 13:44–50.

8. Balthasar, *Theo-Drama*, 9.

9. Ibid., 9.

which adopts it after having first clarified and transformed it and brought it to its true proportions . . . This "dialectic" of nature and grace is based on the fact that man has been given freedom by his Creator and is thus equipped with a certain natural knowledge of his origin. Such knowledge can be obscured in myth, but it is always there in the background. Having given freedom to the creature, God, as Creator, is always "involved" in the world . . .[10]

We can, thus, see a way into our purposes here. We can fruitfully examine the dramas present in our films because of this dialectic of nature and grace, because of the natural dramatic dimension of the Scriptures and the supernatural "involvement" of God in the world. We are free to search for this truth where it can be found.

Kierkegaard also wrote of what he called direct and indirect communication. Our notions of the filmic arts might be informed by such distinctions. The stories told and seen do not always conform to notions of preconceived "holiness"—or how or when it might be found. The indirect line may even be the preferred *modus operandi* in these cases:

One can deceive a person out of what is true, and—to recall old Socrates—one can deceive a person into what is true. Yes, in only this way can a deluded person actually be brought into what is true—by deceiving him. The one who is of another opinion thereby betrays that he simply is not much of a dialectician, which is precisely what is necessary in order to operate in this way. In other words there is a great difference, that is, the dialectical difference, or the difference of the dialectical, between these two situations: one who is ignorant and must be given some knowledge, and therefore he is like the empty vessel that must be filled or like the blank sheet of paper that must be written upon—and one who is under a delusion that must first be taken away. Likewise, there is also a difference between writing on a blank piece of paper and bringing out by means of chemicals some writing that is hidden under other writing. Now, on the assumption that someone is under a delusion and consequently the first step, properly understood, is to remove the delusion—if I do not begin by deceiving, I begin with direct communication. But direct communication presupposes that the recipient's ability to receive is entirely in order, but here that is simply not the case—indeed, here a delusion is an obstacle. That means a corrosive must first be used, but this

10. Ibid., 125–29.

corrosive is the negative, but the negative in connection with communicating is precisely to deceive.[11]

The indirect communicator does something very special—something that the direct communicator cannot. This indirect communicator can, as Emily Dickinson might say, "tell all the truth but tell it slant." The indirect line may be the way to break into the imagination, heart, and mind—and even the unconsciously indirect communicator may stumble upon this truth.

Additionally, films have become the new meaning-giving myths of our culture. Films communicate the "good life" to us—even if it is sometimes done through negative means (e.g., showing us what not to love still aims us away from the thing shown to, presumably, *something*)—and they do so with a power that often goes unrecognized. As James K. A. Smith notes,

> The *telos* to which our love is aimed is not a list of ideas or propositions or doctrines; it is not a list of abstract, disembodied concepts or values. Rather, the reason that . . . the good life moves us is because it is a more affective, sensible, even aesthetic *picture* of what the good life looks like. A vision of the good life captures our hearts and imaginations not by providing a set of rules or ideas, but by painting a picture of what it looks like for us to flourish and live well. This is why such pictures are communicated most powerfully in stories, legends, myths, plays, novels, and films rather than dissertations, messages, and monographs. Because we are affective before we are cognitive (and even *while* we are cognitive), visions of the good get inscribed in us by means that are commensurate with our primarily affective, imaginative nature.[12]

Being such an affective (and effective) art form of sight, sound and story, film has a power to aim us towards certain *teloi*. As such, we are not aimed through mere mechanistic, rationalistic means but more powerful imaginative means that lead our reason. It then becomes an important task to interpret these images, sounds and stories—to tease out meanings and purposes, to find out where we are being aimed. What are these moving images and stories, accompanied by stirring soundscapes, trying to tell

11. Kierkegaard, *The Point of View*, 53–54.
12. Smith, *Desiring the Kingdom*, 53.

us? These are just the sorts of things that our contributors might help us find.

It should go without saying that while the films dealt with in this volume are "theologically analyzed," not all of the films or their makers would have had such concepts and beliefs (at least consciously) in mind. Also, we certainly must be careful, when reading these essays, to be respectful of the films themselves. The irreducibility of the images, sounds, and narratives must be appreciated: when we are attempting to explain the films through some particular lens, we must still realize that the film cannot be once and for all explicated, reduced, tamed—and even the variety of the interpretations within this volume betray this fact. The sounds, narratives, and images spur us on to yet more analysis, more interpretations, more meanings. As Hans Urs von Balthasar warned, "To dispel the charm of beauty by reducing its 'appearance' into some 'truth' lying behind or above it is to eliminate beauty altogether and to show that it was never really perceived in its distinctiveness."[13]

In its broadest sense, this project is a simple attempt to engage film through theology by having the contributors do just this—engage either film in general, one film in particular or multiple films through their particular theological lenses, to tease out theological ramifications. The essays in this volume are grouped together into a loose thematic order (to give the impression of a conversation rather than any kind of cohesive, systematic approach). There is certainly no pretense here of completeness of themes or topics--and while the theological backgrounds of the contributors are obviously not representatively comprehensive, they are, nevertheless, quite diverse. The structure of the book is very loosely held together by simple, broad themes—themes that play with metaphors of light and darkness. With the first section of essays, we move "from the darkness into the light"—grappling with subjects such as evil, violence, and trauma. In the second section, we move "from light to light" with themes of grace, failure, temptation, forgiveness, and community. And lastly, in the third section, we enter into the world of horror, science-fiction/fantasy, and apocalypse—entering into darkness and back out into the light.

The essays in this volume display a depth that, for me, is inspiring. I am humbled by the knowledge and creativity of my fellow contributors. These essays, for me, give a sense of the breadth and profundity of theo-

13. Balthasar, *Love Alone is Credible*, 54.

logical traditions and positions, and they show the intellectual and affective power of film. I hope that this volume entices, excites, and educates. I hope that it does justice to the art form of film making. I hope that it does justice to the power and deepness of theological engagement.

Section I

From Out of the Darkness, Into the Light: Evil, Violence, Depths, and Trauma

1

Representing Evil in *Schindler's List* and *Life is Beautiful*

SIMON OLIVER

To argue for silence, prayer, the banishment equally of poetry and knowledge, in short, the witness of "ineffability," that is, non-representability, is to mystify something we dare not understand, because we fear that it may be all too understandable, all too continuous with what we are—human, all too human.
—GILLIAN ROSE, *MOURNING BECOMES THE LAW*[1]

THE CINEMATIC REPRESENTATION OF the Shoah or Holocaust is prolific, running to several hundred films and documentaries.[2] Of course, depictions of such horrors raise a number of crucial philosophical and ethical questions. Can the Shoah be represented? In what ways do filmic representations of the Shoah contribute to the writing of history? How is the necessarily privileged position of the camera to be negotiated? Should there be limits to such depictions? Is it right to portray the heroic exploits

1. Rose, *Mourning Becomes the Law*, 43.

2. For a comprehensive and critical survey of the Holocaust in film, see Insdorf, *Indelible Shadows*.

of certain individuals or remarkable stories of survival when so many millions died as anonymized victims of industrialized genocide?

For some filmmakers, the question of representation is best answered by returning to key locations, the authority of survivors, and the testimony of victims and perpetrators. Film becomes a vehicle for the transmission of historical witness; the medium is rendered as transparent as possible. The most prominent example of such an approach can be found in Claude Lanzmann's nine-and-a-half hour epic *Shoah* (1985).[3] The impetus towards making films based on survivors' memoirs using painstaking historical detail has been very strong for a number of reasons. First, the number of witnesses is diminishing as the years pass and memories become cold amongst succeeding generations. Our connection to the events of the mid-twentieth century moves from shared memory towards history as an object of study. Film can be a means to preserve the sources. Secondly, the abhorrent specter of Holocaust denial has ensured that filmmakers pay particular attention to the historical record in its various forms. Deviation from, or even lack of attention to, that record is quickly labeled "revisionist." Thirdly, many critics, following the lead of Theodor Adorno who famously claimed that "To write poetry after Auschwitz is barbaric,"[4] insist that the artistic representation of the Shoah is not possible and only survivors' first-hand testimonies and documentary footage should be preserved and disseminated.

Lanzmann's work is sometimes regarded as the culmination of post-traumatic, historical depictions of the Shoah. In its mammoth assemblage of the accounts of witnesses alongside visits to the sites of Nazi murder and genocide, *Shoah* seemed to constitute the final and authoritative historical rendition of the horror of the concentration camps. Alongside, for example, Alain Resnais's *Night and Fog* (1955) and Michel Drach's *Les Violons du Bal* (1974), these films attempt to disrupt the present with the particular and personal memories of tragedy and terror that belong to an inevitably fading past. Nevertheless, many other cinematic approaches have been developed and different perspective on the Shoah have been explored, including those of perpetrators, victims, and children. The

---

3. For an exacting critical appraisal of *Shoah* and *Schindler's List* with further fascinating references to James Ivory's *Remains of the Day* (1993), see Rose, *Mourning Becomes the Law*, ch. 2, especially p. 49.

4. Adorno, "Cultural Criticism and Society," 162.

adaptation of historical novels is a particularly prominent genre. While based on memoirs and first-hand accounts, placing an historical novel on the screen allows the filmmaker greater license to interpret the events and weave together historical and fictional characters in the creation of compelling narratives which are nevertheless in some sense rooted in an historical source. One of the most successful recent examples of this approach is Roman Polanski's *The Pianist* (2002) based on the memoirs of the Polish pianist Wladyslaw Szpilman and his survival in Warsaw during the Nazi occupation.

In this essay, I intend to assess theologically two very different examples of film's approach to the Shoah, the first of which is an adaptation of an historical novel. Measured in terms of box office receipts and awards, Stephen Spielberg's *Schindler's List* (1993) is not only the most successful film to date about the Shoah, it is also one of the most successful films ever made. It is based on Thomas Keneally's historical novel *Schindler's Ark*, the story of the German business man Oskar Schindler and his rescue of over one thousand mainly Polish Jews during the Second World War. Coupled with his "Film and Video Archive of the U.S. Holocaust Memorial Museum" (now including 1,005 hours of archival footage relating to the Shoah), Spielberg has had an enormous impact on debates concerning the representation of the Jewish experience in the mid-twentieth century. Despite receiving criticism for rendering mass extermination "consumable" according to the priorities of Hollywood, *Schindler's List* has been the focus of considerable critical acclaim. Its commercial success suggests that it is by far the most influential film about the Shoah ever made.

The second focus of this essay is Roberto Benigni's *Life is Beautiful/ La vita è bella* (1997). This film has also enjoyed considerable world-wide success: Benigni won the Oscar for Best Actor and the film won two other Academy Awards. The film also won the award for the Best Jewish Experience at the Jerusalem International Film Festival and the Grand Prix at the Cannes Film Festival. Nevertheless, it has proved very controversial because of the use of Chaplinesque comedy in its approach to a horrific period in European history. Gerald Peary, writing in the *Boston Phoenix* in November 1998, states, "Life Is Beautiful isn't just the film title, it's Benigni's reprehensible moral. He dares to assign a transcendent meaning to the Holocaust, which to most Jews resonates with non-meaning, a hollow waste of many millions of lives."[5] Writing in the same month in *Time*, Richard Schickel writes, "Sentimentality is a kind of fascism too, robbing us of judgment and moral acuity, and it needs to be resisted. *Life Is Beautiful* is a good place to start."[6]

I am returning to these familiar, much-discussed and commercially successful films in order to assess them in relation to a particular theological perspective on the nature of theological language and the ontological status of evil. They offer fundamentally different approaches to the questions of representation that continually surround Holocaust film. I will argue that the delicate use of allegory and comedy in *Life is Beautiful* at once resists establishing the Shoah as unrepresentable and therefore definitive of history's meaninglessness while also maintaining the devastating incoherence, and therefore "unspeakable," nature of genocide. Contrary to Peary's assessment, it is precisely Bengini's refusal to assign any transcendent meaning to the Shoah which renders *Life is Beautiful* an insightful approach to the subject. By contrast, the cinematic spectacle of *Schindler's List*, while doubtless heightening public awareness of the terrors of the Shoah and helping to assuage what Gillian Rose calls "knowledge-resistance to the Holocaust," nevertheless renders the experience of Jews and Germans in mid-twentieth century Europe too accessible on a pietistic and literal plain, and therefore "comprehensible." I begin, however, with the theological background against which I will read these films.

Privative Evil

Both the ancient Jewish and Christian traditions, influenced by the legacy of Platonic philosophy, insisted on the supreme reality, and therefore intelligibility, of the Good. According to Plato's famous allegory of the sun in the *Republic*, just as the light of the sun makes all things visible and therefore knowable, so too the "light" of the Good preserves all things and renders them intelligible.[7] By an intensifying participation in the Good, visible created things are more fully themselves. I know the desk at which I am sat is a desk and not a chair or a pile of firewood precisely because it is a *good* desk. When we speak of someone as a true friend, we mean also

5. Peary, "*Life is Beautiful.*"

6. Schickel, "Cinema: Fascist Fable."

7. See Plato, *Republic*, 507b–508d.

that this person is a good friend. So the good and the true are intimately intertwined in Plato's metaphysics. Knowledge of things (epistemology) cannot be separated from what things *are* (ontology). The Good is that which, in itself, is most supremely intelligible. All other things are intelligible insofar as they participate in the Good. This is to say that, the more fully something is fulfilled or actualized, the more intelligible it becomes.

The Jewish and Christian doctrine of creation diverged from the ancient Greek philosophical tradition in insisting that God creates *ex nihilo*. Nevertheless, the Platonic character of theological approaches to creation was maintained in other crucial respects. For example, just as for Plato the Good is the only source of intelligible light and being, so for later theologians there is only one source of being, namely the divine. Created being is a participation in being-itself and has no self-standing ontological status outside of this participative relationship. The insistence on God as the *ex nihilo* source of all things who at once enfolds the transcendentals of the Good, the True, and the Beautiful has consequences for the theological understanding of evil. For the Neoplatonists, Jewish thinkers such as Philo of Alexandria, and the theologians of the early church, evil is a privation of the good. Contrary to Gnostic and Manichean cosmologies, the tradition of evil as *privatio boni* maintains that evil has no "foothold in being": it is a privation that is wholly parasitic on the Good.[8] Some contemporary criticisms of the *privatio boni* tradition point out that viewing evil merely as a privation cannot do justice to its horror and force, not least in the experience of the Shoah. However, it should be remembered that the tradition of viewing evil as a privation of the Good is not an empirical thesis about how we experience evil, but a metaphysical thesis about evil's ontological status in relation to a transcendent reality. It is an aspect of the doctrine of creation.

For Jewish and Christian theologians, the transcendence of God, the source of all being and life, presents a particular problem concerning representation and language. Of course, the second of the Ten Commandments, given in Exodus 20 and Deuteronomy 5, forms the basis of the care that must be taken in referring to God because the specter of idolatry is always apparent. Nevertheless, our speech about God is always

---

8. For a contemporary analysis and defence of the *privatio boni* tradition against the Kantian radical evil school represented by, for example, Jean-François Lyotard, see Milbank, *Being Reconciled*, ch. 1.

regarded as the address of a creature to the transcendent source of all things who exists in unapproachable light. How can words refer adequately to God? The response of Rabbi Moses Maimonides (1135–1204) was that words cannot refer to God, and that we are therefore only capable of saying what God is *not*. To say that "God is good" is not to have any handle on God's goodness; it is merely to say, falteringly, that God is not evil. This became known as the *via negativa*, or "negative way." Thomas Aquinas (c.1225–74), writing in response to Maimonides, insisted that, although we name God from creatures, we do so neither univocally nor equivocally, but analogically. He resisted Maimonides's purely negative approach to theological language and argued that, when we make statements such as "God is good," we do not merely state that "God is not evil." Rather, we name God as good in himself without thereby claiming that we have a grasp on what it is for God to be good. Why? Because what it is for God to be good is not what it is for a human being to be good (just as what it is for a dog to be faithful is not what it is for a husband to be faithful), although a human being is good by virtue of his or her participation in divine goodness. To comprehend divine goodness we would need to know what kind of thing God is, and both Aquinas and Maimonides would insist that we do not know God in himself; we only know God through his creation and, for Aquinas, we name him by analogy.[9]

Against this background, Aquinas, along with much of the Christian and Jewish Neoplatonic tradition, maintained that God is most supremely intelligible *in himself* because God is fully actual.[10] There is, as it were, no ambiguity in God. As being-itself, God is the source of all created being. However, *to us* God is wholly other and transcendent. Our intellects are suited to the knowledge of creatures. We know God by means of his creation and revelation in accordance with the capacities of the human intellect and the constantly arriving gifts of divine grace. On Aquinas's view, contrary to much modern philosophy, the human intellect is not the measure of intelligibility. The fact that we can grasp aspects of the created world but cannot grasp God does not, for Aquinas, mean that the created world is more intelligible *in itself*. It may be more intelligible for

9. For a much fuller explanation of the analogical naming of God in Aquinas, see my introduction to Oliver and Milbank (eds.), *The Radical Orthodoxy Reader*. See also te Velde, *Aquinas on God*, ch. 4.

10. See, for example, Thomas Aquinas's *Summa Theologiae*, 1a.12.7.

us; in itself, however, the created world, in being contingent and subject to change, has its measure of intelligibility by virtue of its participation in the eternal and unchanging Good, which is God.

For a particular tradition, both Jewish and Christian, which finds its deep roots in Platonic metaphysics, the linguistic and artistic representation of the divine always faces the specter of idolatry. Nevertheless, those representations are understood as consummated and yet fully exceeded in the worship of a wholly transcendent divinity.[11] Liturgical mediations of the divine are made possible by *theosis*. However, in the context of this same tradition's view that evil is a privation of that supremely intelligible Good, does not the problem of linguistic representation and intelligibility of evil present itself for precisely the opposite reason? If the Good is, in itself, supremely intelligible, and all creaturely references to the transcendent participate by *theosis* in that surfeit of intelligibility and meaning, what are we to say about representations of evil, which is *precisely* a privation of that intelligibility and meaning? Does evil become unrepresentable? Can any intelligible discourse be maintained?

One answer to this question is, no, evil is unintelligible and not representable. However, this is not quite the response of the tradition which maintains that evil is *privatio boni*. It is crucial to remember that evil's absence of meaning is only revealed with reference to the always-prior intelligibility of the Good. It is not evil which reveals its own unintelligibility, for this would grant to evil the autonomy of self-determination. Rather, it is the Good that reveals evil's unintelligibility. At all times, evil is parasitic on the Good. We do not know evil as unintelligible simply in itself. We only know evil as an unintelligible absence of meaning with reference to the infinite abundance of intelligibility and meaning that we find in the Good. Moreover, the tradition of *privatio boni* continually insists that an *absolute* evil is not possible, for it would dissolve into nothingness.[12] So even an evil as "radical" as the Shoah is in some sense parasitic on a prior good, although in itself it remains blind to its privative nature. For example, Hannah Arendt's report on the trial of Adolf Eichmann in 1961 and 1962 comments that even the Nazi commanders were parasitic on a

---

11. See Pickstock, *After Writing*.

12. For example, see Thomas Aquinas's *Summa Theologiae*, 1a.48.4.

notion of the good in the sense that, in however deranged, depraved, and murderous a fashion, they thought they were doing the right thing.[13]

While maintaining that evil is not utterly unintelligible and unrepresentable—in other words, that it can still, in some sense, be spoken—the tradition of *privatio boni* suggests that evil is only interpretable in relation to a primeval Good, as the lack of that Good. In this sense, we cannot account for evil with reference to a purpose for it is that which, by its very nature, lacks purpose. As Aquinas would put it, evil has no formal or final cause.[14] While we might be able to outline the intellectual and historical background to the Shoah (long-simmering European anti-Semitism, the legacy of nineteenth- and early twentieth-century German philosophy, the humiliation of Germany after the First World War, and so on), we cannot, as the enterprise of theodicy so often attempts to do, provide a *justification* for the Shoah. An example of this kind of justification can be found in the theodicy of the British philosopher Richard Swinburne, for whom certain "higher-order goods" such as extreme bravery or generosity (of the kind shown by Oskar Schindler) depend on certain kinds of suffering for their execution and manifestation.[15] However, Swinburne's theodicy is the precise inverse of the *privatio boni* tradition for it renders the practice of good acts parasitic upon the prior occurrence of certain kinds of evil and suffering. Instead, for the tradition that understands evil as a privation, such evil can have no intelligible justification; if we were able to give a *reason* (in the sense of purpose) for the murder of millions of Jews, or cancer in a single child, we would live in a Satanic world. This is not to say that such suffering is irredeemable or utterly unspeakable. It is to say that suffering calls not for a *justification*, which attempts to render suffering intelligible, but for a *response* borne of the absolute priority of the Good.

We have seen that God, as the transcendent source of created being, is spoken of analogically using words that, from our point of view, also name creatures. It is perfection terms—good, true, wise—that, for Aquinas, are predicated primarily of God and secondarily of creatures.

---

13. See, Arendt, *Eichmann in Jerusalem*.

14. See, again, Thomas Aquinas's *Summa Theologiae*, 1a.49.1.

15. See Swinburne, *The Existence of God*, ch. 11. The most effective articulation of the view that evil is a privation of the good with reference to a recent horrific disaster can be found in Hart, *The Doors of the Sea*.

So in a sense our speech about God will also be speech about other things in their created relation to God. That speech "borrows" its intelligibility from the divine, for God is the ultimate focus of reference.[16] Insofar as we speak of the good of creation, we speak intelligibly of its orientation to the Good. Speech about evil will be compromised by the dissolution of meaning and intelligibility. Nevertheless, for the *privatio boni* tradition that unintelligibility will not be revealed unless such speech is placed by the priority of the Good and its surfeit of meaning. If evil is understood as authenticating its own unintelligibility and non-representability, it is rendered in some sense absolute and ineffable, becoming in Manichean fashion the mirror image of the Good. It is only the transcendent Good, which Jewish and Christian thought name as "God," that is ineffable. Evil is the dissolution of meaning, that dissolution being named by the Good.

It is against this background of the ontological and hermeneutical priority of the Good that I wish to read the approach to the evil of the Shoah in *Schindler's List* and *Life is Beautiful*.

Reading *Schindler's List* and *Life is Beautiful*

In approaching the subject of the Shoah, Spielberg is responding to the widespread concern that awareness and knowledge of Nazi atrocities perpetrated against Jews and other groups in the mid-twentieth century is waning, particularly in his native North America. Nevertheless, he resisted making an "American" film. The actors are European and the locations authentic. The attention to historical detail and fidelity to the visual archives (for example in Ralph Fiennes's depiction of the camp commander Amon Goeth) has been apparent to many commentators and critics. Of course, one important strategy for rendering *Schindler's List* an authentic mediation of events in the 1940s is the decision to film almost exclusively in black and white. Coupled with the extensive use of hand-held cameras, this enables the film to allude simultaneously to a number of different filmic genres: wartime newsreel, 1930s and 40s cinema, *cinema vérité*, and

16. Aquinas adopts Aristotle's *pros hen* (towards a single focus) view of analogy as attribution rather than proportion. We call a diet and a medical treatment "healthy" by virtue of their common focus in the health of the human body. The body is healthy in itself; health is attributed to the diet and the medicine by virtue of their relationship to the body. Likewise, God is good in himself. A human being has goodness attributed to him or her by virtue of a relationship with the divine source of goodness.

contemporary documentary. The use of light, smoke, and close-up por-
trait shots is particularly reminiscent of mid-twentieth century cinema,
particularly *film noir*. More specifically, the frequent use of chiaroscuro
lighting (a common technique before color could mediate relationships
and meaning) heightens the ambiguity in Schindler's character, and the
symbiotic relationship between Schindler (Liam Neeson) and Goeth.
These factors, which feature heavy layers of cinematic nostalgia, combine
to create the impression of reality and authenticity: we are really "seeing"
the Shoah's principal characters, from the victims to the heroes and the
psychotic perpetrators.

Given the aim of presenting the Shoah to a wide audience, it is not
surprising that Spielberg has been thought to adopt what is often called
a classical narrative approach.[17] This approach to cinema, which domi-
nated Hollywood at least until the 1960s, relies on well-delineated character plots in which motivations are clear and the narrative develops in a
linear fashion. Audiences are encouraged to associate particularly with
a single, central character (the "star" of the movie) whose goals define
the seamless development of a unique narrative. In the case of *Schindler's
List*, the goals of the central character, Oskar Schindler, are initially those
of profit-making from his enamelware factory and only later become the
rescue of Jews who are to be deported to concentration camps. The need
to provide a reason why Schindler would risk his profit and life to act
heroically in this way is a particular challenge for the film; to maintain the
classical narrative style the viewer must understand the central character's
key psychological motivations, which govern the plot. The key point concerning the classical approach to cinema is that the viewer is enabled to
"lose herself" in the visual experience. The film becomes almost transparent as the work of interpretation is undertaken effortlessly by a complex
set of filming techniques in which ambiguities are made plain and then
resolved quickly and neatly. For example, the character of Schindler is,
initially, mysterious. During the opening sequences of the film, as he
dresses to attend a party, we see only his hands. The lighting of Schindler's
face again stresses both light and dark. As the story unfolds and Schindler
develops from profiteer to savior, these ambiguities are neatly resolved to

---

17. See, for example, Bordwell et al., *The Classical Hollywood Cinema*; and Hansen,
"Schindler's List is Not Shoah: Second Commandment, Popular Modernism, and Public
Memory" in *Spielberg's Holocaust*, 81ff.

reveal the hero. The worrying aspect of this narrative is that, faced with a choice between the hero Schindler and the psychotic Goeth, audiences departed from cinemas reassured that, if they had been present in Poland or Germany in the 1940s, they, of course, would have acted as Schindler.

As Miriam Bratu Hansen observes, this classical approach eradicates the complexities of the real world because "it relies on neoclassicist principles of compositional unity, motivation, linearity, equilibrium, and closure—principles singularly inadequate in the face of an event that by its very nature defies our narrative urge to make sense of, to impose order on the discontinuity and otherness of historical experience."[18] While Goeth's motivations are interpreted in terms of murderous psychosis and depictions of the brutal murder of Jews scattered through the film add to a sense of the sheer senseless nihilism of these events, nevertheless this narrative as a whole is rendered intelligible and therefore comprehensible through the classical genre. Causal motivations—even those of Goeth and other soldiers—are rendered clear because, we are told, they see Jews as animals, not humans. The narrative of the Shoah is represented within a genre that governs much of classical filmmaking in the mid-twentieth century and allows audiences to believe that they have "seen" or "experienced" the Holocaust in all its authenticity.

A number of commentators have argued that, in other respects, *Schindler's List* subsumes within itself other depictions of the Shoah and thereby develops its credentials as the definitive and intelligible representation. Allusions to previous Holocaust films, notably *Night and Fog* and *Shoah*, abound. For example, the huge piles of suitcases, glasses, shoes, and other possessions once belonging to deported Jews was famously depicted in *Night and Fog* and is repeated in *Schindler's List*. Nevertheless, as Joshua Hirsch points out, the role that such images play in Spielberg's film is quite different.[19] For Renais in *Night and Fog*, the piles of possessions indicate the unimaginable and unrepresentable extent of the loss that constituted the Shoah. Such evil is unintelligible in its depth, extent, and deprivation. Similarly, the throat-cutting gesture made by a bystander as a trainload of Jews makes its way to Auschwitz is used by Lanzmann in *Shoah* to depict the moral complicity of the bystander. Spielberg uses both in *Schindler's*

18. Hansen, "Schindler's List is Not Shoah," 81.
19. Hirsch, *After Image*, 147.

List, but not to indicate the unintelligible and the privative; rather, these are events of history that are, as Hirsch states, quite representable.

While *Schindler's List* is unambiguously a "Holocaust film" with a single, linear narrative, the same cannot be said for *Life is Beautiful*. Beginning in Italy in 1939, the film begins by stating very clearly that it is a fable. Crucially, we are told that the story is difficult to tell. There is no pretence to speak literally or historically, and one might say that the film is only tangentially about the Shoah. The Shoah is placed by other more fundamental narratives, rather than assuming its own definitive priority. The film is saturated in comedy, allegory, layered narratives, and magic. Divided into two parts, the first half of *Life is Beautiful* focuses on the growing and magical romance between Guido Orefice (Robert Benigni) and Dora (Nicoletta Braschi). As their romance unfolds, so the specter of fascist anti-Semitism gradually emerges as an aspect of the film. However, at no point is that anti-Semitism allowed to stand alone as if it might interpret itself; it is interpreted as ludicrous by the admittedly daring use of comedy. For example, when a government inspector comes to visit Dora's school, Guido takes his place and, via slapstick and farce, provides a devastating critique of Italy's anti-Semitic laws of the late 1930s in a fashion that renders those policies quite literally laughable.[20]

The magical narratives that Guido weaves into everyday events as he seeks the love of Dora point to the multiple meanings of life beyond its purely material significance; there is always more to be seen.[21] These hidden meanings are explored with particular poignancy in Guido's relationship with Lessing, a German doctor staying at the hotel where Guido works as a waiter. Other than Guido, Dora, and their son Giosuè, Lessing is the only character to appear in both halves of the film.[22] Strangely, he is fixated on riddles that he cannot solve. In one scene in the first half

20. It is important to note that this scene, one of the funniest in the film, critiques an Italian government policy rather than brutal murder. At no point in the film is murder and genocide—to which only allusion is made—the subject of specifically comic derision.

21. For an excellent and more detailed reading of these narratives, see Viano, "*Life is Beautiful*. A detailed analysis of *Life is Beautiful* is also available in Celli, *The Divine Comic*, ch. 11.

22. It is beyond the scope of this essay to discuss the significance of the names of certain characters in *Life is Beautiful*, but the importance of references to the German philosophers Arthur Schopenhauer (1788–1860) and Gotthold Lessing (1729–81) should be noted.

of the film, Guido solves a riddle that had been perplexing Lessing for eight days: "The bigger it is, the less you see it." The answer: obscurity. In the second half of the film, when Guido and Giosuè are together in the labor camp (while Dora, a Gentile who has voluntarily followed her husband and son, is in the women's section), Guido once again encounters his friend Lessing who is now working as a doctor in the camp. While Guido is waiting on the tables of the Germans in the camp mess, Lessing states that he must talk with Guido urgently. Needless to say, Guido is full of expectation; he believes that his friend, the doctor, will aid his family's escape. The expectation is allowed to mount through a number of vaguely comic but tense scenes. Finally, the meeting takes place in a corner of the dining room. Lessing has a ludicrous riddle he cannot solve: "Fat, fat, ugly, ugly, all yellow in reality. If you ask me what I am I answer 'Cheep, cheep, cheep.' Walking along I go, 'Poopoo.'" Throughout the scene, Guido is silent. As Benigni portrays Guido's reaction, his comic persona appears wholly crushed. His face conveys utter incomprehension and the total unintelligibility of his circumstances. Guido departs the shot leaving Lessing banging his fist on the sideboard in deranged frustration. This exchange, one of the very few that mirrors the first half of the film, becomes a metaphor for the unintelligible and nihilistic nature of the Shoah. Unlike the representation of *Schindler's List* and its voyeuristic approach to brutal murder, this reference is wholly tangential and "unreal," yet it nevertheless does not leave Nazi psychosis uninterpreted; Guido, the master of narrative and the discloser of secret meanings, is crushed. Still, he returns to his son who, despite the hidden murder of his father later in the film, will eventually emerge alive from the labor camp to tell a more primitive story.

A key aspect of the second part of *Life is Beautiful*, in which Guido is interred in a labor camp with Giosuè, is "the game." In one of the most comic scenes in the film, Guido pretends to translate the yelled instructions of the German guard concerning life in the camp from German into Italian. Guido, to the astonishment of his fellow inmates and Giosuè, tells of a game in which prisoners compete to win a tank. By means of this game, Guido attempts to lift the spirits of his son and preserve his innocence. While commentators have observed that Giosuè is more aware of his circumstances than Guido allows, there remain competing narratives at work in this part of the film. Which will win? As sober and realistic observers, we know that Guido's account of "the game" is pure fantasy and that tragedy is near. Indeed, for Guido, this is what comes to pass; he is shot dead, unseen, as Giosuè hides from the fleeing German soldiers. Yet as Giosuè emerges from his hiding place into a new day amidst the abandoned camp, an American tank with liberating soldiers enters through the gates. Giosuè climbs aboard and enjoys his "victor's ride." We are left with the question, which narrative was more fundamental for Giosuè? It is this final scene of apparently joyful and wholly sentimental survival with former prisoners running into sunlit countryside that has incurred the scorn of many critics of *Life is Beautiful*. Yet it is in no sense *realistic*. This is a commentarial metaphor. The competing narratives of the film unfold in a fashion totally unlike the single linear narrative of *Schindler's List*. For *Life is Beautiful*, despite the devastating incoherence and unintelligibility of the camp (again, a *metaphor* for the Shoah) a narrator in the form of Giosuè lives to tell a more fundamental story, which nevertheless *places* the Shoah and marks its privative unintelligibility. Can the Shoah be represented? Yes, but only as the privation of a more ontologically fundamental Good. In this sense, it is not "ineffable." As the film closes, we finally learn that the narrator at the beginning of the film, who announced the fable as "a simple story, but not an easy one to tell," is Giosuè with whom the film closes.

The allegorical significance of *Life is Beautiful* was ignored by many critics, who derided its historical inaccuracies and revisionist tendencies. This is to misunderstand Benigni's purpose, which is to convey both the Shoah's privative unintelligibility and its place within a more fundamental narrative that refers to a transcendent Good. He does this by means of metaphor and allegory. Can we nevertheless regard the fantastic stories of *Life is Beautiful*, such as "the game" in the labor camp, as childish and sentimental escape from the brutal reality of the Shoah, which simply repeats the violence of the camps? Not if a proper understanding of allegory is maintained. Allegory does not displace other readings of texts; it supplements them and points to unforeseen realities and symbolism. The allegories of *Life is Beautiful* do not displace the material reality of everyday life, whether of mundane events or the horrors of a concentration camp. Rather, they point to other possibilities, wider frames of reference, and more primitive meanings. This is not to suggest that the Shoah has a hidden meaning; quite the contrary, for Begnini is careful to highlight the unintelligibility of the camp—if you like, its "untranslatable" nature.

Rather, it places the Shoah within the wider context of *other* and deeper narratives that are more primitive, and thus resists the tendency to make *absolute* and *ineffable* the tragic, horrific, and unimaginable story of mid-twentieth century European Jewry.

I began this essay with reference to the tangential nature of language about divinity. To speak of God is to speak analogically with reference to creatures. In being created, those creatures are symbols of the creator. It is as created that they gain their meaning. For the tradition that understands evil to be the privation of the Good, which is God, evil dissolves meaning and intelligibility. Yet that dissolution is only made apparent by reference to the more fundamental and "real" story of transcendent goodness. Because of *Schindler's List*'s self-enclosed and all-encompassing realism, it does little to reveal the incoherence and nihilism of the Shoah beyond the literal portrayal of brutal murder, which it renders visible in unproblematic fashion. The problem with such depictions of brutality is that, in their simple literality, audiences become over-familiar with such scenes. At some point, it becomes apparent that one must leave the theatre; one is watching a film. For *Life is Beautiful*, the narrative extends beyond the movie theatre's doors. If spirituality is the faithful search for as yet undisclosed or unrealized meanings, *Life is Beautiful* is of greater theological import than its realist counterpart *Schindler's List*.

2

Imagining a Better Way

Ben X and Marjorie Suchocki's *The Fall to Violence:*
Original Sin in Relational Theology

J. RYAN PARKER

OVER THE PAST DECADE, the Internet has brought people closer together
and strengthened relationships through email, blogs, and social networks
like Facebook and Twitter. Grandparents can see their grandchildren's
first steps moments after they take them. Parents who lose children in
childbirth can experience the love, support, and prayers of friends and
family members around the world, around the clock. I could fill this entire
chapter with examples of how this virtual connectedness benefits our lives
emotionally and spiritually. Unfortunately, I could also do the same with
a list of the ways in which these connections have provided avenues for
violence, hatred, bigotry, and separation.

The rise in cyberbullying in the past few years reveals yet again that
violence is a key sin that plagues the human experience. It has characterized every relationship we have ever developed, be it broadly political
or deeply intimate. It has even polluted our virtual relationships. Viral
videos of embarrassing moments at school make them eternal rather than

momentary. Insults are no longer simply exchanged between individuals or overheard by a few onlookers but are posted online for millions to see. Rumors spread at a destructive speed through texts and social network posts. The shocking and disturbing news of teen suicides by victims of cyberbullying again reveals what we have known, but denied, all along. Words (and images) do indeed hurt us. They can even kill us.

In an article on cyberbullying and suicide for the Cyberbullying Research Center, Sameer Hinduja and Justin W. Patchin found that cyberbullying victims were "almost twice as likely to have attempted suicide compared to youth who had not experienced cyberbullying."[1] Of the youth who have committed suicide, Hinduja and Patchin found that "many of the teenagers who committed suicide after experiencing bullying or cyberbullying had other emotional and social issues going on in their lives."[2] Of course, it is not a stretch to imagine that bullies exploited these issues in the first place. The rise of cyberbullying has had an especially traumatic effect on gay teenagers, often outing those who were previously closeted. The rash of successful gay teen suicides, which almost certainly pales in comparison to attempted suicides among members of the same population, have inspired a virtual retaliation as concerned celebrities, politicians, parents, and friends created a viral video campaign assuring these teenagers that "It Gets Better."[3]

As with violence in any aspect of the human experience, cyberbullying demands creative, imaginative responses to it in order to break its hold on our relationships. In this chapter, I want to highlight key points in what has been, for me, a transformative text: Marjorie Suchocki's *The Fall to Violence: Original Sin in Relational Theology.* I am particularly concerned with her emphasis on unnecessary violence as the central sin in the human experience, her radical notion of forgiveness as willing the well-being of both victim and violator, and finally her emphasis on imagination as a key ingredient in breaking cycles of violence. I will conclude this chapter with a discussion of the Belgian film, *Ben X* (2007), by director Nic Balthazar, which embodies both the violence inherent in our

---

1. Hinduja and Patchin, "Cyberbullying Research Summary," 1.
2. Ibid., 2.
3. For more information on this campaign, visit http://www.itgetsbetter.org.

real and virtual worlds and Suchocki's recognition of the importance of imagination in combating it.[4]

In *The Fall to Violence*, Marjorie Suchocki moves the definition of sin away from traditional understandings of "rebellion against God" to "rebellion against creation." She argues that maintaining an understanding of sin as *primarily* "rebellion against God" is problematic on a number of levels: it (1) often confuses divine "law" with cultural mores; (2) keeps the poor and oppressed powerless because rebellion against authority is equated with rebellion against God; (3) levels the severity of sins; (4) makes the victims of sin invisible; (5) devalues creation; (6) elevates and separates humanity from the rest of creation; and (7) simply does not fit with the experiences of most people in the world.[5] Yet Suchocki does not imply that sin has no affect on God. Rather, given a relational understanding of creation and God, God has a "feeling of connectedness" to creation; any harm or violence that creation feels, God feels. God suffers with the world and feels its brokenness.

For Suchocki, sin is any act of unnecessary violence that violates the well-being of any member of creation. Unfortunately, Suchocki's emphasis on well-being is perhaps the most nebulous part of her theology. While we might envision it from a political perspective, i.e., the Constitution's guarantee of life, liberty, and the pursuit of happiness, it goes much deeper than that. In fact, creaturely well-being has its origins in God's well-being. Suchocki writes, "In considering the criterion of well-being relative to God, we are led to an understanding of an ultimate truth, love, and beauty pertaining to all things."[6] Suchocki's definition of God's well-being helps point to a clearer understanding of creaturely well-being. She defines divine well-being as such:

> Truth, in this context is God's absolute knowledge of every entity in the fullness of what it has become . . . Love, in this context, is God's absolute acceptance of every entity in the fullness of what it can be, both within God's transforming action within the divine reality, and within the ongoing world . . . Beauty, in this context, is God's ability to integrate every entity not only with all others in

4. Balthazar based the film on his novel, *Nothing Was All He Said*, which is also based on a true story of a young boy with autism who committed suicide as a result of being bullied at school.

5. Suchocki, *The Fall to Violence*, 17–18.

6. Ibid., 76.

a "reconciliation of all things" within God's own nature, but also with the infinite resources of the divine harmony.[7]

Thus, if we were to take this definition and apply it to the human experience, we might come to the conclusion that creaturely well-being entails the pursuit of the fullest knowledge and acceptance of the other in the fullness of who they are and will become and the willingness to cooperate with one another in the healing of the world. It seems that to ensure, for example, the well-being of a neighbor, we must strive to know them as fully as possible, to support them in what they can be, and to work with them to bring about God's kingdom on earth. Of course truth, love, and beauty, Suchocki's criteria for well-being, are culturally loaded terms, a point that Suchocki recognizes and to which I will return below.

Nevertheless, we can all agree with Suchocki that violence destroys well-being, and when it is unnecessary and avoidable, it is sin.[8] Suchocki points to other more traditional understandings of original sin and its origins, particularly pride and anxiety, and argues that they actually flow from violence. Violence produces pride and anxiety.[9] The interconnectedness of creation, a key point in relational theology, only exacerbates the effects of violence. Suchocki writes, "Evil anywhere is mediated everywhere through the relational structure of existence." Furthermore, it is unavoidable: "We are each participants in every act of violence, whether or not we are aware of these acts."[10] In fact, the social structures that we create often transmit sin. Suchocki continues, "Through our social heritage the particular forms of sin that are embodied in a society's institutions to protect the privileges of a dominant group deeply influence the structures of consciousness and conscience of each new generation."[11] To that end, we all bear responsibility for the violence and sin in our world, however, we do so to varying degrees.

Suchocki's understanding of sin as primarily offense against creation keeps the victims of sin at the forefront of our minds while also helping us properly understand the varying gravity of those sins and our complicity in them. To the degree that we are free and able to *not* participate in sinful

7. Suchocki, *The Fall to Violence*, 78.

8. Ibid., 85.

9. Ibid., 97–98.

10. Ibid., 104, 106.

11. Ibid., 113.

acts or, conversely, to the degree in which we *do* participate in them, we are or are not guilty. As such, our violent tendencies, interconnectedness, and sin-perpetuating social structures mean that we are all, to varying degrees, both victims and violators. Suchocki writes, "Guilt is involved when the freedom to transcend the structures of ill-being is present, and one does not transcend those structures."[12] As a result, Suchocki distinguishes between two types of guilt, ontological (that of simply being part of the human race) and felt (the emotions we feel, rightly or wrongly, when we either remain in or transcend social boundaries). Though Suchocki argues that guilt can be a roadblock to transformation (we can be mired in regret and depression), she also notes its positive influences, especially when it "functions as pain does in signaling a dysfunction in the body. Feelings of guilt can be the catalyst toward transformation."[13]

While Suchocki argues that violence is part of our evolutionary history and results from our inherent aggressiveness and is enhanced by our interconnectedness and social structures, we can still overcome it given our capacity for self-transcendence. In fact, Suchocki claims that "God's continuing creative call is toward a transcendence of unnecessary violence."[14] This self-transcendence can take place in one of three ways, "in relation to one's own past through memory; in relation to others in the present through empathy; and in relation to the future through imagination." It is important to understand these modes of self-transcendence because, as Suchocki claims, "the human act of [violence] always involves a failure of one or more of the modes of transcendence."[15] While all of these faculties are necessary, Suchocki argues that memory is most important because empathy and imagination require it. To empathize, we must remember similar past experiences, and to imagine a better future, we must remember the past that we want to change.

Suchocki argues that there is no isolated self and writes, "The personal is social."[16] As a result, empathy is vital to the human experience. We can never fully know or grasp the other because our relationships are constantly changing, or, as Suchocki refers to them, they are "infinite

12. Ibid., 129.
13. Ibid., 142.
14. Ibid., 87.
15. Ibid., 36.
16. Ibid., 39.

dynamism." Because of this, we should be open to others in ways that can be mutually transformational, constantly resisting the selfish urge to close ourselves off to the other. Yet if empathy recognizes infinite relationships, then imagination recognizes infinite possibilities. Suchocki writes, "Through imagination, one transcends one's present circumstances and envisions a future . . . Imagination transcends the present self through its vision of a different state of affairs. Through this vision of the future, the self participates in the transformation of the present."[17]

Practicing these modes of self-transcendence—memory, empathy, and imagination—also involves the act of naming sin, which is, at its heart, a prophetic act. Naming an act as sinful asserts that "1) these actions should not have happened, 2) there is human responsibility for these actions, and 3) there is an alternative vision for how interdependent human beings can resolve disputes."[18] Naming sin is just the first step in transcending it; it is one that we must continually take. This naming is also an act of memory that we undertake throughout our lifetime. However, Suchocki emphasizes the importance of remembering rightly. We can remember sins that we committed or that were committed against us in ways that leave us feeling angry or guilty. On the other hand, we can remember them in ways that open up paths for the transformation of the present into a better future. Guilt can help us recognize the problem, but we must even break through it. Suchocki argues that guilt and anger "must give way to forgiveness."[19]

Suchocki's understanding of forgiveness is radically different from the popular notion of forgiving and forgetting, which often devolves into forgiving *as* forgetting. Again, like naming sin, forgiveness requires a lifetime of remembering the violator and violation, but in a way that does not lead to resentment but to the development of the well-being of the victim and violator. Furthermore, Suchocki's definition of forgiveness does not necessitate good, positive feelings toward the violator on the part of the victim, which is most certainly a reassurance for victims of rape or domestic abuse for example. Suchocki writes, "[Forgiveness] is fundamentally a matter of intellect rather than of emotions . . . [One] *can* deliberately

17. Ibid., 41.
18. Ibid., 45.
19. Ibid., 142.

will well-being, even over against feelings of revulsion and antipathy."[20] It simply, yet quite profoundly, requires the victim to will the well-being of the violator, an act that breaks the cycle of violence that would inevitably continue should the victim desire violent revenge on the violator. Suchocki writes, "Remembrance of sin in the context of forgiveness is quite different from remembrance of sin in the context of vengeance. The critical difference is the will toward well-being or ill-being. In the case of forgiveness, one remembers in order to transform; in the case of the vengeance, one remembers in order to destroy."[21] Furthermore, Suchocki's emphasis on the interconnectedness of all creation should remind victims that at times they too have been violators. Finally, Suchocki's notion of forgiveness requires the practices of self-transcendence that I discussed above. She writes, "[Without] memory, empathy, and imagination there can be no forgiveness."[22]

Rightly remembering a past violation and empathetically willing the well-being of the violator are just the first steps of forgiveness. We must put those memories and that will to action. For Suchocki, imagination is the key. She writes, "In and through imagination, the will to well-being moves into visions of well-being, which themselves empower one to work toward well-being . . . Forgiveness as the active will toward well-being is the creation of a new human future, and thus forgiveness is the substance of human hope."[23] Suchocki's use of the words "work" and "creation" reveal that the act of forgiveness is not only intellectual but active, requiring both victim and violator to build a better world made possible first through that act of forgiveness.

Finally, Suchocki's discussion of violence, sin, well-being, transcendence, and forgiveness all have deep implications for our understanding of God. She writes, "God, as the fullness of truth, love and beauty is memory, empathy, and imagination carried to maximal form. In God the criterion of well-being (truth, love, and beauty), and the elements that make for forgiveness (memory, empathy, and imagination) merge, so that in a sense one might say that the divine character *is* forgiveness."[24] This is indeed a

---

20. Ibid., 145.

21. Suchocki, *The Fall to Violence*, 151.

22. Ibid., 144.

23. Ibid., 152–53.

24. Suchocki, *The Fall to Violence*, 158.

powerful and inspirational claim. Yet if we, as children of God, have been created in the image of God, what implications does it have for our own character? How much more should we be creatures of forgiveness?

As important and convincing as Suchocki's argument is, even she recognizes its inherent difficulties. While the violation of well-being might be a fitting criterion by which to judge acts as sinful, the notion of well-being itself does have two prominent problems. First, life depends on the destruction (ill-being) of other life. Quite simply, human beings need to eat to survive, and this act of eating requires that we harm other life, be it plant or animal. Second, well-being is a culturally dependent concept.[25] Even though all of life is interconnected, we often view our needs and experiences from a perspective that most values that upon which we most immediately depend. What happens when these needs, or perceived needs, leads to the ill-being of others? Less severe, perhaps, but no less controversial are questions of competing notions of truth and beauty. That well-being, as Suchocki ultimately argues, is a "culturally dependent concept," the possibility of universal well-being is all but impossible. Yet, she argues, it is a challenge that we must ever hold before us. As a result, universal well-being, Suchocki argues, is tenuous at best, yet it is a challenge, providing "an ideal that calls our more limited ideals ever into question."[26]

Suchocki fills her book with news accounts of inexplicable, horrific violence that provide perfect examples of the brokenness of our world and of sin as the violation of another's well-being. Unfortunately, she does not provide the alternative; examples of what her notion of forgiveness looks like in practice. What do exercises of transcendent memory, empathy, and imagination look like in the face of the Holocaust, genocide, environmental degradation . . . or even cyberbullying? Thankfully, after first reading *The Fall to Violence* in 2005, I have seen a number of films that embody elements of her theology, particularly imaginative responses to violence. I want to turn to one of those films, *Ben X*, that shows what an imaginative, creative response to violence looks like. It is my hope that placing *Ben X* in conversation with *The Fall to Violence* will reveal the power of filmmaking and film-watching to enhance, and be enhanced by, our act of doing theology.

25. Ibid., 67.
26. Ibid., 73.

Ben X tells the story of Ben (Greg Timmermans), a high school student with Asperger's syndrome, a form of autism, which, throughout his life, has complicated his relationships with family members and made social interactions at school all but impossible. Passed around from doctor to doctor, all of whom pronounce a variety of explanations for his condition (he's either stressed, special, or mildly psychotic), his mother (Marijke Pinoy) and father (Pol Goossen), struggle with whether or not to keep him in a mainstream educational system once they finally learn that he is indeed autistic. His mother believes alternative educational opportunities are necessary, but his father disagrees, citing Ben's intellectual superiority over his peers. His father wins out, but, unfortunately, school becomes a living hell for Ben. The teachers are ill equipped to meet his needs while the students brutally bully him.

Ben's life becomes especially difficult in high school when two bullies, Bogaert (Titus De Voogdt) and Desmet (Maarten Claeyssens), take a particular interest in him. They tease him mercilessly, calling him a faggot and a retard. They constantly shove and hit him. After class one day, they take the punishment to another level, lifting him up onto a desk and forcing him to stand there while they pull his pants down. The rest of the students join in the jeering and break out their cell phone cameras to capture all the "fun." The videos immediately go viral. The school is essentially powerless because Ben will not tell on Bogaert and Desmet for fear of violent repercussions. Ironically, the school forces Ben's mother to take him for further medical evaluation. A few days later, not satisfied with their domination, Bogaert and Desmet take Ben to a park where they continue to harass him, physically attack him, force him to take a hallucinogen, and spit on his face and in his mouth. This pushes Ben to his breaking point

As a means of escape from his daily torment, Ben plays ArchLord, a massively multiplayer online role playing game (MMORPG), for hours each day. He has mastered the game on two levels. First, as a gamer, he has reached level 80, earning powerful abilities and the respect of other players, and second, as a participant in a social network, he has befriended a female avatar/player, Scarlite (Laura Verlinden). In this respect, contrary to popular fears about the danger of violent video games, ArchLord serves a therapeutic function for Ben. He can escape to this virtual world to take out his anger and frustration on orcs and dragons. However, while playing, he develops and is nourished by his friendship with Scarlite. Back in the "real world," the structure of the game helps him make sense of his day-to-day experiences. He views Bogaert and Desmet as over-powering orcs that he must avoid, but when he has finally had enough of their bullying, he crafts a weapon like the one his in-game character, Ben X, uses. However, unlike his virtual prowess in ArchLord, he realizes that violence will not solve his real world problems.

After learning of his troubles at school, Scarlite tells Ben that she wants to meet him and will be arriving at his train station the next day. Although Ben goes to the station and sees Scarlite from a distance, he cannot bring himself to talk to her. However, her willingness to reach out to him empowers and moves him. Having seen Scarlite in person, she becomes an imaginary friend with whom Ben converses about his experiences and his desire to put an end to his suffering. The two hash out a plan to take revenge on everyone who has wronged him. Scarlite reminds Ben that he cannot succeed on his own and convinces him to form a guild like they do in ArchLord. Having worked out the details of his plan with Scarlite, he finally tells his parents that he wants their help to commit suicide. However, this will be no ordinary suicide. Inspired by the Jesus narrative, his video game experiences, and Scarlite, Ben plans a death and resurrection that will not only convict the violators but also teach a powerful lesson to the community in the process. With the help of his parents, Ben stages his suicide and funeral. With family, teachers, students, and members of the press gathered at his funeral, Ben interrupts his headmaster's eulogy with a pre-recorded video. In this video, he includes footage of his humiliation in the classroom. The students in attendance, many of whom were caught in the video making fun of Ben, cannot hide from the on-looking adults and news cameras. Ben emerges from the church balcony and walks among his tormentors, triumphant at last.

Throughout *Ben X*, director Nic Balthazar weaves images of the story that I have just recounted with documentary footage of interviews with Ben's parents, teachers, and doctors, all of whom reflect on Ben's life, his "suicide," and the events that lead to it. We are to take these images as part of a documentary on teen suicide and bullying that a journalist created after Ben successfully staged his death and resurrection. These scenes reveal the toll that Ben's abuse took on his parents and even a couple of his teachers. On the other hand, in terms of the latter, the interviews reveal the school system's inability (or unwillingness?) to address the brutal environment in which Ben lived. Throughout the documentary footage, Ben's mother says, "Someone always has to die first. Then everyone wakes up. But by then, it's too late." Here, she sums up the school system's delayed reactions to acts of violence, particularly bullying. Moreover, in flashbacks to Ben's childhood years at school, teachers constantly scream at him, "What's wrong with you?!" None of them, even in the interviews, ever pause to consider what is wrong with an educational system that allows such bullying to take place. The doctors that "treated" Ben along the way are just as ineffective. Most of them simply dismiss his experiences of school violence. The doctor that finally makes the Asperger's syndrome assessment says, "Bullying. That shouldn't happen, but it does."

Ben X is a perfect conversation partner for Suchocki's *The Fall to Violence* for a number of reasons. In fact, Suchocki even selected it as one of the films for the 2008 Whitehead International Film Festival, which she chaired. First, it reveals the complexity of sin in the human experience and the lack of well-being as a criterion for it. Second, it highlights our capacity for self-transcendence through memory, empathy, and imagination. Finally, it reveals a complex understanding of forgiveness that, while not naming it as such, involves the imaginative creativity necessary, as Suchocki argues, to break cycles of violence.

Violence is the central sin in *Ben X*. Bogaert and Desmet mercilessly bully Ben. The violence they enact is both verbal and physical. They consistently call him a "fag" and a "retard" while they shove, hit, and spit on him. In their most humiliating act, they strip him in front of the class for all of his classmates to see. However, the effects of their violent behavior towards Ben transcend the actual moments in which they take place. Their bullying creates an oppressive atmosphere that forces Ben to live in fear, even when Bogaert and Desmet are nowhere to be seen. This ever-present fear further complicates Ben's already heightened discomfort in social settings as a result of his autism. Although we do not see it in the film, if Bogaert and Desmet are this unforgivingly ruthless towards a peer that suffers from a social disorder, there must be no limits to the objects of their bullying.

Bogaert and Desmet's torturing of Ben reveals a singular aspect of violence, that is to say the ability of one person to harm the well-being (physical, emotional, psychological, or spiritual) of another. However, it also reveals the complicity of society, both as a group of people and institutions, in those singular acts of violence. When Bogaert and Desmet force Ben to stand on the desk in class before they pull down his pants, nearly everyone in the room cheers them on. When his pants come down, they cheer even louder. In this scene, Balthazar turns his camera on two other students who stand on the periphery of the activities. They do not join the other students in taunting Ben, but they do not attempt to stop them either. One of the non-participants records the events, keeping his camera on the students making fun of Ben, an act that will help Ben in the future. His reluctance to attempt to physically stop Bogaert and Desmet could result from the fact that they consistently bully him too, frequently calling him a "faggot." Doubtless he fears the retribution that would most certainly follow should he try to intervene. Nevertheless, every student in the classroom is guilty of participating in the humiliation of Ben; however, their levels of guilt must vary given the lengths to which they participate in it. So while the two students might not be guilty, explicitly, of humiliating Ben, they are complicit in it because they do not attempt to stop it. The other students, especially those whose camera phones create the videos that go viral, must account for a higher degree of guilt. Furthermore, their use of this technology, which increases the social aspect of this sin by spreading a confined event to the broader world through emails and blog posts, makes their participation even more egregious.

There is yet another social aspect to the violence that Ben endures. The social structures/institutions of medical, psychological, and educational systems fail Ben miserably. Though it might be more tenuous to do so, we could suggest that Ben's family structure fails him as well. Ben's father fails to see that his son requires a specialized educational system and that, while he many be intellectually superior to his peers, his inability to function highly on a social level makes the ordinary educational setting a living hell for him. His father vetoes his mother's attempts to stand up for him and ensure his well-being by having him change schools. At the same time, Ben's mother seems to be far less pro-active than the situation requires. She too easily kowtows to inept medical and educational systems. Though she is highly defensive and protective of her son, she never puts that to "productive use" until the end of the film.

The real culprits here, along with Bogaert and Desmet, are the participants in the medical and educational systems, doctors, teachers, and administrators. None of them are especially intelligent or imaginative, and all of them seem to take the easiest path in "dealing with" Ben. In fact, they all attempt to simply "deal with" rather than help, treat, or protect Ben. In flashbacks to Ben's younger days at school and experiences at hospitals and clinics, the doctors and teachers are often as violent and insensitive as his peers who mercilessly tease him. Doctors poke and prod him or yell at him when he does not respond to their questions. Teachers yell at Ben when he will not participate in group activities. As Ben ages, though teachers are less violent towards him, their complicity in his ill-being is perhaps heightened. Apathy and ineptitude rule the (school) day. The doctor that finally realizes that Ben has Asperger's simply dismisses the fact that he is bullied at school. He never imagines a specialized future for Ben, encourages his parents to seek alternative educational systems, or confront the school administrators about Ben's situation. Though one or two of Ben's teachers stand up for Ben, this only heightens his awkwardness and fuels the bullies' fire even more. Moreover, they never effectively punish Bogaert and Desmet. In fact, these teachers seem to be afraid of them too. Ben's headmaster simply turns a blind eye to Ben's tormenters. He knows full well that Bogaert and Desmet have been tormenting Ben, but he "needs" a confession from Ben to fully prosecute them, a confession he will never get because it would only enhance Bogaert and Desmet's hatred of Ben. To make matters worse, the headmaster even suggests that Ben's mother take him for further psychological evaluation.

Taken together, Ben's experiences at the hands of his abusive peers and apathetic "guardians" underscore the prevalence of violence and sin, and the complexity of them, in so many high school students' experiences today. Yet, like Suchocki, the author and director of *Ben X* is not without hope. For Suchocki, this hope is the human capacity for self-transcendence that can lead to forgiveness. Though *Ben X* does not name it as such, the film includes elements of Suchocki's emphasis on self-transcendence, namely through memory, empathy, and imagination, that leads to forgiveness.

To put it quite bluntly, Suchocki's emphasis on empathy does not apply to Ben. It is almost unimaginable to ask Ben to be empathetic towards his tormentors, especially since he has such difficulty with social relationships in the first place. However, Bogaert and Desmet's abuse of Ben is as clear an example of the failure of empathy leading to violence as one could ask for. Bogaert and Desmet are the epitome of non-empathetic individuals. They never once ask or imagine what it would be like to be in Ben's shoes. Because they never empathize with him or imagine the effects of their abuse, they are "free" to continue in it. That it could or would ever lead to Ben's suicide never crosses their minds. In fact, even when it appears that Ben has committed suicide, they express no remorse or guilt. At the funeral service, they seem to be there out of a sense of obligation, as if they have been forced to go on another boring field trip.

Though Ben has difficulty in social situations, he does have an active memory and a vivid imagination. He keeps his past experiences of doctors, students, and teachers at the front of his mind and both rightly and wrongly remembers how he has been treated. That is to say, these memories haunt him as his mental repetition of past abuses further enhances their violent effects upon him. On the other hand, they help him navigate his day-to-day existence. He knows to be skeptical of teachers and doctors, especially when it is apparent that they are taking the easy way out. He knows which students to avoid and which (precious few) students he can trust.

We could also see Ben's participation in ArchLord as a form of self-transcendence. While the gameplay allows him to take out his frustrations in a virtual world, while in that world, he establishes a relationship that his physical limitations would prohibit in person. Furthermore, he is able to transcend and navigate his daily experiences by recalling time spent in this virtual world. As theologian Marion Grau commented, "What is especially powerful is the fact that the dying and rising of characters in the video game becomes something [Ben] can translate into social reality."[27] He can envision his daily preparations for school as equipping his avatar to go into battle. He views certain school settings as game worlds where he must avoid larger opponents (orcs/bullies) rather than fighting back. Of course, the game has a negative influence when it inspires him to enact violence himself by making a dagger from a crucifix. Yet his attempted use of this weapon is purely out of self-defense and not a preemptive attack.

It might also be possible to view Ben's staged suicide as an act of self-transcendence. In discussing how he plans to kill himself with Scarlite,

27. Grau, "Comment post on 'Creative Gaming.'"

she tells him that he is too intelligent to simply throw himself in front of a moving train and even makes fun of the ways in which other people kill themselves (drinking poison or hanging themselves). She tells him that he has to "rise above it all" and to even "rise above [himself]." She knows that his death can mean so much more and that to make it meaningful he must devise a creative plan. In the process, he seeks out the help of his parents and turns his oppressors' strategies (particularly viral video) against them by filming his own "suicide."

Ben X does not include the word "forgiveness" nor does it portray Ben or his family forgiving his tormentors. In fact, it would have seemed trite to do so. Yet what *Ben X* does offer is a glimpse of the necessary steps toward forgiveness, ways to break the cycle of violence in which Ben has suffered and naming that suffering and identifying those complicit in it. First, the entire stretch of documentary footage is prophetic in that Ben's mother, primarily, names what happened. Although she never uses the word sin, she does assert, like Suchocki, that the events did not have to happen, people were responsible, and there could have been an alternative way. Other participants in the documentary confess their complicity, or at least shortcomings, in those events. This video is likely to become a viral reaction to the viral abuse that Ben endured.

The suicide stunt that Ben dreams up with Scarlite is itself a creative response to violence. It brings attention to the suffering-unto-death that many teenagers experience without actually resorting to suicide, an ultimate act of violence against the self. We could easily envision ways in which Ben could imagine and enact violent responses to Bogaert and Desmet, perhaps fueled by his participation in ArchLord. As I have already discussed, he tries to meet violence with violence but fails . . . it is not for him. His fake suicide brings the failures of the medical and educational systems to light in vastly more effective ways. His singular voice from "beyond the grave" demands a transformation of the social structures that sent him to his "death" in the first place.

Like Suchocki's *The Fall to Violence*, *Ben X* leaves lingering questions and is open to some criticism. Though we hope that Ben's imaginative plan will change things at his school, we should remain skeptical. In the film's conclusion, it appears that Ben has been removed from this school. While this will no doubt promote his well-being, what of Bogaert and Desmet? Are they still free to terrorize their weaker classmates? Furthermore, why do Bogaert and Desmet bully other students in the first place? Are they victims of abuse themselves? Finally, how have the medical and educational systems responded to the documentary video that recounted all of these events? Of course, we could also see these "shortcomings" as strengths. The film offers no explanation for Bogaert and Desmet's behavior, because, oftentimes, evil is inexplicable. While creative responses to violence might break one cycle of it, another cycle somewhere else will begin to spin out of control.

The film also inspires questions that will no doubt contribute to fruitful discussion in both the congregation and the classroom. Who or what is God for Ben? How do school systems deal with mental differences within the same schools; within the same classroom? What caused Ben to strike out, or attempt to strike out, against Bogaert and Desmet? Are video games the culprit or was Ben simply re-enacting the violence under which he had suffered?

While the idea of refocusing sin as primarily an offense against creation and secondarily against God might unsettle more conservative believers, in a frequently more interconnected world, this view is increasingly important. "Someone had to die or you wouldn't have come. It had to stop," says Ben's mother in one of the concluding lines of the film. With ever-present news of teen suicide and (cyber)bullying, we wonder when the violence will ever stop in our own schools. Furthermore, we can no longer ignore the ways in which our virtual connections intensify this violence. Nor can we ignore or dehumanize the real victims of our behavior by claiming that this violence is first and foremost an offense against God, because when watching *Ben X*, it is difficult to view anyone other than Ben as the chief victim in his experiences. *The Fall to Violence* and *Ben X* remain fitting texts in both the classroom and the congregation, especially among adolescent and teenage viewers who need both fresh visions of the implications of their behavior and hope for a better future. The narrative of Ben's experiences of violence and his creative response to it, born out of a sacred narrative, an MMORPG, and an "imaginary friend" is an inspirational alternative to the world in which he, and so many like him, live.

3

De Profundis . . . Out of the Shallows . . . Enter the Void

PETER MALONE

BEFORE THE WARNER BROS logo has faded at the beginning of *The Rite* (2011), a voice asks, "Do you believe in sin?" In a film about demonic possession, that seems a reasonable question. But, what of films that are not quite so religiously explicit, or not explicit at all? Does the question apply?

In the early 1990s, a group of German theologians associated with OCIC, the International Catholic Organization for Cinema (established 1928), tackled this issue of films that portrayed the darker areas of human nature, questions of sin and possible redemption, even when characters were groping for it, sometimes without quite realizing what they were crying for. Was redemption possible and were these films authentic and serious human dramas? One of the key films in the discussion was Abel Ferrara's *Bad Lieutenant* (1992).

The German discussions led to the rediscovery of the opening of Psalm 130, already used by Oscar Wilde for the title of his Letter from Reading Prison. The psalm begins,

> Out of the depths [Latin: *de profundis*], I cry to you, O Lord,
>
> Lord, hear my voice!

O let your ears be attentive
to the voice of my pleading.

If you, O Lord, should mark our guilt,
Lord, who would survive?
But with you is found forgiveness,
for this we revere you.[1]

Bad Lieutenant is a useful film for discussing the De Profundis theme. Director Abel Ferrara has a Catholic education background. There is explicit Catholic imagery in the film. A nun from Poland has been raped in the sanctuary of a New York Church. Harvey Keitel plays the bad lieutenant of the title. He is a corrupt man, alcoholic and drug-addicted, a gambler who is in debt to criminals. Frustrated when the nun will not name her assailants, he comes to a peak moment of desperation. He hallucinates in the aisle of the church, howling his despair in four-letter frankness. He sees an image of the crucified Jesus (whom the audience has seen when the crucifix moves into live action during the nun's rape ordeal, clearly showing her as a suffering Christ-figure). The lieutenant demands to know where Jesus was in all his troubles, screaming and whispering, "Where were you?" He crawls towards Jesus, weeping and repeating, "I'm sorry." It is a hallucination because the figure is actually a church cleaner. It is a cinematic equivalent of Eduard Munch's The Scream. But, this sequence, especially for OCIC and for its successor, SIGNIS (The World Catholic Association for Cinema, established 2001), has become an emblem sequence for what can be called De Profundis films.

This discussion and use of De Profundis terminology and ideas became important not only for Catholic theologians and film students but also for the inter-church collaboration for juries at international Film Festivals. While OCIC and then SIGNIS have their own juries (for example in Venice, San Sebastian, and in Latin American countries), since 1973 in Locarno and 1974 in Cannes, Catholics and Protestants have worked together in Ecumenical Juries in Berlin, Montreal, Karlovy Vary and further afield in Ukraine and Armenia. Some jurors began to ask whether ecumenical awards should be made to films that could be characterized as De Profundis films.

1. Richards, *The Psalms: A New Translation*.

One of the earliest examples of this context for discussion was *Bad Boy Bubby* (1993) in the OCIC jury in Venice in 1993. An Australian drama, the film won the international jury's director's award. It also received a commendation from the OCIC jury. But, not without some wrestling with the film. An Italian member of the jury, who assumed he had some Vatican authority, went immediately from the critics' screening to complain to the festival director that the film was "beastly" and "unethical." However, the other members of the jury wished to consider it for an award. On reflection, one sees that there was a desire for some compromise because the prize went to Kieslovski's *Three Colours: Blue* (deservedly) and the commendation to *Bad Boy Bubby*, some members of the jury praising the film but feeling it was still not the kind of film to give the top prize to. Interestingly, three years later, the 1996 jury (including the Italian member again) worked a different compromise. They made an award "ex aequo" to another Abel Ferrara film, *The Funeral*, and to Jacques Doillon's more obviously worthy story of a grieving child, *Ponette*. Two years later, another Italian was complaining to Church authorities about the OCIC juries' choices of dark films for awards.

In 1999, John Paul II made a telling contribution to the discussion: "Even when they explore the darkest depths of the soul or the most unsettling aspects of evil, artists give voice in a way to the universal desire for redemption."[2] This makes it clear that De Profundis applies to film about sin and redemption:

> Because with the Lord there is mercy
> and fullness of redemption.
> Israel indeed he will redeem
> from all its iniquity.[3]

However, the case of *Bad Boy Bubby* widened the discussion. The Bad Lieutenant himself was responsible for his own depths situation. Bubby was not. He was a victim of a slatternly mother who had imprisoned him in a basement from childhood, threatening him with God's punishment if he moved out. This time the person in the depths was innocent but still needed saving from the viciousness and ugliness of the depths. Bubby does emerge and find a happier, more grace-filled life.

2. John Paul II, "Letter to Artists."
3. Richards, *The Psalms: A New Translation.*

Before considering the biblical background for exploring the De Profundis films, it is worth noting a further reflection, a clarification of the depths of such films. Not all films are as dark as *Bad Lieutenant* or, say, the *Godfather* trilogy or some of Martin Scorsese's films like *Cape Fear* or *The Departed*. People do live their lives, which can have many miserable moments, in a less profound way. This is not to underestimate the pain and suffering, but it is a reminder that so many lives are lived in the shallows rather than the depths. But, from those shallows, there is a similar cry.

The film that suggested this distinction between depths and shallows was *Waitress* (2007). It is a film about women who worked in local diners. One of them, played by Keri Russell, is subjected to physical abuse by her husband (Jeremy Sisto). Again, she was the innocent victim who needed salvation rather than redemption. It seemed useful to include, "Out of the Shallows" with "Out of the Depths."

A further development of these considerations came with the very grim film from Gaspar Noe (who had made one of the most De Profundis French films, *Irreversible* (2002)). His long and tortuous drama, *Enter the Void* (2009), made reference to the Tibetan Book of the Dead, the Japanese belief in ghosts and a pessimistic view of life. The Void was the name of a Tokyo nightclub where much of the action takes place. *Enter the Void* was a reminder that some films are so pessimistic about life and human nature as to be nihilistic. Characters do not get out of the depths, they are not redeemed. Their destination is the void or, as will be seen, in Graham Greene's *Brighton Rock*, Hell.

With the use of Psalm 130, the range of biblical stories and references becomes important for interpreting the De Profundis films, whether the central characters have made moral choices which have led them into the depths or whether the central character is a victim in depths. A useful starting point is the parable of the Prodigal Son (Luke 15:11–32). Jesus, in his storytelling, seems to be keenly aware of the depths.

The younger son is clearly the character who makes the poor moral choices. He is willful in demanding his inheritance, seemingly ungrateful as he leaves home, a licentious wastrel (according to the final accusation of his older brother) with little sense of responsibility. Jesus describes his "depths" as complete personal degradation. Not only was he doomed to feeding the unclean animals, the pigs, but he was willing to eat pig's slop but no one would give him any. Then, out of the depths, comes the realization that his father is a good man and that he can return and throw himself on his father's mercy. The lavish treatment of his lost son by the father who becomes prodigal in his abundant gifts of love and reconciliation becomes the paradigm for Christian forgiveness of those who come out of the depths. It is not as if the younger brother is the only one who cries out. The older son is, in view of his depiction, expresses an angry anguish "out of the shallows," without his quite realizing it. He is resentful, jealous, single-mindedly narrow in his outlook towards his father, his brother, his work and even the servants. His prodigal father is no less loving in coming out of the house to plead with him for love and for kindness and the lavish phrase, "everything I have is yours." Redemption is certainly possible, according to this story and so many like it (the woman who was a sinner in the city in Luke 7:36–50, Zacchaeus in Luke 19:1–10, the woman taken in adultery in John 8:1–11 and even Peter himself after his denials in John 21:15–19). And Jesus himself is the perfect symbol of those who cry from the depths even though they are innocent. Whether it be the different versions of Jesus' temptations in the wilderness, his agony in the garden of Gethsemane or his cries of abandonment on the cross, Jesus endures De Profundis experiences.

In fact, the Old Testament offers many stories where (generally) men turn against God but their cry of repentance is heard. In the Deuteronomic history, two examples stand out. The first is Samson (Judges 13–16) who succumbs to the wiles of Delilah but whose prison experience and change of heart are symbolized by his growing his Nazarene hair again and, in the rather wild times and moral certainties of the period of the Judges, brings the temple of Dagon down on the Philistines and on himself. Many filmgoers have vivid images of this via Cecil B. De Mille, Victor Mature and Hedy Lamarr in the 1949 epic film, *Samson and Delilah*. There was a remake with Belinda Bauer and Anthony Hamilton (1984) and it was reprised for the biblical series by Elizabeth Hurley and Eric Thal (1996). John Milton immortalized this struggle in his Samson Agonistes.

The other personality who brought to life an awareness of profound sin, accepting responsibility and profound repentance was David. The sentiment of Psalm 51, attributed to David, is one of the most profound expressions of this De Profundis cry. The details of David's lust and adultery, his conniving to have Uriah killed in battle, are not shirked. His grief at the death of his child and then the revolt by his son, Absolom, indicate that one does not come out of the depths unscathed. A winning characteristic of Hebrew storytelling is that there is no false honoring of those in authority and command as being beyond sin. All are sinners and that must be acknowledged. David's story is also familiar from screen versions, from that of Gregory Peck in *David and Bathsheba* (1951) to Jeff Chandler in *A Story of David* (1961) to Richard Gere in *King David* (1984), to Nathanael Parker in the biblical series (1997).

This heritage was brought to bear in the Creation narrative in Genesis with the emblematic story of the sinful nature of human beings with Adam and Eve, temptation, the serpent, the apple and the desire to eat of the tree of the knowledge of good and evil. Adam and Eve are thrust out of the Garden of Eden into the depths of self-consciousness, awareness of sin, and a life of pain and toil. John Huston's *The Bible: In the Beginning* (1966) offers a literally quaint vision of Adam and Eve.

In the light of this heritage, we move into the New Testament. As has been noted already, the narratives, which seem to be variations on the prodigal son theme, mean that key figures of the Gospels have De Profundis experiences, which their choices have brought on themselves. The woman of John 8 faces stoning for being caught in the act of sinning but Jesus makes the point that only those who have not sinned have the right to cast stones. This scene is shown in most of the Jesus' films. In *The Greatest Story Ever Told*, rather a more austere presentation of Jesus than most, Jesus actually makes his statement—and then throws a stone, but not at the woman. He is entitled to throw stones but he does not throw them in punishment or vindictiveness. The sequence in Zeffirelli's *Jesus of Nazareth* where the woman intrudes into Simon's banquet has Robert Powell showing genuine amazement at the woman's behavior and a profound expression of love and forgiveness.

But, one of the people closest to Jesus illustrates this theme. It is the brash Peter. After proclaiming loudly that, even if everyone else were to run away from Jesus, he never would. Within a short time, he has denied Jesus three times. He is in the depths, weeping bitterly. John's Gospel dramatizes his repentance. He dives from his fishing boat in haste to swim to Jesus on shore and is asked three times to affirm his love for Jesus. Jesus, like the father in the parable of the prodigal son, reaches out to prodigal Peter. Franco Zeffirelli and his writer, novelist, Anthony Burgess, understood these links well. In *Jesus of Nazareth*, Peter is taxed by Matthew and resents him. When Jesus goes to eat with the tax collectors and the prostitutes, Peter refuses to accompany him. However, he does come to the door, hears the parable, spoken beautifully by Robert Powell, is moved and then comes in (like the older brother in the parable) and is reconciled.

While these biblical stories indicate the reality of sin and cries from the depths of the heart as well as the infinite capacity for loving forgiveness by God, it is the stories of those who suffer for others that reinforce the awareness of this love.

Going back into the Old Testament, we appreciate the suffering of Job, his faith being tested as he is reduced to the bottom of the depths in terms of his possessions, his status, his health, and his humble place before God (expressed in his final prayer of submission and silence in the face of God, Job 42:1–5). Perhaps his story served as a model for the experiences of the prophet, Jeremiah. Jeremiah is mocked, ridiculed, put down a pit and spat on. He is bewildered because he is the prophet who was consecrated by God in the womb and, though young and inexperienced, was given God's words on his mouth. He was able to speak of the heart of flesh that would replace the heart of stone in the people. He could not understand why he should suffer and why "sinners' ways prosper." Yet, all the while, no matter his despair, he could always say to God, "I commit my cause to you."

This kind of trust is reprised in the stories of Tobit, Esther, and Daniel. It is also the emotional words of Psalm 22 (which Jesus repeats on the cross). But, "I commit my cause to you" is also the cry of the archetype of innocent suffering, the Servant of the book of Isaiah. The progress of faith and commitment through the four 'songs' of the servant illustrate how the innocent servant, called and beloved by God and offering God's message in gentleness, who is listened to but who becomes the butt of insult and injury and who is led by the hand, finally, like a lamb to slaughter. But, the fourth song brings in the key theme (almost 600 years before the coming of Jesus) that this suffering is vicarious suffering. The servant's suffering is for all, in the place of all. While the people of that time did not have a clear idea of life after death, they could still express hope that there would be some kind of "resurrection" and "glorification" for the servant. This comes to a peak in Daniel 7, when the glorious Son of Man comes into the presence of the Ancient of Days to receive the reward of total fidelity.

It is these themes that pervaded the minds of the early Christians. When they began to find ways to write down descriptions of Jesus, they went to the Servant Songs and the Son of Man passage from Daniel. They used direct quotations, during Jesus' trial for instance, from the songs and 1 Peter reprises the quotations about Jesus suffering for our sins. In the Acts of the Apostles, the story of Stephen's martyrdom is modeled on the Old Testament stories of martyrs (Eleazar, the seven brothers in the book of Maccabees) as well as on the passion narrative of Jesus—which means that, from a Christian perspective, there is a repentance perspective and a redemption perspective that can be brought to films which can be described as out of depths as well as out of the shallows. With the realization that a number of stories, novels, plays and films, do not include repentance or redemption but are, to that extent, nihilistic, we come those stories where the characters "enter the void."

Again, it is worthwhile to go back to the biblical narratives because there are stories there where the characters seem to have nowhere to go but into the void. In returning to the Deuteronomic History, we find that the principal void character is Saul. Chosen to be the first king of Israel, beloved of Samuel who anointed him, he is a man of moods, grudges, and superstitions. When he does not obey God's injunctions through Samuel, especially about the treatment of enemies (which seems brutal in the light of later understandings of vengeance and punishment), he consults the witch of Endor. He becomes jealous of David and tries to kill him with his javelin, resents the military triumphs of David and the people's acclaim. Finally, defeated in battle that he brought on himself, he requests that his servant kill him. There are no words of redemption even though David mourns him.

Still in the Deuteronomic History, we have the history of Solomon. Solomon's fate is all the more regrettable since he began his reign so well and faithfully. In his dream, Solomon is rewarded with a wise and discerning heart (1 Kgs 3:5–15). The queen of the south comes to Jerusalem to acknowledge his renown. It is Solomon who is able to build the temple (something his sinning father, David, was not able to do) and dedicate it. But, as time went on, he becomes more "worldly." He makes trade agreements, which included as one of the ratifications, the taking of a bride from the foreign nation (and which included her bringing her gods to Jerusalem), a kind of practical apostasy. His death is spoken of in brief but deadly dismissive words, "his heart was not wholly with Yahweh his God" (1 Kgs 11:1–8). Solomon went into the void achieving immortality only in the heritage of his wisdom and the attribution of so many books to him. A reputational redemption but not a personal redemption.

These issues had been well understood by the time that Genesis 1–11 was written. While Adam and Eve could find redemption, the themes of depth and void became clearer with the stories of their sons, Cain and Abel. Abel is the innocent victim. Cain, on the other hand, refuses to repent, is branded with his "mark," and is exiled to the void, popularized in twentieth-century literature and film, "east of Eden."

In these same chapters, there are stories of faithless people who refuse to acknowledge God and suffer fates that could be described as voids. The men and women of Noah's time are drowned in the floods of the deluge. Later, the presumptuous people will try to build a tower to reach God at Babel, but God confounds them with the void of confusion of tongues. Again in *The Bible: In the Beginning*, John Huston dramatized both the deluge (with himself as a kind of ringside Noah with the animals) and Babel with an effete Stephen Boyd firing an arrow into the air to reach God and failing. There is a more sober presentation of these events in the Bible series, *Genesis* (1994), with Omero Antoniutti as Noah.

There are several characters in the New Testament who enter the void, the void being described as Hell or Gehenna, where there is wailing and gnashing of teeth. The rich man, Dives, in the parable in Luke 16:19–31, finds himself in Hades with no hope of crossing into the bosom of Abraham, and not even the hope of a drop of cold water on his tongue to relieve his torment. The man without the wedding garment suffers a similar fate (Matt 22:1–14) as do those on the left of Jesus, the goats, who have refused kindness and service to those in need. They go to the place reserved for the devil and his angels (Matt 25:46). In The Acts of the Apostles, 5:1–11, Ananias and Saphira, lying about their fraud are struck dead with no possibility of repentance.

But the New Testament personality who embodies going into the void is, of course, Judas. Better if that man had never been born. After betraying Jesus, flinging back the thirty pieces of silver at the disdainful Sanhedrin, he hangs himself. Although it is so familiar, this story of Judas, a man so close to Jesus himself, is one of the most powerful enter the void stories.

Because it is so dramatic, even traumatic for Jesus and the disciples, the film versions of Judas explore all kinds of motivations from greed (the Gospel of John's interpretation, John 12:4–7), to political and religious disillusionment with Jesus not being the kind of leader he expected (like the attitudes of the disciples on the road to Emmaus, Luke 24), to a controller of Jesus. This latter is evident in Scorsese's *Last Temptation of Christ*. Mel Gibson portrayed Judas' death, after his clash with the children, in graphic style in *The Passion of the Christ* (2004). Judas has a film of his own, *Judas* (2001, released 2004 after the success of *The Passion of the Christ*) and was immortalized, rock opera style in both the film (1973) and concert performance (2000) of *Jesus Christ, Superstar*. His lyric is, "Damned for all time." A variation on this damnation was the surprising and inventive screenplay of *Dracula 2000* where Dracula is, in fact, the embodiment of Judas, with flashbacks to his betrayal of Jesus.

What remains is to look at some key Out of the Depths, Out of the Shallows, Enter the Void films in the light of the biblical background. It is not fanciful to be linking a film, even a commercial Hollywood movie, to Christology or to be using it as a source for theological understanding. A short statement made by the bishops present at the First Vatican Council, 1869–70, highlights this (though a more modern translation is desirable): "Reason, indeed, enlightened by faith, when it seeks earnestly, piously, and calmly, attains by a gift from God some understanding, and that very fruitful, of mysteries; partly from the analogy of those things which it naturally knows . . ."[4] The other ways for fruitful insight are from the relations the mysteries of faith bear to one another and to our final destiny.

Our stories, our cinema stories, relate and dramatize "analogies" (metaphors, images, symbols) of those things which reason naturally knows. What follows is a reflection on several films that illustrate the cries from the depths and the shallows and entering the void.

From a religious and theological point of view, Graham Greene has shown himself a master of desperate religious cries. Film versions of two of his most profound cries were released in the first half of the 1950s soon after the publication of the novels. They were *The Heart of the Matter* (1952) and *The End of the Affair* (1955). *The End of the Affair* was remade in 1999.

---

4. Neuner and Roos, *The Teaching of the Catholic Church*, 36.

In *The Heart of the Matter*, District Inspector Scobie is a convert to Catholicism with a Catholic wife. When he begins an affair with a young woman, he does not want his wife to know or to be hurt so he accompanies her to Mass and receives communion sacrilegiously. He has gone to confession but has not been given absolution because of his unwillingness to end the affair. He goes to communion in a state of mortal sin. He is prepared to risk damnation because of his feelings for both his wife and mistress. His situation does not get any better and he commits suicide, prepared to go to hell rather than hurt those he loved.

In the present state of a theology of sin, repentance, and grace in Catholic teaching, there would be greater nuances than Greene drew on in the 1940s and 1950s. This makes his De Profundis cries the louder and more harrowing. Since Scobie's choice is for hell, it means that he is prepared to enter the void of Hell, the same destination of choice for Pinky Brown, a far more callow character, as will be seen with *Brighton Rock*.

But, in his next novel, *The End of the Affair*, the De Profundis cry turns towards God instead of Hell. Sarah Miles has been in a relationship with writer, Maurice Bendrix. She is married and knows that she is betraying her husband. Her crises comes (in an event that seemingly Greene himself experienced) when a bomb hits the building where she and Bendrix have met. These events take place during the war. When Sarah discovers Maurice dead, her De Profundis cry is for him. She asks God for his life. Her pledge is to break off the affair when he recovers. God hears the prayer.

Bendrix meets Sarah's husband who thinks she is seeing someone. Bendrix hires a detective to follow her. In fact, she is seeing a priest and receiving instruction in the Catholic faith. When Sarah dies, she is perceived as a kind of saint and exercises miraculous powers of healing, especially for the son of the private detective.

Scobie goes to hell. Sarah Miles goes to heaven. The affairs end in opposite directions. Greene is offering in these two novels, possibilities for desperate cries to be heard and the choices the protagonists make. The screenplay for Neil Jordan's 1999 version of *The End of the Affair* goes a Greene-like step beyond the novel. Sarah risks damnation for breach of promise to God by agreeing to begin the affair again. This version acknowledges the realities of human weakness and sin. It is out of these depths in the newer version, that Sarah finally makes her decision for God.

This can be seen in *Get Low* (2009) where an old solitary man (played by Robert Duvall) decides he wants to celebrate his funeral while he is still living. But the deep reason for this is his sense of shame for what he did forty years earlier. He wants to confess to the townspeople and ask their forgiveness, a positive cry from forty years of depths.

With these De Profundis films, the central characters have made deliberate choices to enter the depths. With so many films, as with the archetypal Job story, the characters are victims of the behavior of others.

Hitchcock made a somewhat dour film in 1956 with Henry Fonda, *The Wrong Man*. Fonda is mistakenly identified as a criminal, arrested, imprisoned, and seemingly trapped though innocent. The title, *The Wrong Man* (woman), could be seen as archetypal for this kind of story. There are Catholic overtones to this film. Fonda's character and his wife are Catholic, so the cry is made to God. A film with a similar theme but secular is *The Fugitive* (1993), with Harrison Ford as a man wrongly accused of crime, who, out of the depths, has to listen to his own cries and pursue truth and his justification himself. This leads to a personal and secular justification. But, the depths can be no less profound than the more explicit depths.

Another kind of De Profundis story is found when the individual does not make sinful choices with a need to repent or when the individual is victimized. This is the kind of story where individuals and/or communities are overwhelmed by traditions and customs that they have inherited and need (whether they are explicitly aware of it or not) that they are oppressed and need to be freed from these depths. This is the enslavement or exile experience reminiscent of the Hebrew people trapped in Egypt and experiencing an Exodus or of the later exile of the people in Babylon needing mountains being laid low, valleys filled and straight paths being made through the desert for a return home and liberation.

There are not many films that come from Albania. American Joshua Marston read of the centuries old traditions of feud amongst the population, heard of stories of how the feud impositions controlled some villages and families and created a story of people longing for some breakthrough and freedom from these murderous traditions. His film was called, symbolically, *The Forgiveness of Blood* (2011).

We hear accounts of how the unwritten law of feuds has been handed down orally since the later Middle Ages. There are prescriptions for punishment of offenders by the offended family and the community. *The*

Forgiveness of Blood has a contemporary setting, the years after the collapse of Communism. The youngsters at high school with their mobile phones, taking photos and texting is not the way of the previous generations.

When the father of the central family attacks the son of another family and he dies, the whole family comes under feud laws. The father is banished. The male children are confined to their house. The women are free to move about and the livelihood of the family depends on them. In fact, the young daughter of this victim family discovers her talents for management and selling. But, the little boy has to stay at home, receive tuition from a teacher who comes to the house. The older boy, of senior high school age, finds his home imprisonment too much to bear. His is the articulate De Profundis cry on behalf of the whole family.

The film is about his maturing and trying to find other ways of bringing the feud to an end and having his father able to return to the family. His solution is that he must give up his family and his way of life and go into exile himself. Once again, he hears his own cry and opts for a desperate solution to the situation.

Another very powerful and complex film with these themes is the Oscar nominee for Best Foreign Language Film, *Incendies* (2010). Set in an unnamed Middle East country (a thinly disguised Lebanon), the film operates in two time zones. In the first, a woman is almost killed for shaming the family (Christian) by having a baby out of wedlock. Later, the woman joins a rebel group, assassinates a right-wing leader, is imprisoned where she is raped and gives birth. The film opens with the reading of her will to her twin children. She sets them a mission to find their father. This is the culmination of her cry from her depths. The children discover more than they ever want to know, horrifying for the audience as it is for them. But, the final letter to her children is not a cry for vengeance (as well it might) but a deep plea for forgiveness and reconciliation.

In moving to a consideration of cries "from the shallows," we see the same categories of stories: the cry of the person who has made the willful choice, the victim of another's wrong choices, the pressure of tradition and community that people have inherited.

A useful example, but one which many audiences could find tedious, is Sofia Coppola's *Somewhere* (2010). Actually, the title could be *Anywhere*, or even, *Nowhere*. This is where the character of Johnny Marco, a famous Hollywood movie star, lives or, sometimes, just exists. Johnny's life is the

Hollywood dream and nightmare. He is popular. He has wealth. He has easy access to women. Despite turning up for press conferences, for publicity jaunts to Italy, for make-up tests, he is a lazy and idle man. But, he has opted for this kind of glamorous drifting life. As the film progresses, and Johnny seems merely to grow in self-indulgence, there is increasing niggling dissatisfaction. The person who hears his unarticulated or subconscious articulation of his shallows plight is his young daughter, Cleo. Though separated from his wife, he does make time for his daughter. There is a bond between the two. If he has a lifeline that will draw him out of his shallows, it is his daughter, a common-sensed and practical little girl who is shrewder than her father thinks.

Sofia Coppola, daughter of Francis Ford Coppola, knows what she is filming about. She had been caught up in it since she was a little girl. The Hollywood emptiness of *Somewhere* serves as a microcosm of shallow cries of discontent and for help.

The Thanksgiving holiday in the United States is a time not only for gratitude for benefits but a time for family gathering and reconciliation. This is a theme that is used as the occasion for many a family film. An appealing Thanksgiving film is *Pieces of April* (2003). With its theme of preparation of a Thanksgiving dinner and celebration of unity through shared food and drink, it also echoes Eucharistic themes.

April is a young woman living in an apartment in New York City, somewhat alienated from her parents. She is one of those victims (not desperately so) of parental disapproval and critique that leads to the young people moving out. The preparation of the dinner is April's cry from the shallows for some approval from her parents, some acceptance. When things go wrong with the cooking, with the stove, and with the preparations, April enlists the help of her multi-ethnic neighbors and grows a little in maturity herself. The reconciliation takes place.

To return to the theme of cries that come from those who are burdened by the traditions and cry out to one another and beyond, this is the experience of everyday life in suburbia or in a country town. British director Mike Leigh is a master at this kind of film. His titles indicate this: *Secrets and Lies* (1996), *All or Nothing* (2002), *Happy Go Lucky* (2008), *Another Year* (2010). Leigh takes into the depths and shallows of humdrum. *Another Year* is a fine example of this kind of film. Gerry and Tom have been married for forty years. She is a social worker. He is an engineer. Their son is about to be engaged.

It is because Gerry and Tom are good people, dependable in their work, devoted at home, that desperate people tend to gravitate towards them, expecting the couple to listen, to take them in, to solve their problems. "Oh, God," is a commonplace response. Gerry has worked with Mary for twenty years. Mary makes messes of everything, especially relationships, misreading responses, overdoing her emotions and dependency, driving most people away except Gerry. Tom is visited by an old friend who is out of work, overweight, ageing, and a drinker wanting to be dependent. Later they have to cope with Tom's brother and his bitterness, his wife's funeral and his irascible son. These are the shallows of everyday life. Gerry and Tom's way of responding is through basic human decency and kindness.

A different religious response is seen in *Le Grand Voyage* (2005). A Muslim family, originally from Morocco but settled in France, is at the centre of the film, especially the grandfather who decides he wants to make the Haj. *Le Grand Voyage* reminds audiences that it is not only the younger generations in Christian families that live a-religious lives with a-religious attitudes. It can be the same for the younger men and women of Muslim families and those of other world faiths.

In this story, it is one of the grandsons who is designated to drive the grandfather to Mecca. Not only is the young man resistant, he has no feel for the pilgrimage at all or its meaning. Grudgingly he drives the car. They get lost. They are robbed by a con man. The roads are difficult. As we expect, the young man changes. He does not necessarily undergo a conversion experience, but he learns some respect for his grandfather and observes what the pilgrims do and feel. His life is the equivalent of a Muslim "Somewhere." And his grandfather has recognized the unarticulated cry from the shallows.

The nihilistic films where there is an anguished cry, either shallow or deep, often indicate that the storytellers think that evil can triumph over good. We see so many gangster and crime films where the conscienceless characters exit this world violently seemingly without any hope, through the gates to hell.

Returning to Grahame Greene, there have been two versions of his *Brighton Rock,* one in 1947 where Greene himself, with playwright

Terence Rattigan, wrote the screenplay, a second in 2010, written by the director, Rowan Joffe, who wanted to offer a new interpretation rather than a remake.

Pinky Brown is a petty criminal in England's holiday coastal town, Brighton, famous for its pier and its confectionary, Brighton Rock. Greene wrote in 1938, highlighting crime in the 1930s. The film was released in the immediate aftermath of World War II and its continued rationing and austerities. The new version has located the action in 1964, the era of Mods and Rockers and bikers.

The other character is Rose, a waitress in one of the many cafes in Brighton. She seems a mousy type and is easily attracted to Pinky who is a charmless go-getter in the 2010 version and has been commissioned by his bosses to recover a photo of Rose taken on the pier which has a picture of the boss. Pinky uses Rose's Catholic devoutness as a means to lead her on. He proposes that they marry. She is torn between her conscience and Catholic teaching and her love for Pinky. Like Scobie who was yet to come, Rose is prepared to go through a marriage ceremony in a registry office risking hell, even though she has gone to church and prayed.

When Rose and Pinky talk about their faith, Pinky's grim outlook is that there is a hell and that is most probably where he is ultimately going. He has no truck with ideas of heaven. Pinky dies at the end without any redeeming features whatever. His cry is directed towards himself and his need for success and survival, but he goes into the void that is hell.

In the novel, Pinky's detestation of Rose is finally revealed to her, deliberately trying to make her life on earth her hell. In the film version, Pinky has made a record at Rose's insistence on the pier. He encourages her to think that it is a declaration of love. When she is confined in the home for unmarried mothers, she borrows a record player. The audience, in anticipation, dreads what will happen when she hears it. But the needle sticks on the words, "I love you," part of Pinky's taunt that he did not. Rose, despite the record, is not voidbound.

The person who chooses to go into the void, like Pinky Brown, must be to some extent what we call mad, insane. Possibly one of the best known of such characters in popular writing and popular films in recent decades has been Hannibal Lecter. Played three times by Anthony Hopkins (*The Silence of the Lambs* (2001), *Hannibal* (2000), *Red Dragon* (2002)), his image comes into people's imaginations when the name is mentioned. (Brian

Cox played him earlier in Michael Mann's *Manhunter* (1986) and Gaspard Ulliel in a prequel to his adult career in *Hannibal Rising* (2007)).

The sinister calm and clarity of Hopkins' Lecter, his meticulous use of logical argument, his outward courtesy to Clarice Starling were all the more shocking because of his conscienceless relish in describing the physicality and detail of his killings and cannibalism. Hannibal Lecter is one of many in the gallery of cinema villains and unrepentant opters for evil who remind us that the only place where they will be at home is Hell or the void.

A living hell is the destination and destiny of Rosemary in *Rosemary's Baby*. Seduced by her husband and impregnated by Satan, Rosemary is the victim of the New York coven and their Satanic worship. Her cry when she discovers what has happened to her is from the most harrowing depths. But, at the end of the film, she goes to the pram draped in black and looks at the demon baby and finds that she must love the child she bore. Her hell has come to earth in a mockery of the incarnation of Jesus.

These films illustrate the emptiness or darkness of the void. However, there is a strand of storytelling that is positive in the face of nothingness after death. This might be an ultimate void but the path through life is where nobility and excellence is to be found. The existentialists of the 1950s and 1950s faced this question. A fine example of this in a novel, and in Lucchino Visconti's film version, is Albert Camus' *The Outsider* ("*L'Etranger*"). Life should end, so to speak, with a dignified bang rather than a whimper.

To return at the end to the words of John Paul II, "Even when they explore the darkest depths of the soul or the most unsettling aspects of evil, artists give voice in a way to the universal desire for redemption."[5]

---

5. John Paul II, "Letter to Artists."

4

Recalling Jesus

Form, Theory, and Trauma in Jesus Cinema

MICHAEL LEARY

Trauma and Memory

A RECENT STUDY AT Washington University in St. Louis has demonstrated that viewing emotionally traumatic images after taking a test increased participants' ability to remember newly learned information.[1] We generally assume that our minds shield us from trauma by erasing shocking or burdensome details from our memories, and would expect that such imagery would dull the process of recall. But surprisingly, this research indicates that there is a formative link between traumatic emotion and the process of remembering. Identical studies using positive images did not yield the same results. While this research is about the actual process of information retention and retrieval, it is a handy illustration of a few of the basic assumptions at play in a subset of memory theory that focuses

---

1. Fitzpatrick, "Shock and Recall."

on the way traumatic events are stored, recalled, and translated into cultural artifacts.[2]

A dominant trend in trauma studies has claimed that "massive trauma precludes all representation because the ordinary mechanisms of consciousness and memory are temporarily destroyed."[3] From this perspective, recollections of trauma are impossible to represent and events like the Holocaust or 9/11 are doomed to persist in history without any authentic witness. The trauma itself eclipses our ability to recollect and represent it in any accurate fashion; what may appear to be collectively therapeutic is really just a form of dissociation. However, a more recent alternative approach to the representation of trauma in literature, film, and the arts argues that "A more innovative approach is to re-insert history into the psyche and try to understand trauma as a cultural and historical phenomenon."[4] It may be the case that representations of past trauma are not only possible, but they are actually an organic feature of the development of culture through a history littered with tragedy.

Trauma and Cinema

This growing body of theory is particularly relevant for the study of cinema, which has expanded our critical ability to understand the psychological and historical forces at work in representations of the Holocaust, but also has become relevant across multiple genres.[5] And more significantly, trauma theory has provided tools that enable us to distinguish between good and bad examples of historical memory. In such cases we find things like *Schindler's List* opposed to *Shoah* as bad and good examples of remembering the Holocaust.[6] We tend to think of traumatic experiences as private affairs that reveal themselves in later in spasms of our psyche that can only really be interpreted by psychologists. The classic image is one of Freud's patients that survived a horrific train crash only to suffer later from various psychological ailments, the trauma in this case represent-

---

2. A few representative examples include: Bennett and Kennedy, *World Memory*; Felman and Laub, *Testimony*; and Caruth, *Unclaimed Experience*.

3. Leys, *Trauma*, 266.

4. Kaplan and Wang, "From Traumatic Paralysis to the Force Field of Modernity," 8.

5. Such as Kaplan, *Trauma Culture*; and Lowenstein, *Shocking Representation*.

6. Hansen, "'Schindler's List' Is Not 'Shoah,'" 292–312.

ing itself after the fact in unrelated, inaccessible terms. But the central concern in this recent critical discourse is a recovery of representations of trauma as a valid space in which we can individually and collectively remember tragedy. It critiques the private, dissociative understanding of processing trauma as "considerably impoverished as a tool of critical historical analysis by being relegated to an exclusive ineffable privacy on the one hand, to the mystery of fate on the other."[7] In this essay, I would like to draw together a number of these recent theoretical themes and argue that they provide promising avenues for progress in the study of Jesus cinema.

Trauma, Cinema, and Jesus

The connection between the study of Jesus and the study of historical memory is a burgeoning field of study at the moment.[8] It is a natural progression to begin applying some of this focus beyond the representation of Jesus in the Gospels to representations of Jesus in the cinema. Jesus cinema is, after all, the act of recalling specific social, theological, and narrative elements of the life of Jesus as recorded and/or reframed in the many Gospels circulating throughout the first and second centuries. But it is a very specific form of recall in that it is shaped by passage through the traumatic memory of Jesus' death, which has given the passion narrative its profound theological gravitas. According to Kari Syreeni, "What in the Gospels seems grief work for Jesus, is actually a multilayered and mixed phenomenon. The writing of the Gospels was not directly occasioned by the original, concrete bereavement, but by a more recent *symbolic* loss, which set off a secondary, both *ideological* and *literary* grief work."[9] In the same way that the canonical Gospels are burdened by the historical memory of Jesus' trial and death, so is Jesus cinema inherently framed by this trauma of loss and absence and its array of possible representations.[10]

7. Kaplan and Wang, "From Traumatic Paralysis to the Force Field of Modernity," 8.

8. Two good entry points into this large body of literature are Thatcher, *Jesus, the Voice, and the Text*; and Dunn, *Jesus Remembered*.

9. Syreeni, "In Memory of Jesus," 194.

10. A common objection is related to the way that the Gospels modify this trauma by concluding with the resurrection. But Syreeni's essay tracks the various ways in which the Gospels process the grief of Jesus' death and subsequent absence, which are a necessary prelude to the more triumphant conclusions of Luke, Matthew, and John. It argues that the absence of Jesus following the ascension was a significant emotional component of the development of early Christian theology.

It is also a very specific form of recall in that it takes place in the cinema, thereby subject to the broader theoretical discussion about how things are filmed. It is a bit difficult to think of Jesus cinema this way, as it forces us to talk about it as cinema—as a matter of pacing, composition, and structure. Excepting discussion of films like *The Passion of the Christ* or *The Gospel according to St. Matthew*, Jesus cinema is rarely subject to this kind of film-theoretical scrutiny. I think this is the case because discussion of Jesus cinema has struggled to find a point of access to actual aesthetic discourse. But the potential connection suggested in this essay is provided by trauma studies, which has been successfully applied to other forms of cinema dealing with issues of history, memory, and representation. This critical discourse is fitting in this context because it enables us to engage the formal elements of Jesus cinema with an eye toward understanding how we recall traumatic experiences, and more specifically, how we reframe them within the formal elements of cinema itself.

In order to interact with the language of trauma studies, a brief reading of two relevant films will follow. Neither of these films are what are typically considered Jesus films, in that neither specifically derive from the text of the canonical Gospels. And frankly, at a surface level, they have little to do with the life and times of Jesus of Nazareth. But I have selected these examples because of their oblique relationship to the canonical narrative. They are themselves stories about trauma that happen to refer to Jesus as a formative, parallel paradigm of trauma. In this process of recalling the death and absence of Jesus as an iconic form of trauma, we can see a few interesting facets of what it means to remember Jesus in cinema terms. Not simply to remember him in the sense that we are reciting points of historical detail contained in the canonical Gospels, but to actually recall the great weight of tragedy that permeates the passion narrative.

La Vie de Jesus (Bruno Dumont, 1997)

Despite the directness of its title, Bruno Dumont's *La Vie de Jesus* is not a Jesus film. And if it weren't for the title, there is no way that even an informed viewer would connect this to the life of Christ in any fashion. Over the last decade, critics have rightly interpreted Dumont's penchant for confrontational imagery in the context of his overall humanistic concern with intimacy, loneliness, and the raw poetry of human relationship.[11] *La vie de Jesus*, which caused quite a stir, falls neatly within such a reading.[12]

In an interview, Dumont explained that he took the title from Ernest Rénan's book of the same name, saying: "I had the desire to tell the life of Jesus. Not to repeat what everybody knows . . . I invented a story to regenerate the meaning, to show that there is a humanism in Christianity that they don't teach in the Church, in the schools."[13] For Rénan and Dumont, Christ is a "poetic expression of the human tragedy."[14] This vaguely rewritten "Life of Jesus," attempts to retread Jesus' expression of humanity in the life of Freddy, an unemployed French teenager who divides his time between caring for his pet finch, playing in a local marching band, and hanging out with a girl that lives in this same lower class provincial French neighborhood. There is a scene in a hospital toward the beginning of the film during which someone points out a faded medieval print of Jesus raising Lazarus. This brief flicker of divinity, one of few direct references to the biblical narrative, soon peters out beneath the slow pace of Dumont's gravely meditative filmmaking.

Freddy eventually kills a boy who has been flirting with his girlfriend and the film ends as quietly as it began, leaving one to wonder where Jesus was other than the flat image medieval image in the hospital. Yet Dumont claims: "Without the title, the film loses something. It is a very mystical film. Film has the power to touch something mysterious in the body, its secrets."[15] Beyond the materialist context posed by Rénan's reading of Jesus' life, there is a very film theoretical background to Dumont's statement. Dumont sees film as a way of regaining contact with the body, with the physical, in such a way that contradicts the disembodiment that has come to characterize commerce and advertising in the information age.

Dumont's representation of Jesus serves as the background against which Freddy's tragedy occurs, thus merging this trauma enacted by Freddy with a greater sense of historical gravity. But this complex form of Jesus remembrance takes place within the context of Dumont's inter-

---

11. cf. Falcon, "*La Vie de Jesus/The Life of Jesus*," and Hughes, "Bruno Dumont's Bodies."

12. *La vie de Jesus* includes a few brief sequences of an erotic nature that were very controversial when the film was released.

13. Walsh, "Interview with Bruno Dumont."

14. Ibid.

15. Ibid.

est in disembodiment. In essence, the title creates a certain expectation for the presence of Jesus in the film, which never actually occurs. As a result, the slow movement in the film towards murder is attended by the formal disembodiment of Jesus, as we move from the title of the film to the realization that Jesus is not actually going to return. This interplay between secrecy and revelation put into play by the title calls to mind the work of Kelber and Kermode on the Gospel of Mark. On Mark, Kelber says: "the gospel encourages experimentation with a new logic in defiance of received opinion. Secrecy, or as I prefer to call it, mystery results from a disorienting-reorienting narrative which forestalls closure."[16] Likewise, Dumont's film ends darkly, in a shadow, disconnected from the expectation of its title. The viewer is invited to consider the traumatic implications of this absence, which have been embodied in the film by Freddy and his girlfriend. This is not to say that Freddy's story recapitulates the narrative of Jesus, but that it serves as the contemporary circumstance within which the grief of the Gospels can be recalled and observed as an emblematic trauma for the information age.

To return to the description of a dominant brand of trauma studies above, Lowenstein notes the modernist trend in trauma studies is to achieve representations of trauma that serve as monuments to historical tragedy. But these monuments are always a shell game, as they are ultimately forms of dissociating from the raw details of the actual events. He goes on to point out that, "When this desire reaches its extremes, however, when traumatic experience becomes solely equated with the 'unrepresentable,' then this respect for victims/survivors transforms, paradoxically, into a silencing of both experience and representation."[17] What makes Dumont's film so interesting as an example of recalling the trauma of Jesus is that Jesus is never even represented in the film. But this does not mean that Dumont is expressing Jesus' trauma as something "unrepresentable," and thus stripping it of its ability to actually speak. Rather, Dumont's film capably transfers the core of the Jesus trauma, which is his Markan absence, directly into his film. Jesus is not unrepresented here, he is completely absent. Here, this absence can only be perceived by considering the overall form of the film itself.

16. Kelber, "Narrative and Disclosure," 1–20.
17. Lowenstein, *Shocking Representation*, 4.

Last Days (Gus Van Sant, 2005)

A loosely fictional account of the day before the suicide of Blake, the lead singer of a famous grunge band, *Last Days* is an extended meditation on the death of a thinly veiled stand-in for Kurt Cobain. It is a passion play in the truest sense of the term, each scene the stop on a walk through the "stages of the cross." Van Sant's methodical pacing follows Blake in a series of dramatically lengthy tracking shots set in and around a ramshackle mansion owned by him and group of hipster musician friends currently sponging off Blake's celebrity. But sown throughout, there are hints of Veronica, the Garden of Gethsemane, and the paralyzing fear of the disciples after the death of Christ. At the end, Blake commits suicide, and in the one non hyper-realist image of the film, his wispy soul can be seen leaving his body and climbing a window frame into heaven.

In previous films, Van Sant has explored the narrative quality of prime-time media images and CCTV footage. The epilogue of *Last Days*, which grafts the famous MTV coverage of Cobain's suicide over Blake's death, links this theoretical tendency in Van Sant to the references to Jesus' life made throughout the film. The point of comparison between Blake and Jesus is the hagiography that has developed around both in the wake of their death. Van Sant films Blake within the narrative framework of Jesus' passion and resurrection not because he wants to impose a redemptive significance on Kurt Cobain's life, but because just as our readings of Jesus as a man get lost in the shuffle of the Christology vindicated by the resurrection, so did the media fail to penetrate Cobain's personal suffering. This image of ascension signifies Blake's worth as a person over and against his worth as a cultural icon. It is an utterly human image, an iconography of pathos that robs Cobain's death of its purely cultural overtones and recasts it in the dignity of anonymous suffering. And, of course, this is all very early Albert Schweitzer.[18] Here we see a different

18. Referring to the famous passage: "There is silence all around. The Baptist appears, and cries: 'Repent, for the Kingdom of Heaven is at hand.' Soon after that comes Jesus, and in the knowledge that He is the coming Son of Man lays hold of the wheel of the world to set it moving on that last revolution which is to bring all ordinary history to a close. It refuses to turn, and He throws Himself upon it. Then it does turn; and crushes Him. Instead of bringing in the eschatological conditions, He has destroyed them. The wheel rolls onward, and the mangled body of the one immeasurably great Man, who was strong enough to think of Himself as the spiritual ruler of mankind and to bend history

iconography of Jesus being developed, in which he is co-opted as a first-century media figure who presages fallen media figures of our age.

But there is a great deal of trauma in this film that derives from the raw shock of Cobain's suicide. We referred earlier to a famous patient of Freud that survived a tragic train accident only to experience a number of psychological issues at a later point in time. This disconnection between the traumatic event and its actual effect were part of Freud's overall description of the dissociating effect of trauma. While I have been resistant to accepting this sense of dissociation as the key factor at play in the process of recalling trauma, there is a sense in which this formal dislocation is an important part of the process: "The shuffling between individual psychic trauma and historical shocks (suggested by Freud) needs to be read as symptomatic of the modern process in which the individual is atomized, cut off from an active role and stripped of agency in history."[19]

Here in *Last Days*, this atomization occurs. It occurs first within the Blake's suicide narrative, and then in the flight of his friends from the mansion upon this discovery. But it is represented as a form of trauma by Van Sant in three ways. First, the minimal form and careful composition of the film depict Blake within each frame as disconnected from the background. Excepting one unexpected musical interlude, he passes through the film as if already dead. Second, the final transcendent image that contradicts the preceding naturalism of the film disconnects Blake as a meaningful agent in history from history itself. His ascension is a recovery of value, dignity, and substance that from Van Sant's perspective only exist outside of the confines of his film. But third, Van Sant explicitly connects Blake and Jesus by framing these as Blake's *Last Days*. From the very beginning of the film the cultural memory of Cobain's suicide and the memory of Jesus' death are intermingled, and we do little other than wait for the Blake/Jesus parallels to tragically align. As with Dumont's film, *Last Days* becomes a formal space in which a specific aspect of the tragedy of Jesus' death is recalled and woven into the fabric of its overall effect.

---

to His purpose, is hanging upon it still. That is His victory and His reign." (Schweitzer, *The Quest of the Historical Jesus*, 368–69).

19. Kaplan and Wang, "From Traumatic Paralysis to the Force Field of Modernity," 8.

Recalling Jesus

The preceding is posed as an invitation to consider the presence of Jesus in cinema in a different way. By borrowing from a critical discourse that has emerged as a way to talk about the representation of trauma we can begin to talk about Jesus films in a way that allows us to refer to cinema itself, and the odd forms by which cinema recalls the history of Jesus. This approach to the presence of Jesus in film has several benefits:

First, it focuses the discussion. Trauma and memory studies enable us to coordinate representations of Jesus in cinema with relevant conversations in film theory and history. There is little discussion of formal film issues in Jesus cinema, which would assess the different ways Jesus' story is composed, structured, and paced in film. This discussion becomes possible when we can understand these basic cinema elements as formal strategies of recalling the emblematic trauma at the center of his biography. The great struggle of Jesus cinema is the same struggle that directs trauma studies—it is the struggle to represent something that we feel is not able to be represented. The Markan shape of Jesus' absence is hard to comprehend in both historical and psychological terms, but cinema seems to be able to comprehend it in an effective way.

Second, it broadens the discourse. Jesus cinema should not be limited to the current canon, which is largely populated by rote translations of the Gospel accounts into film. There are many films that think of Jesus as a tragic figure that haunts our representation of personal and historic trauma, and as exemplified by Dumont's and Van Sant's films, these films can recall important elements of the canonical Gospels that are difficult to represent in other terms.

Third, it does justice to the material. In the same way that the application of memory theory to the study of the Gospels and the historical Jesus have opened up the way we understand the transmission of his biography, so can the application of trauma studies to Jesus cinema expand our ability to understand and engage contemporary acts of Jesus recollection. These acts of reference and remembrance may occur in unexpected cinema forms, but thinking of these appearances of Jesus as a form of traumatic recall is a critical activity faithful to the experience of the Gospel authors. If the representation of tragedy in cinema often verges on a form of dissociation from the historical reality of trauma, it is intriguing to think that the forms of Jesus in cinema serve a space in which the horrors of history can be addressed in culturally transformative ways.

Section II

From Light to Light:
Grace, Forgiveness, and Community

5

Embracing Failure and Extending Grace in a Digital Age

Viewing *The Social Network* and *Catfish* Theologically

J. SAGE ELWELL

MY FIRST ENCOUNTER WITH a social network was at a Kansas funeral home in 1986. I was ten years old and my grandfather had just passed away. In the days that followed, I learned that a social network is a group of family and friends that help organize estate sales, go to the grocery store for you, walk your dog, water your plants, and bring you casseroles. These were the people that held us when we cried and laughed with us when crying was too hard.

Back then a social network was a small community of people that surrounded and supported you. It included neighbors, aunts and uncles, little league coaches, pastors, and teachers. We saw the people in our social network at the store, at school, and at church. We trick-or-treated at their houses, had pizza parties together after games, and complained about their lawns. The social network was an emotional and spiritual base where horizontal relationships branched upward toward a greater whole, perhaps even something sacred. Much has changed since then.

In 1986 Mark Zuckerberg was two years old. Seventeen years later he would create one of the most popular web sites in the world and revolutionize the idea of the social network.[1] Now, with more than 600 million users from around the globe, Facebook is the face of our network culture. We have traded the holiness of human contact and the spiritual sustenance of authentic communion for the ease of constant connection and the safety of weak-ties and performative identities. This chapter explores the theological dimension of this exchange of one social network for another in two films about Facebook.

The Social Network is a fictional retelling of the birth of Facebook in the dorm room of Harvard undergrad Mark Zuckerberg (Jesse Eisenberg). The film gained popular and critical acclaim, earning an Academy award nomination for best film due in part to director David Fincher's layered cinematic storytelling and screenwriter Aaron Sorkin's slinging dialogue. *Catfish* is a low-fi independent documentary about a real-life long-distance romance between New York City photographer Nev Schulman and Megan Faccio, a small town girl from Minnesota who only ever existed as a Facebook profile. *Catfish* did well on the festival circuit, but drew only marginal popular attention in the box office and was thus significantly overshadowed by its fellow Facebook film.

These two movies invite conversation and comparison. Thematically, both films are about inclusion and connection in the age of the digital network. Inclusion here describes the experience of being a part of a whole, a member of something bigger than one's self. Connection refers to the unique inter-personal relationship that develops between two people.[2] Unfortunately, the protagonists of these two films mistake the one for the other. In *The Social Network*, Mark mistakes the inclusivity of Facebook for real connections with other people. And in *Catfish*, Nev mistakes his Facebook connection with Megan for inclusion in the dynamic whole of a real relationship.

1. Throughout this chapter I use social network in the singular to describe Facebook in particular, but also the entire matrix of today's digitally networked culture that Facebook represents.

2. I acknowledge that inter-personal connections occur between more than two people, however in the films (and therefore in this essay) the focus is on a single individual's ability to connect to another person.

Mark and Nev thus model a typical confusion in today's digital culture. That is, on the one hand, being included in a digital network without any actual connections to the people that make up that network. And on the other, being digitally connected to someone via the network without the authenticity of inclusion in the greater flow of actual human relationships. The cause for the confusion is an absence of failure and grace. Unlike the social network I experienced after the death of my grandfather, today's digital network is valenced against an ontotheology that embraces human failure and encourages ameliorative grace.

The following unfolds these ideas in three sections. The first section addresses *The Social Network* and how we mistake digital inclusion for authentic connection. The second presents *Catfish* and how we mistake digital connection for genuine inclusion. The third section brings these first two together for a concluding comparison that penetrates to the broader theological and cultural dimensions these films suggest. In this section I conclude that the digital nature of today's social network refuses to embrace the fallible being of human being and the concomitant grace this calls for, an embrace, which I claim is essential to the integration of connection and inclusion at the heart of a genuine social network.

The Social Network

Aaron Sorkin's screenplay for *The Social Network* was inspired by Ben Mezrich's unauthorized and libelous book, *Accidental Billionaires*. Though the film does follow a basic arc of agreed-upon events surrounding the creation and popular explosion of Facebook, it remains a work of fiction. And perhaps the film's biggest invention is Mark's girlfriend, Erica Albright (Rooney Mara), who we meet in the theme-establishing opening scene.

The film opens in a dark Harvard bar with a five-minute volley of rapid-fire insults between Mark and Erica. The dialogue between them patters like a pinball as Mark opines over which of Harvard's exclusive blue-blood final clubs he'll join until Erica finally dumps him. She baldly explains that "Dating you is like dating a stairmaster." As she storms out of the bar and Mark is left sitting awkwardly alone, the thematic tone of the movie is set. The breathless headlong pacing, the cold staccato of back and forth insults, and the vertigo-like sense of a near total collapse, all coalesce in Mark's obsessive insecurity and desperate hunger for inclusion.

Jesse Eisenberg plays Mark with his unique brand of soft-faced, head-down, shuffling shyness that has made him a go-to actor for loveable geeks. But here his usual nebbish posture is saddled with a brilliantly unforgiving arrogance that suffers the ignorance of others with only red-hot contempt. The combination makes for a Mark Zuckerberg that is at once a horrible jerk and yet lovably vulnerable in his complete social ineptitude. As a stand-in for today's networked everyman, this lends both his anxiety and callousness a familiar sense of insecure humanity in a digital age.

Fincher wants his audience to see the limits of life in the network embodied in its most celebrated creator, a shifty and awkward Eisenberg. Beneath the shadow of his perpetual hoodie, Mark's eye contact is spotty, he lacks a sense for the flow of genuine dialogue, he talks in the stop-go mechanics of unfiltered blog-speak, and he refuses to acquiesce to subtlety or nuance, insisting instead on interpreting everything absolutely literally.

Every moment for Mark is a zero-point, an isolated blip of thought or line of code without any sense of connection to anything else. In this, his tetchy personality mirrors the antiseptic utility of the binary logic he works in. Not surprisingly then, the social network he creates is similarly sterile and reflects his impulse for inclusion, but at a distance.

This distance is captured cinematically as Mark hurriedly shuffles back to his dorm room after Erica dumps him. In a series of drawn-back wide shots that frame the darkened Harvard campus, Mark is isolated and alone as he muddles through clumps of socializing students. He is clearly one of them and yet also clearly not. As he walks up the steps to the entrance of his dorm the camera captures him from behind with a shallow depth of field, figuring him in focus and yet removed, like one of Caspar David Friedrich's *rueckenfiguren*, where presence is always an absent presence. And as he walks into his dorm, Trent Reznor and Atticus Ross's dark soundscape begins to rise like a storm.

In the film, the social network functions as the symbolic counter to Mark's Harvard experience. Harvard, with its ex-girlfriends and final clubs, is elite, hierarchical, historical, location-specific, and private. The social network, with its linked-loose construction, anywhere and everywhere geography, and digitally open ethos, represents Mark's challenge to the exclusivity of all that that passed him over. The network's sprawling web of links undermine the rigid grid of walls that make exclusion possible.

In *The Moment of Complexity* Mark C. Taylor contrasts this webbed network with the walled off grid. He writes "Whereas walls divide and seclude in an effort to impose order and control, webs link and relate, entangling everyone in multiple, mutating, and mutually defining connects in which nobody is really in control. As connections proliferate, change accelerates, bringing everything to the edge of chaos. This is the moment of complexity."[3] As Taylor explains, networks are defined by the fluidity of ever-expanding connections whereas grids form rigid structural divisions that isolate and exclude. However, in excluding all that falls outside its walls, the gird simultaneously includes all that is within. Thus the grid is a model of inclusion/exclusion and the network is a model of connection. To claim then, as I am, that Mark mistook inclusion for connection is to claim that he mistook the network for a grid.

It is easy to mistake the network for a grid. We do this when we stand in relation to the network as a whole, but not in relation to any of the people that constitute that network. Here, the network exists as a single entity, an object that we stand in a one-to-one relationship with, rather than an organic complex of discrete and dynamic relationships. Sherry Turkle's book *Alone Together* features an interview with a college student who, when asked about his sense of the network, explained, "I feel that I am part of a larger thing, the Net, the Web. The world. It becomes a thing to me, a thing I am part of. And the people too, I stop seeing them as individuals, really. They are part of this larger thing."[4]

This kind of total inclusion is incredibly seductive. It offers the promise of involvement without the demands of intimacy or vulnerability. When we do this our friends become fans and our profiles become a performance of our identity. We can join any number of different groups without ever actually knowing any other members and conversely we can organize our friends into groups they will never know they are in. As Taylor points out, grids offer order and control, and taking the network itself as a grid puts us in the center of a massive matrix of inclusion. However, when we do this the connectivity and transparency promised by the networked culture of web 2.0 dissolves into digital anonymity.

3. Taylor, *The Moment of Complexity*, 23.
4. Turkle, *Alone Together*, 168.

For Mark, and many like him, this combination of inclusion and anonymity is comforting. Over dinner at a swanky California restaurant, the snakey Sean Parker (Justin Timberlake), creator of Napster and web entrepreneur, embodies a new future of inclusion without connection. He knows everyone, but is known by no one, he is the life of the party, included in everything, yet connected to nothing. And like Brad Pitt to Edward Norton in Fincher's *Fight Club*, Sean's slick and easy way with everyone and everything radiates as Mark's alter ego. Over dinner Sean dazzles Mark with what Facebook could become, with who he could become, and persuades him that "private behavior is a relic of a time gone by" and Facebook is the natural progression in the "true digitalization of your life." Digitization, however, is a move away from the truth of life in which we need both connectivity and inclusion.

To actually digitize something involves two steps. First, whatever is to be digitized must be sampled. Sampling is usually done at regular intervals to convert continuous, analog material into discrete data. For example, pixels converts a continuous image into a pixilated grid. Once sampled the image exists as distinct units. In the second step, each unit is quantified by assigning it a numerical value from a predetermined range. In the case of a 16 bit color image, that range is 0–65,536. Once sampled and quantified, the image is digitized. Appreciating this is important because it shows how digitization is essentially an act of abstraction.

Digitization is abstraction in that it involves abstracting from the particularities of the real, which exist as contiguously given, in order to realize their idealization as bits of data. Whatever is digitized then exists as an abstraction from the real in that it is perfected through the universality of quantification. Once fixed, numbered, and coded all differences fall away in the totality of the grid. As Taylor observes, "the figure of this all-encompassing logic is the grid."[5] It is all-encompassing in that its economy of straight lines and right angles transforms the complexity, subtlety, or ambiguity of any particularity into discrete parcels of a totalizing whole. In the 16-bit color range there is no difference between the 4 bits for red in a Van Gogh and the 4 bits for red in a McDonalds ad.

Digitization brings both unity and uniformity to its object in the form of the perfect, error-free precision of digital code. Thus the "true digitalization of your life" means comporting the complexity of analogue

5. Taylor, *The Moment of Complexity*, 30.

being to the intimacy-free security of technological inclusion. For a generation that would rather text than talk, this is an easy choice.

In the film, Mark, who clearly serves as a token stand-in for this generation of net-natives, mistook inclusion for connection and regarded the network as a grid. Unlike the heavy Harvard reality from which he was excluded, the inclusion that Mark realizes is simple and precise without the burden of other people. And just as the brightness of Silicone Valley contrasts with the darkness of Boston, so too does the weight of connections with actual people contrast with the light paucity of inclusion in a gridded network. This is because inclusion in the digital age is as easy as the click of a button. There are little to no demands of time or energy, to say nothing of vulnerability or faith. Part of this is because, as Mark experienced in the film, inclusion in the social network is consuming and total.

There is nowhere where the network is not and thus exclusion is impossible. In the film, when Facebook programmers are writing code they are described as being "jacked-in." There is nothing else, only the code. Increasingly, we live our entire lives "jacked-in." Through smart phones, texting, email, Skype, and instant messaging, we live our lives inside digital social networks in a state of perpetual inclusion. This could be likened to the agapic love of God that is total and absolute, all encompassing and without distinction. This is a love of the whole without regard for the parts. A love that is always on. Inclusion, or love, on these grounds is comfortable and reassuring but it lacks the elements of particularity that constitute real connection. It is like the digital code that reduces and abstracts all details through digitization, covering everything in a blanket of encoded sameness. There is no sense of genuine knowing and being known as "this one here." There is only the easy inclusion of the digital embrace.

Section II: *Catfish*

Where Mark mistakes the inclusivity of the digital network for real connections with other people, *Catfish'* s Nev Schulman mistakes his Facebook connection with Megan for inclusion in the dynamic whole of a real relationship. However, Nev's willingness to accept fallibility, both his own and others, redeems his mistake and points to an integration of inclusion and connection in a deeper embrace of an ontotheology of human failure and retributive grace.

Catfish begins with the arrival of a package for Nev. Nev is a thirty-something photographer from New York City where he lives and works with his brother Ariel and their mutual friend Henry Joost (who co-directed the film). Together they have been documenting one another's lives non-stop for years. The package Nev received contained a painting from eight-year old Abby Wesselman from rural Michigan. The work was an ungainly reproduction of one of Nev's published photographs. Flattered nonetheless, Nev and Abby find one another through Facebook and Nev eventually befriends Abby's entire family, including her mother Angela and her attractive older half-sister, Megan. The connection between Nev and Megan was immediate. Thus what began as Ariel and Henry's record of a quirky relationship between a New York City photographer and a child-artist turned into an accidental documentary about Nev's cross-country love affair with Megan.

Unlike *The Social Network*, a film about Facebook that intentionally did not feature the actual website in any meaningful way, *Catfish* impressively combines Facebook posts and tags, Youtube clips, and Google Earth to tell a twenty-first century new media story. Other than these imported online features, the film is shot almost entirely on hand-held cameras, which often makes for a jarring inbreaking of an analogue element in an otherwise digital tale. This, and the soundtrack of ambient noise, lends an immediacy to the events that play out as scenes are neither framed nor staged, but rather spill out in an unpredictable collage.

Throughout the film we see only what Nev sees. Like voyeurs, we peer over his shoulder, knowing only what he knows. There is no storyteller or omniscient perspective. We learn about Megan along with Nev as he scrolls through her Facebook profile, clicks on her photos, and "likes" her links.

Early in their courtship, Nev sits on a couch and candidly talks about his growing connection with Megan. He explains:

> She works as a vet, so she likes animals a lot. I like animals . . . She's a musician. I think she plays the cello, maybe also the guitar, and she sings. I'm not really a musician, but I guess you could say that we have a similarity there. She's a dancer. She takes ballet and does belly dancing. Again, not that I do either of those, but dance is a

big part of my life. I mean, I guess I don't know that much about her. Yet.[6]

Mediated through Facebook, Megan is little more than a database of personal information. She is a collection of likes, preferences, tags, and drop-down boxes. She is flattened into a collection of multiple-choice options.

This flattening of identity that accompanies the conversion of self-hood into a database is the result of two things. First, a database is not a robust medium. The term was coined in a 1963 memo by the System Development Corporation that read, "A database is a collection of entries containing information that can vary in its storage media and in the characteristics of its entries and items."[7] By design then, a database is intended to be a starting point—quite literally, an "entry" into something more. In constructing identity as a database however, the network takes the beginning as the end, the final product. The profile pictures, the posts, the relationship status, the likes, and preferences are the sum total of identity on the network. The result is a flattening of identity such that complex emotions, mixed feelings, ambivalence, nuance, and subtlety—in short, analog being—are all excluded by design.

Jaron Lanier succinctly captures the situation writing that, "information underrepresents reality."[8] Thus, in the same way that there is no difference between the 4 bits for red in a Van Gogh and the same 4 bits in a McDonalds ad, when identity is digitized it is reduced to a series of predetermined states such that my selection of "single," "in a relationship," or "it's complicated" is the same as any one else's selection. When we embrace an information-only model of reality or identity, all that remains are these singular contact points that are shared without context.

The second reason selfhood is flattened in the network is because it is identity designed and packaged for consumption. Unlike what Sherry Turkle calls "life in the real," in the social network selfhood has an intended audience. We know who will see our status updates, the pictures we post, and the things we like. In this respect, it is not identity, it is a performance of identity. What we put on the network is an edited version of ourselves, designed to reflect and represent specific life qualities in a

6. Joost and Schulman, *Catfish,* Universal Pictures, 2010.

7. Simpson, "Database."

8. Lanier, *You Are Not a Gadget,* 69.

give-and-take with an audience of friend-fans that review and comment upon it daily, even hourly. If who we are on the network gets negative reviews, we can change it in a feedback loop that propels us away from our ontological fallibility.

Thus Nev's connection with Megan is as much a product of Megan's performance of identity as it is Nev's response to that performance. Just as we take time to carefully craft the image of ourselves that we put on the network, so too is that database of identity often carefully studied by others. Whereas identity and relationships "in the real" play out in the dynamic whole of real time, in the network relationships and identity are static objects. This affords a degree of control that is absent in analogue life. In the network we can choose when to respond to someone, we can linger over their words, analyze them, read into them, and parse their information-identity.

Nev for instance connects with Megan by filling in the blanks to construct himself as an ideal match. What he knows of her are a string of particulars that he in turn connects to his own matching set.

There is a banal horizontality to this mode of connection. Grounded as it is in the static and timeless particulars of a flattened informational-identity, this connection only expands outward according to a point-coun-ter-point logic of identification. Consequently, one-to-one connections existing solely, or predominately, in the network tend to lack the integrity of inclusion in the dynamic whole of relationships in the real, where a history together roots the relationship downward while it also branches upward to transcend the digital immediacy of the here and now. This immediacy is a product of the direct particularity of purpose-oriented information that the network caters to.

The favored form of the networked communiqué is brief, simple, and particular—and likewise for interpersonal connections. Neither emotional nor intellectual complexity plays well in the network and neither does any other form of protracted engagement. When limited to a 140 character Tweet or a 420 character status update, subtlety and complexity are difficult to achieve. This velocity toward efficiency is built into the algorithmic structure of a network that favors product over process. Relationships that are formed in the network thus tend toward expeditious connection (or rejection) without context or *telos*. The result being connection without inclusion. That is, a connection between particulars (likes, dislikes, profession, musical taste, etc.) without a sense of the whole to which one is connected.

Nev experiences this as his relationship with Megan moves increasingly offline and he begins to sense that he is indeed missing something of the bigger picture. While in Vail, Colorado with Ariel and Henry to film a dance festival, Nev discovers that a song Megan claims to have sung is actually a recording by professional singer Suzanna Choffel. Investigating things a bit further Nev discovers that a number of songs Megan posted to Facebook and claimed as her own were in fact lifted directly from Youtube, MySpace, and other sites. While Nev reels from the discovery, asking "Why should I even waste my time with this?," Henry calmly interjects "Don't you want to get to the bottom of this?" And when the trio is at a loss as to how exactly to accomplish this, Henry again provides, "I think we finish up with Vail, and we drive to Michigan."

Nev is initially opposed to the idea. He wants to simply be done with the situation, to leave the "Facebook family" as he calls them, on the Internet where he found them. For Nev, there is no point in going forward; all roads lead to humiliation. Megan clearly is not who he thought she was and he has no idea who he has been sharing the most intimate details of his life with for the past eight months. The only outcome for him is the embarrassment of the dupe. Nonetheless, he is persuaded. Nev sees that the only way forward is to risk failure by embracing the whole he has been missing.

In Michigan, Nev meets Angela and discovers that Megan never existed. Angela, a lonely middle-aged housewife, created Megan as a Facebook profile by cobbling together images and information culled from the Internet and her imagination. She peopled Megan's life with fake friends, gave her false hobbies, and took her to fictitious events. Upon discovering the truth, Nev is initially angry and appalled, but as Angela apologizes and owns up to her offenses, and as Nev gains a sense of her life in rural Michigan raising two severely mentally handicapped children, he comes to see her as a fellow flawed human being who was just trying to make a connection with someone else. He offers her grace instead of indignation and as Nev heads back to his life in New York, he and Angela part as friends.

Nev mistook a digital connection for inclusion in a real relationship. The only thing Nev knew about Megan was what Angela told him and what he gleaned from Facebook. Bits and pieces; scraps of information. There was never a larger context, a relational *lebenswelt*, in which to situate her or their relationship. As a result their relationship played out like a series of Facebook posts and status updates. It lacked the continuity and rhythm of a real relationship and instead pulsed to the sporadic beat of text messages and Facebook comments. And like text messages, tweets, and Facebook posts, their whole relationship had an air of striving, of aiming for amusement with missives defined by the velocity of information and not the natural flow of genuine inclusion in the life of a relationship.

Connection *and* inclusion do however finally come together at the end of the film. Nev did not have to go to Michigan. He knew that Megan was not the person he thought she was. Yet he went all the same. And once there, he did not have to accept Angela. Nonetheless, he chose to face the incongruity between the network and the real, between his expectations and reality, and he forgave her. The integration of connection and inclusion is only realized by embracing failure and extending grace.

Section III: Social Catfish

In *The Social Network* Mark mistook digital inclusion for real connection and in *Catfish* Nev mistook a digital connection for real inclusion. Frustrated with the exclusivity of Harvard and rejection from his girlfriend, Mark believed that the inclusion of the network, reconceived as a grid, could fulfill the basic human need to actually connect with another person. Surprised by his bullet-point connection with Facebook Megan, Nev pursued digital romance only to be disappointed by who was at the other end of the connection.

These films offer Mark and Nev as examples of two ways of living in today's wired world of the social network. We can, like Mark, use the network as a way to feel included without having to risk the vulnerability that genuine intimacy and real connection demand. Or, like Nev, we can use the network to pursue precisely this kind of intimacy and connection only to discover that without the deep and visceral context of analog inclusion, the connection rings false. In both instances, the integration of connection and inclusion is absent.

The explosion of social networks of all kinds and their accompanying technologies has created a culture that favors digitally mediated interpersonal relationships. Many of us would rather send a text message of instant-message than make a phone call, which is increasingly considered "intrusive" and overly personal. As one of Turkle's teenage interviewees notes, with communication via the network, as opposed to a call, "there is a lot less *boundness* to the person."[9] In this, the social network promotes a paradigm of interpersonal interactions that discourage presentments of fallibility. Because when we are not bound to people, we needn't risk vulnerability.

The network lets us connect, but at a safe distance. Our feelings are protected by the screen that mediates the relationship by allowing us to put people on hold, compose and edit our emotions, feign nonchalance, and ultimately turn the relationship off and walk away. More and more we live in the social network and yet we remain solitary and alone behind our screens. We are alternatively included but disconnected and connected but not included. Bringing these two together means embracing the very things the network discourages: failure and grace.

Failure is unique to the human experience and it is more complex than it might appear. It entails an assessment of an object or objective, a determination that that object or objective is desirable, an effort to attain it, the ineffectualness of that effort, and the subjective recognition of that ineffectualness. Animals and machines make mistakes, but only humans fail. We alone have the existential capacity to understand and appreciate what it is to miss the mark. It is more than recognizing or being distraught over not obtaining a desired end. It is a reflexive state that dwells inside the broken middle term between desire and end. It is our natural state.

As Heidegger would have it, we are thrown into the world as beings-unto-death. Our entire existence is played out in that space between being and non-being, where non-being is the final terminal failure and negation of being. Thus the ontology of our being is freedom within protracted failure; perpetual fallibility. The Christian story affirms this inasmuch as the being of human being is understood to be essentially broken by virtue of its ontological and moral separation from God. My aim here is not to set out an entire ontotheology of failure, but rather to simply note that there exists a robust philosophical and theological tradition of conceiving of our being as possessed by a lack, an absence, and a projection toward nonbeing such that this nonbeing is equally constitutive of our being as

9. Turkle, *Alone Together*, 190.

both possibility and inevitability. And if this is the case, then grace at an equally fundamental level is required. The integrity of connection and inclusion in a digital culture rests in embracing this.

If fallibility and failure constitute a key dimension of our ontology, grace is the operative moral obligation that emerges from that ontology. Grace typically describes a relation of undeserved favor or forgiveness from a superior to an inferior. There is then an implied verticality to the traditional grace relation such that, for instance, within the Christian tradition, God above bestows grace upon humankind below. Early in Christian theology we see this formulation in Augustine's prevenient grace, and in the twentieth century a similar model appeared in Barth and Rahner. However, grace as such need not entail a bestowal from superior to inferior to preserve relational verticality.

Grace is premised on the undeserving character of the recipient. When grace is given between the equally undeserving—the equally fallible and failing—the grace-relationship itself is vertically extended. Without the roles of superior and inferior, the grace-relationship stretches between an embracing descent into the human ontology of failure and an extending ascent of recognition of the mutuality of that ontology. Whereas grace traditionally redeems humanity from sin, here grace redeems humanity from digital perfection.

We are analog creatures living in a digital culture that is ill suited to our fallible being. Digital technology is premised on a rigid system of binaries—one or zero, on or off, open or closed. The result is a seductive precision that eliminates the noise and clutter of complexity. We, however, are not precise and we thrive in the fuzzy realm of the real. We have flourished as a species precisely because we are able to draw conclusions that surpass the given data. We tolerate enormous amounts of ambiguity and uncertainty and we generate very little in the way of precision and accuracy. Yet we live in a culture that is structured by the requirements of a technology that demands precision and accuracy and expects to be treated on its own terms, not ours. And the social networks we increasingly live within are constructed according to these digital parameters. As Jaron Lanier observes, "The binary character at the core of software engineering tends to reappear at higher levels."[10] Thus from programming to platform, the web of technologies mediating our relationships, from

10. Lanier, *You Are Not a Gadget*, 71.

inclusion to connection, require us to acquiesce to a binary perfection that is fundamentally at odds with our fallible being as analog creatures.

The popular online dating site OKCupid provides a instructive example of this. OKCupid was launched in 2004 as a free dating website that used member-created quizzes to match its now more than 3.5 million users. The combined data from user profiles and quiz responses constituted an enormous amount of information about human relationships. In 2009 the site's founders created a tandem website, OKTrends, as a way to share their findings. Among their discoveries, they found that, on average, people list themselves as 2 inches taller, they inflate their salary by $20,000, and the more attractive the profile picture is the more likely it is out of date.[11] Even in a (virtual) space such as this, designed for interpersonal connection and relationship inclusion, vulnerability apparently remains anathema.

As we navigate within the digital strictures of a technology built culture that prizes the absolute metrics of quantification above all else, we, like Mark and Nev, are bound to be disappointed. Thus, when we encounter the blunt reality that the person at the other end of the network falls woefully short of their digital promise, we must realize that they are likely thinking the same thing of us.

In this respect, Mark and Nev are our representatives in the network. In *The Social Network* and *Catfish* we watch as they, like us, struggle to navigate the complexity of being analog in a digital culture. Put in conversation with one another we see the flaws of each of their paths as they find themselves uniquely unfulfilled. Mark flees from the real into the network while Nev flees from the network into the real. And ultimately, Mark is *included but alone* while Nev is *connected but disillusioned*. However, in the conversation between the two films there emerges an implicit agreement that if we truly want to connect with another person and experience the dynamic whole of inclusion in a real relationship, then we must break free of the horizontal gravity of the network and embrace the depths and peaks of failure and grace.

11. Rudder, "The Big Lies People Tell in Online Dating."

6

There Will Be Frogs

P. T. Anderson and the Strangeness of Common Grace

ALISSA WILKINSON

PAUL THOMAS ANDERSON'S 1999 film *Magnolia* is populated by broken, confused, twisted-up characters, but two stand out as what we'd call the "good guys": big-hearted beat cop Jim Kurring and gentle hospice nurse Phil Parma. In an essay called "The Judgment of Grace," in Alan Jacobs' *Shaming the Devil: Essays on Truthtelling*, he wrestles with the question these two characters pose to the thoughtful. Kurring is the only obviously religious character in the film, and Jacobs wonders aloud if he's good because he's a Christian, or if he'd be good regardless. The issue is complicated by Parma, who is, to all appearances, simply a thoroughly decent guy who cares about his dying patient and his family.

"Some people are [good]; what can we offer by way of explanation but a shrug?"[1] Jacobs asks. But a shrug is not enough for him. The answer, he says, gets at the very heart of our understanding of the world, of the

---

1. Jacobs, *Shaming the Devil*, 81.

"mystery of virtue as well as the mystery of iniquity."[2] Jacobs, a Christian, says that Christians need to "press our audiences to see the strangeness of goodness, the extraordinary unexpectedness of love and grace."[3] Then he asks: "Why is anyone good to anyone else? That we're cruel to one another doesn't surprise me in the least; I want an answer to the problem of goodness."[4]

Ah, the problem of goodness: not a small one, and—contrary to its cousin ("the problem of evil") and perhaps counterintuitively—one that has a way of troubling the faithful the most. Those of us who expend a great deal of effort in the hard work of repenting and believing for our share of grace might be excused for our difficulty. In orthodox Christian theology, God's saving grace is extended to believers, but the full measure of his grace is not restricted to the work of saving souls, nor is it confined to those who exercise (or are permitted to exercise, depending on your theological flavor) some of their own agency in the process of salvation.

For that very reason, this broader sort of grace—common grace—can be tricky to swallow. Bestowed on *all* creation, it's what keeps the world from spinning into oblivion, what lets those who haven't experienced saving grace still do good, love their spouses and children, build good businesses, wrest life-saving medications from the created world, and craft life-giving stories. So thoroughly unmerited is common grace that each human is its recipient from birth. Chance and destruction are not given free reign in this world; unexplainably good things happen quite apart from any explicit recognition of Christ. It's what accounts for the air we breathe and the water we drink: James reminds us that every good thing comes from God, and in Matthew, Jesus points out that God makes the sun to shine and the rain to fall on both the evil and the good—whether or not they "deserve" it is largely beside the point.

You'd think we'd rejoice at the idea of common grace, but the idea that our neighbors who live quite apart from Christian practice—like, apparently, Phil Parma—receive grace to do good can irk us. As a child, I struggled, with no answer, to find a reason that my friends and relatives who did not go to church, memorize Bible verses, and pray seemed often

2. Ibid.

3. Ibid.

4. Ibid.

to be happier than my church friends, and just as able to be kind and loving. It felt unfair, but the answer I most often received was that yes, people who were not Christians could do good things, but it didn't matter, because they were doing them for the wrong reasons. They weren't doing them for Jesus. So that somehow, in my mind, negated their good deeds. It was a common, but deeply unsatisfying answer that left me without a framework for evaluating or rejoicing in much of the good I saw around me.

As Jacobs points out, Christians are not the only ones in history to have difficulty with this strange doctrine. We tend, he says, when reading the book of Exodus, to forget that God did not destroy Egypt at once when Pharoah refused to let the enslaved Israelites go. He could have simply obliterated Egypt. But why did he send plagues instead? Because he loved the Egyptians. The plagues were a "judgment which is also a gracious gift. They comprise a terrifying act of love."[5]

Why do we forget this? Jacobs says we are usually busy focusing on how much God loved *Israel* that we ignore the Egyptians: "It is as though we believe that he loved them because they agreed to his proposed covenant. Or as though we believe that he made a covenant with them, made them his 'peculiar treasure,' because he loved them instead of loving others made equally in his image." Israel felt the relative injustice, too. Isaiah 19:24 pegs not just Israel, but Egypt and Assyria in God's blessing: "Blessed be Egypt my people, and Assyria the work of my hands, and Israel my inheritance,"[6] but it was translated in the Septuagint (a Greek version)—by rabbis who found this bizarre—as "Blessed be my people who are in Egypt and Assyria, and Israel my inheritance."

Chosen folks—whether Israel or the church—find it hard to believe God also loves the non-chosen, or, in a sense, chooses them too, to experience his blessing and grace. But it is a story told over and over in the Scripture, in Jonah's experiences with the wicked Ninevites, Jesus' kindness to Samaritans, the centurion who offers the suffering Christ relief for his pain.

Goodness, then, unexplainable goodness found in and enacted outside the church walls, finds its root in common grace. Goodness becomes a "problem" because we struggle against the common grace, against the

---

5. Jacobs, *Shaming the Devil*, 65.

6. Isa 19:24, NRSV.

idea that despite all our holy striving to be good and choose the right, some seem to be just *born* that way: good, kind, thoughtful, seeking the betterment of others, talented and loving. The "wicked" prosper, and not always through wickedness. And something in our hearts wants this not to be so.

So returning to *Magnolia*: Jim is good, and Phil is good, and both bring goodness to those around them quite apart from a specific faith commitment. The strangeness of common grace is that it is extended to the righteous and the wicked. It is a strange fact that—as in the plagues— God's common grace sometimes looks like what Jacobs calls a "terrifying act of love," a plague that sends us straight into the refining fire.[7] And it is a stranger fact that sometimes God's common grace means we escape that fire, even when we deserve it. We rarely receive our full punishment in this life.

And perhaps most strangely of all, a non-religious, biblically-illiterate, God-haunted filmmaker from the San Fernando Valley shows us both sides of this coin.

Though he'd made a number of shorts and a feature film (called *Sydney* or *Hard Eight*, depending on who you talk to), wunderkind Paul Thomas Anderson had his proper burst-onto-the-scene moment at age twenty-seven with *Boogie Nights*, his 1997 tribute to the porn industry in the 1970s. It begins with a five-minute continuous shot that winds through a club and introduces the characters whose spectacular rise and fall we're about to witness. It also introduces Anderson as an upstart master of the medium with an uncanny, intuitive grasp on what makes for a good movie.

For a film about the porn industry, the movie isn't really about porn—"If you were a porno fan going to see 'Boogie Nights,' you'd be really disappointed," Anderson said in a 1999 *New York Times* profile.[8] From the get-go, it's clear that Anderson's theme is parents and children, both biological and adoptive, and the connections people try to make with one another that run deeper than mere acquaintance. Everyone works and plays too hard; everyone makes their fortune; and everyone falls spectacularly in the end, but not without hope, because they have one another still, a sort of motley, weird, mildly disturbing family.

7. Jacobs, *Shaming the Devil*, 65.

8. Hirschberg, "His Way," 8.

Boogie Nights earned Anderson the chance to make *Magnolia*, followed by *Punch-Drunk Love* in 2002 and the epic *There Will Be Blood* in 2007. (His next film, about a Scientology-like cult led by a character played by Anderson regular Philip Seymour Hoffman, is due out in 2012.) Each returns to the question of parents and children: how we deal with the ones we've got, and how we make new ones, too.

Not to wander too far off the path, but: families, it seems to me, are one of the truest examples of real, non-Hallmarky common grace at work. This is a complicated grace. It doesn't let us contentedly reflect on the glories of safety and comfort in the love of a good mother for her child, the care of a good father for his offspring. Common grace includes the good family, but also the wicked one.

To be sure, bad families inflict horrendous pain and damage on their members. Those examples are all too numerous and all too public, and Anderson does not shrink from them, apparently not without reason: he "has a troubled relationship with his mother that he won't discuss and was very close to his father, who died in 1997."[9] The family at the center of *Punch-Drunk Love* is one of those huge, loud families that are the source of and, occasionally, the remedy for the main character's neuroses. In *Magnolia*, the parents range from neglectful to overbearing to profoundly abusive. But in real life, even good parents screw up, and some who were damaged by bad families grow into good people, capable of loving and having families of their own. God's terrifying act of love can mean we are inflicted, beyond our own power, with a bad family. Or with a good one. And we might get past it, too.

In *There Will Be Blood*—which has a darker worldview than its predecessors—the two families around the narrative destroy themselves. Twin brothers Paul and Eli Sunday tear their world apart in pursuit of money and power—and power for Eli, it should be noted, comes in the form of leading a church. But Eli's nemesis is one of the most disturbing antiheroes in American cinema: Daniel Plainview, a calculating oilman who adopts the son of one of his workers, who he calls H.W., when the worker dies in an accident—not from pity, love, or a sense of duty or kindness, but in order to help him build his business through portraying himself as a "family man." Later, a man claiming to be Plainview's half-brother Henry

9. Hirschberg, "His Way," 6.

appears, seeking work and eventually prompting Plainview to ship H.W. off to boarding school after the suspicious boy sets Henry's bed on fire.

H.W., especially, has had a rough time of it: his family stripped from him, he's given an unloving father whom he believes to be his own, who raises him through childhood and then sends him away. But one can sense a sort of severe mercy behind the expulsion, particularly when he returns to request that their partnership be dissolved so he can start his own oil company. Plainview scornfully tells him of his origins and sends him away again, this time permanently. But who would want to be the son of Daniel Plainview? Who would want to spend formative adolescent years in the company of such a man? And what better training to run one's own oil company than a childhood watching Plainview in action?

Anderson's movies are bound to one another by his continual re-flections on families, and by another thing: they always go off the rails somewhere, usually in a profoundly weird way, infuriating and delighting audiences. In the hand of a lesser director, *Boogie Nights* probably could have ended right around the second act. *Punch-Drunk Love*, weird and wonderful from beginning to end, unceremoniously and unexplainably hurtles a harmonium off a truck at the beginning. It spends the rest of the movie threatening to take off for Hawaii—and entirely unexpectedly, it *does*. Audiences new to Anderson were mystified by the bizarre, bloody bowling alley scene (with its instant pop-culture meme refrain, "I drink your milkshake! I drink it up!") that wraps up *There Will Be Blood*, but everyone else knew better: That's just P.T., being P.T.

Magnolia has two off-the-rails moments. At one point it suddenly turns into a musical. And at the end of the film, a plague of Biblical proportions drops, quite literally, from the sky.

Which was not a very popular choice with some people. On its release, *New York Times* film critic Janet Maslin declared that "when that group sing-along arrives, 'Magnolia' begins to self-destruct spectacularly . . . As the desperate reach for some larger meaning begins, the sheer arbitrariness of his approach is laid bare. So bare, in fact, that when 'Magnolia' finally does come in for what is quite literally an amphibious landing, it actually invokes a biblical plague to create a sense of resolution. Even in the Bible, that kind of maneuver was a last resort."[10] Ironic criticism, perhaps. The film spends quite a bit of time—perhaps, really, its entire

10. Maslin, "Entangled Lives on the Cusp of the Millennium."

narrative—on whether or not "arbitrariness" even exists. The film's open-ing sequence narrates three strange and cruel (non)coincidences from history, punctuated by a refrain: "And I would like to think this was only a matter of chance . . . and I am trying to think this was all only a matter of chance . . . and it is in the humble opinion of this narrator that this is not just 'something that happened.' This cannot be 'one of those things . . . ' This, please, cannot be that. And for what I would like to say, I can't. This was not just a matter of chance."[11] Nobody wants to live in a world of arbitrary cruelty—least of all, Paul Thomas Anderson.

Magnolia won scads of awards and was nominated for three Oscars, and it has an 83 percent rating on Rotten Tomatoes. Today it stands out as one of the finest films of its era, mostly because despite Maslin's protesta-tions, it persists in leaving the audience with a lot to chew on. In the *New York Times* profile, Anderson says, "You have to sit in the movie and really absorb it . . . I am always looking for that nuance, that moment of truth, and you can't really do that fast."[12] Furthermore, he says, "I was trying to say something with this film without actually screaming the message . . . Although three hours may be something of a scream, I wanted to hold the note for a while."[13]

Still, Maslin is not wrong in being unsettled by those two shark-jumping moments. They are twin expressions of that strange common grace that manifests in both welcome and terrifying mercies.

Like animals on the ark, everything in *Magnolia* comes in pairs. The most developed evil and good characters in the film share a name: TV game show host Jimmy Gator and cop Jim Kurring. Jimmy Gator is old and dying, as is Earl Partridge, their last names perhaps belying their relative capacity for redemption. Their two maligned wives are named for flowers: Rose and Lily. The estranged children of these men, drug-addict Claudia and sex-addict Frank, have taken on aggressively flora- and fauna-less last names (Wilson and Mackey) to separate themselves from their fathers. There are two quiz-show contestants, one kid and one who is just an overgrown kid, complete with braces and a cockeyed self-awareness. There's more, too. There are no arbitrary choices in Anderson's world.

11. Anderson, *Magnolia*, New Line, 1999.
12. Hirschberg, "His Way," 2.
13. Ibid., 2.

So it's not surprising that the moments of grace come in a pair, too. First, as the characters hit their loneliest moments of despair, they are covered by a single song, which each sings in turn: Aimee Mann's song "Wise Up," with the chorus: "And it's not going to stop / it's not going to stop / it's not going to stop / till you wise up." Some despair and some find strange comfort in the song's conclusion—"so just give up"—but though they're all alone, separate and isolated in this scene, they are joined together by the music. It's like the sunshine and rain Jesus speaks of in Matthew (and on this note, it's probably no accident that the film is drenched in a persistent and unusual Southern California downpour).

The other moment of grace—the amphibious moment of judgment—did not, interestingly, originate as a last resort reference to a biblical plague, as Maslin implies. In the interview that accompanies the shooting script for *Magnolia*, Anderson explains that he'd written the reference into the script because he read about it in the work of Charles Fort, a

> turn-of-the-century writer who wrote mainly about odd phenomena . . . I just went, Wow! How cool and scary and fun to do that would be—and what does it mean? So I just started writing it into the script. It wasn't until after I got through with the writing that I began to discover what it might mean, which was this: You get to a point in your life, and shit is happening, and everything's out of your control, and suddenly, a rain of frogs just makes sense. You're staring at a doctor who's telling you something is wrong, and while we know what it is, we have no way of fixing it. And you just go, so what you're telling me, basically, is that it's raining frogs from the sky . . . The frogs are a barometer for who we are as people. We're polluting ourselves, we're killing ourselves, and the frogs are telling us so, because they're all getting sick and deformed.[14]

Most surprising is this admission: "And I didn't even know it was in the Bible until Henry Gibson gave me a copy of the Bible, bookmarked to the appropriate frog passage."[15]

Alan Jacobs' musings on the plagues and the problem of good are prompted by this very sequence in the film, and in some key ways this cinematic frog-shower matches the terrifying, merciful grace of the plagues that God sent to try to keep the Egyptians from destroying themselves—because he loved them.

14. Anderson, *Magnolia*, 206–7.
15. Ibid.

Even in *Magnolia*, the frogs raining from the skies and splattering onto car windshields and asphalt, and crashing through skylights, and thumping cacophonously onto roofs and gas station canopies, are portrayed as a way for God—or Someone, Something Up There—to arrest the attention of people who are ruining their own lives and the lives of those around them:

> It's not his disgust that moves him, it is his horror at our self-disgust; he doesn't destroy us, but tries to stop us from destroying ourselves . . . no one seems to notice the conditions; they always have their backs to the windows; turned inward, eyes downcast or vacant, they continue to eat away at their own guts, oblivious to the external world, muttering the lyrics to a song they seem not to feel the force of. Only the crashing of frogs onto windshields and roofs and through windows and skylights—and in one case, right onto a man's upturned face—is sufficient to shake them from their self-referential stupors.[16]

But the frogs change all this. In the course of the loving plague, children reunite with parents, lives are saved, crimes are halted, rights are wronged, sins are confessed. Redemption is coming to everyone, in fits and starts. Everyone, that is, except the father who has molested his daughter. The severity of common grace leaves him surrounded by glass and frogs in a burning house, with two months left to live in his cancer-infested body.

Yet everything is not fixed: the frogs leave a mess. Men are still going to die. Wives and children will still live with guilt, addiction, and hurt. The children of Israel may have gone in search of freedom, protected by their God, but the Egyptians are still left without a means to make bricks, with destruction, without their firstborn sons, and they've just given their valuables away to the nation that left them behind. If God loves them, could he not have made life a bit more bearable?

Strange grace, indeed, that keeps us from our own destruction, that holds the world together, that gives us the ability to start new relationships and renew old ones, but still leaves us picking up the pieces, struggling with the consequences of what we've done. Strange grace that loves Israel, but loves Egypt too, after wronging the chosen folks. Strange grace that lets us join the work of picking up the pieces of the mess we've made.

16. Jacobs, *Shaming the Devil*, 67.

Anderson's narrator probably says it best: "And it is in the humble opinion of this narrator that these strange things happen all the time, and so it goes and so it goes and the book says, 'We may be through with the past, but the past is not through with us.'"[17]

17. Anderson, *Magnolia*, New Line, 1999.

7

Solitude, Search, and Forgiveness in *Paris, Texas*

An Augustinian Turn

JEFF SELLARS

WITHIN THE WORK OF director and writer Wim Wenders, one can discern a theme that continually emerges: namely, the theme of the searcher or the pilgrim.[1] Quite possibly there is nowhere that this theme is more

1. "The central metaphor in nearly all his films is that of a lone figure on a journey, even if the destination is not known. Like Walker Percy's character Binx Bolling (from *The Moviegoer*), Wenders's protagonists are on a "Search," find a direction, a dimly sensed goal, even if more time on the road is necessary. Whether it is [Travis in *Paris, Texas*, or Damiel in *Wings of Desire*, or Howard Spence in *Don't Come Knocking*, something] has propelled them onto a path . . . each character starts as a wanderer and becomes a pilgrim" (Wenders, "Artist of the Month."). Furthermore, Wim Wenders also speaks of his own search for the divine: "During those twenty years when, though I always remained a believer, I went as far away from the Catholic Church as possible, I thought that all churches were the same. The Catholic Church had made some tremendous mistakes, and I had taken these mistakes too personally. For twenty years I never attended church anywhere. I had left the church in 1968, and at the time I was very involved in socialist politics. During the seventies, I was involved in psychoanalysis, another substitute religion, like socialism, which strangely enough has religious roots. Then in the eighties I was involved with Asian philosophy and Buddhist ideas, although that never really showed in any of the work I did then. When I came back to the Church, it was a return to the beginning

readily apparent than in his film *Paris, Texas*. In *Paris, Texas*, Travis, our protagonist, is first seen walking through the desert. The metaphor cannot be lost: the desolate landscape reveals the inner landscape of Travis' soul. He has been lost for four years. He has amnesia.[2] He is alone. He is searching for something. Travis is on a quest, and, at least at first, it has been a fruitless search through the desert. But Travis's search soon takes an Augustinian turn. Of course, Augustine, too, wrote of a search: "to praise you is the desire of man, a little piece of your creation. You stir man to take pleasure in praising you, because you have made us for yourself, and our heart is restless until it rests in you."[3] Much like Travis' lonely search through the desert, Augustine's own story implies that the search must be done in solitude (though, of course, not necessarily without thrusts from surrounding events, circumstances, communities and individuals): Augustine's quest for God moves forward through introspection, through an internal search for wisdom. However, the search is not to end in solitude—for community must be found—nor is it necessarily done without our help. But it is ultimately the searcher who must take up the journey.

---

after going through a long circle—and *Until The End of the World* marks the end of the circle. At the end of that film, the writer character says that he has started to pray again. He quotes the gospel of John, 'In the beginning was the Word,' when he rediscovers the word against the image. In the twenty years I had been absent from church, my films' main subject was alienation, being on the road, being on some sort of pilgrimage toward understanding, or realization, or fulfillment. Even though most of those characters didn't know what it was they were after, they were on the way somewhere. For twenty years, being on the road itself became the topic, as the destination was so uncertain. Looking back, I was like a pilgrim who didn't believe in the marked path anymore, but still believed that being on the road had to lead somewhere as long as I was relentless about it" (Wilson, "Excerpt.").

2. Walker Percy noted that the amnesiac-plot device is a common one: "In all soap operas and in many films and novels, a leading character will sooner or later develop amnesia" (Percy, *Lost in the Cosmos*, 17). Why is this? What is the pay-off on this plot device? Percy observed that we get an extra dividend from watching and identifying with such a character—and it is (only) when the character is "on the track of who he is (who you are)" (ibid., 18). Percy then asks a series of questions pertaining to the plot device, each referring in some way to the nature of human boredom or the intolerable-ness of life. Why is it that Travis has decided to take his journey? We are first given scant clues in the narrative: e.g., he has purchased a lot (an empty lot) of land in Paris, Texas; it is the place his mother and father first made love, and possibly the site of Travis' conception. We see in this the real sense of a (new) birth, of a beginning: this is where Travis "began," and it is where we begin as viewers. Thrust into the world, not knowing our way, we must find our path through the narrative, finding meaning, interpreting events.

3. Augustine, *Confessions*, 3.

Even though Augustine undertook his search in solitude, he found his path in and through community. Similarly, Travis finds his path through his reorientation to his friends and family, through the recognition of his past. In *Paris, Texas*, we see solitude, search, and forgiveness portrayed vividly and expressly through the characters and the landscape. One might suspect that the themes of solitude, search, and forgiveness in *Paris, Texas* would give rise to a standard resolution. However, the story resists the trappings of a traditional denouement. There is, no doubt, a resolution—if only implicitly. The story's denouement is ultimately found through the search of Travis—which is an Augustinian project at heart. It is through the search in solitude that we see a possible path of continuation for Travis; and it is through this search that Travis confesses, finds the path to forgiveness and attempts to reconnect a son and mother.

The idea of search and solitude permeates the film: the landscape is one of desolation, isolation. Travis is a man alone, one who must find who he is: he is the searcher, the wanderer. But he is not yet a willing pilgrim, not yet one who is actively and knowingly searching for meaning. He is, instead, attempting to find a complete solitude, a sort of ignorant bliss. In one of our first introductions to Travis, we find that his desert wandering is an act of running away—it is not the serious search that he finds he must begin towards the end of the film. His search is exhausting—taking all of his life and energy. But it is, as Augustine noted, in "desiring to find their delight in externals" that we "easily become empty and expend [our] energies on 'the things which are seen and temporal' (2 Cor 4:18). With starving minds [we] can only lick the images of these things."[4] In contrast, the true search, the longing for the divine, is an energizer: the pilgrim will be renewed and revitalized for his or her searching; the joy of the infinite, of the divine, replaces the weariness of the finite. Travis has been wondering for four years, exhausted. His search has left him lifeless. He is finally "caught": he collapses in a run down bar in Terlingua and is taken to a medical clinic. Travis does not talk; indeed he refuses to talk. He is in self-imposed isolation: as the clinic doctor states, "He has something to hide."[5] His brother, Walt, is called and comes to find him. Yet, even here,

4. Augustine, *Confessions*, 161.

5. Shepard and Wenders, *Paris, Texas*, Twentieth Century Fox, 2004. Augustine also noted that we often attempt to deceive ourselves: "It is certain, then, that all want to be happy since there are those who do not want to find in you their source of joy. That is the sole happy life, but they do not really want it. But perhaps everyone does have a

Travis resists the call to return to his former life, to give up his fruitless search and confront his past. And, so, he attempts to leave again.

Once again Travis sets out to search for "blissful nothingness." Travis is walking along train tracks—having left Walt—towards the vast expanse of desert landscape. Walt finds Travis and asks him, "You mind telling me where you're headed, Trav? What's out there?"[6] Walt gestures toward the desolate landscape and they look to the horizon. Walt continues: "There's nothing out there."[7] Walt asks Travis if he trusts him. There seems to be a clear philosophical subtext here: Walt is asking Travis to commit to an authority of experience. We certainly do not know if Walt has experienced the desolation of fruitless solitude. Augustine maintained that it is more "modest and not the least misleading to be told by the Church to believe what [cannot] be demonstrated—whether that was because a demonstration existed but could not be understood by all or whether the matter was not one open to rational proof . . ."[8] These issues of authority lie in wait for us all: whether it be individual or personal authority, proclaimed rational authority, or some other traditioned authority. This is not, however, an unthinking, blind acceptance of authority; it is rather like a warning against a particular kind of rational certainty—simply because we can not provide an argument that will convince all rational beings does not put us in any worse of a position than other philosophies or theologies. According to Augustine, we believe many things on authority, numerous things in life that we believe to be true and do not see for ourselves, "such as many incidents in the history of the nations, many facts concerning places and cities which [we] have never seen, many things accepted on the word of friends, many from physicians, many from other people."[9] There is no necessary fault in believing on authority (even though critical

desire for it and yet, because 'the flesh lusts against the spirit and the spirit against the flesh so that they do not do what they wish' . . . they relapse into whatever they have the strength to do . . . For if I put the question to anyone whether he prefers to find joy in the truth or in falsehood, he does not hesitate to say he wants to be happy . . . This happy life everyone desires; joy in truth everyone wants . . . Why then do they not find their joy in this? Why are they not happy? It is because they are more occupied in other things which make them more wretched than their tenuous consciousness of the truth makes them happy. . ." (Augustine, *Confessions*, 199).

6. Shepard and Wenders, *Paris, Texas*, Twentieth Century Fox, 2004.

7. Ibid.

8. Augustine, *Confessions*, 95.

9. Ibid., 95.

engagement must be maintained), and questions of doubt in regards to the authority of the church or Scripture had to do with matters of belief and not rationalistic, "raw," "factual" proofs:

> How do you know that these books were provided for the human race by the Spirit of the one true and utterly truthful God?' That very thing was a matter in which belief was of the greatest importance; for no attacks based on caviling questions of the kind of which I had read so much in the mutually contradictory philosophers could ever force me not to believe that you are (though what you are I could not know) or that you exercise a providential care over human affairs.[10]

The weakness of human reasoning necessitates, for Augustine, the need for authoritative Scriptures and traditions, which are themselves either the experiences of those who have gone before, the "reasonings" of those who have gone before, or the epiphanic/revelatory "reasonings" of those who have gone before. These things reveal the mystery of God for Augustine. And Walt is asking Travis, who is in a state of weakness himself, to commit to his certainty that there is nothing "out there" for Travis. The fruitless solitude that Travis craves needs to be replaced (though, of course, this is not explicitly shown as recognized by Walt) by a recommitment to, and a recognition of, his past. Essentially, Travis is on a search to find himself—even if he does not at first recognize it as such. He leaves and isolates himself, but the things he wants and needs cannot be found in his fruitless search: it leads, ontologically, to nothing, no-thing, non-being. He really only begins to find himself when he recommits to communion—to the world, to his family, and to love. The outward journey into the desert is replaced by the inward journey of the soul.

Travis knows he must begin a new search, and to usher in his newfound quest he is literally given new clothes. Travis cleans up, shaves, and puts on these new clothes. Walt asks him, rhetorically, "Bet it feels good to be in new clothes, huh?"[11] However, there is still an emptiness that he cannot hide, a desire to 'check out' and enforce, once again, a self-imposed deception. The empty lot that Travis has purchased is another metaphor we are meant to appreciate. Travis states, "It's mine."[12] Walt remarks, "There's

10. Ibid., 96.

11. Shepard and Wenders, *Paris, Texas*, Twentieth Century Fox, 2004.

12. Ibid.

nothing on it."[13] We hear Travis chuckle, happily, and rejoin, "Empty."[14] He is still drawn to his idealized life of fruitless wandering, of the emptiness and the abdication of love, community, and responsibility.

Soon after this aforementioned episode, Walt asks Travis why he would want to buy a vacant lot in Paris, Texas. Travis pauses, thinking deeply, and replies, "I forgot." The Augustinian-Platonic tradition of anamnesis (that learning is remembrance, recollection) raises its head here and with it the connection to the search, to longing—we long for that which, in some sense, we already know.[15] The search is present because we cannot love that which is unknown, but in our pursuits of knowledge, for example, there is great love: the "student . . . already knows the value of . . . knowledge in general: his love is directed to an ideal present to his mind. He seeks to know the unknown for the sake of something that he already knows."[16] Augustine, clearly referencing the Platonic tradition, argued that learning is remembering—and as we see in the *Meno* dialogue, Plato attempted to demonstrate just such a thing. While discussing the matter with Menon, Socrates' interlocutor, Socrates counters the argument that humans cannot really attempt to find something out when they have no notion of what it is they are searching for and will not search for something they already know: "Will you lay out before us a thing you don't know, and then try to find it? Or . . . how will you know this that which you did not know?"[17] Socrates replies that it is obvious one does not attempt to find what one already knows: for clearly one already knows it and no search is necessary. He also replies that one cannot attempt to find

13. Ibid.

14. Ibid.

15. For example, Augustine noted that "there is another kind which is more similar and nearer to remembering and receiving the truth. An example of this is when we see something, think for certain that we have seen it before, and even say that we know it, but as for where or when or how or in whose presence it came to our notice, we are hard pressed to recollect and remember. For example, if this happens to us with a person, we ask him where we met him; and when he tells us, suddenly the whole event floods back into our memory like a light and it is no longer a chore for us to remember. Those who are well educated in the liberal arts are like this. While learning, they uncover and in some way dig up things which were undoubtedly buried in forgetfulness. Nevertheless, they are not satisfied and will not stop until they gaze fully and completely at the face of truth, whose splendor shines faintly in those arts" (Augustine, *Soliloquies*, 94).

16. Augustine, *Augustine: Later Words*, 72.

17. Plato, *The Great Dialogues of Plato*, 41.

something that he or she does not know for the simple fact that he or she does not know what to attempt to find. So, the idea of anamnesis is offered as a possible solution: when one remembers, one already knows but has simply forgotten; then, the attempt to remember avoids the problem of discovering what we already know and the attempt to find that which we do not know. This is also reflected in the scene where Walt invites Travis to view Super-8 images of his life. The film viewing rekindles memories and feelings, reconnecting Travis through moving images to his son (and his estranged lover and past deeds). We soon learn that Travis has abandoned his family, but, eventually, this is replaced by the realization that Travis and Jane, his lover, have really left each other (and, as a result, their son). Travis hints that his rage is the reason Jane has left—that she could no longer be a mother after what happened between them. As the story unfolds, we find in addition that his jealousy is why Jane has left him (along with her feelings of captivity--the trappings of marriage and a child for the young woman). And it is here that the search evolves: Travis' must also find Jane.

Furthermore, Walt insists on knowing what has happened between Travis and Jane. He's "sick of this fucking mystery!"[18] Walt displays a common modern malady: the malady to eradicate mystery. Augustine warned us that God, too, is a mystery, the ultimate mystery: If anyone finds God to be "beyond his understanding, it is not for me to explain it. Let him be content to say 'What is this?' (Exod 16:15). So too let him rejoice and delight in finding you who are beyond discovery rather than fail to find you by supposing you to be discoverable."[19] The push to eradicate mystery can be dangerous, hasty. Travis's mystery at first glance appears to have an easy remedy: Walt's "sickness" could be resolved by Travis being forthright and telling his full story. But Travis' story is complicated and even he does not know how to begin to tell it. If Travis' story is complicated and cannot be reduced in this fashion, how much more complicated then is the mystery that is God. It is often that we seek to tame mystery, to confine it, to define it. As Wendell Berry notes, in broadly modernist terms, mystery is

> attributable entirely to human ignorance, and thereby [appropriated to] the future of human science . . . the unknown = the to-be-known . . . [This modernist approach] has no ability to confront

18. Shepard and Wenders, *Paris, Texas*, Twentieth Century Fox, 2004.

19. Augustine, *Confessions*, 8.

mystery (or even the unknown) as such, and therefore has learned none of the lessons that humans have always learned when they have confronted mystery as such . . . [The modernist] cannot bring himself to say that scientists do not know something; he must say that they do not know it *yet*; he must say that one thing cannot be known *until* another thing is known . . . This "not yet" forthrightly appropriates mystery as future knowledge. It takes possession of life and the future of life in the names of its would-be explain-ers—and, it follows, of its would-be exploiters. As soon as mystery is scheduled for solution, it is no longer mystery; it is a problem.[20]

We often see a mystery not as a proper meeting with the unknown, and certainly not the miraculous. Thus, mystery is the result of ignorance: it is only that which we have not yet understood. Mystery is, then, not mystery: it is a problem; and if it is a problem it can be solved; and if it can be solved it can be quantified, categorized, tamed, demystified, and put away (or instrumentalized). Walt's attempt to know what happened also presupposes some sort of immediacy—the idea that there is some "raw" account and experience of the event that is not interpreted (and needs no further interpretation). The psyche of Travis is surrounded in mystery, too, and the mystery of the psyche is, according to Augustine, "the most intense, complex and reflexive" sites of the past which is left in traces of the future.[21] These events are not merely "once for all" events but are continuing events that can be altered and mutated (within limits) by future happenings. Just as Augustine argued, in *De Musica*, that "a note . . . is only situated and defined by its place in a sequence, such that the end of a musical composition still to be heard can change the nature of what we have already heard," so it is that a past event can be changed when viewed from another future vantage point.[22] Nonetheless, "the note remains this note, however far the new relations it enters into may re-disclose it."[23] The past events are still those same events: Travis still beat Jane and treated her horribly; Travis' actions are absolutely not excusable, and they remain. But Travis has yet to figure out his future story, i.e., where his search is tak-ing him and how it relates to his past. So, he cannot disclose and define the meaning of his past until he figures out his situation in his new narrative.

20. Berry, *Life is a Miracle*, 27–36.
21. Milbank, *Being Reconciled*, 53.
22. Ibid., 53.
23. Ibid.

Or, in a like manner, he cannot answer Walt yet because he is currently in the process of understanding and re-working his narrative.

Walt's insistence comes at a time when Travis cannot divulge what has happened. He must first come to terms with it himself. He starts, in part, by leaving a message to his young son, Hunter. He has started his journey by reuniting his family, by reconnecting to the world, and once he does this he can then continue (really start anew, start right) his search. But he must still reconcile his past life with his current search, and he must allow Jane and Hunter to move on properly, to allow healing to take place. This is revealed in Travis' tape-recorded message to Hunter:

> I was afraid I'd never be able to say the right words to you, in per-
> son, so I'm trying to do it like this. When I first saw you this time,
> at Walt's, I was hoping for all kinds of things. I was hoping to show
> you that I was your father. You showed me I was. But the biggest
> thing I hoped for can't come true. I know that now. You belong
> together with your mother. It was me that tore you apart, and I
> owe it you to bring you back together. But I can't stay with you. I
> could never heal up what happened. That's just the way it is. I can't
> even hardly remember what happened. It's like a gap. But it left me
> alone in a way that I haven't gotten over. And right now, I'm afraid.
> I'm afraid of walking away again. I'm afraid of what I might find.
> But I'm even more afraid of not facing this fear. I love you, Hunter.
> I love you more than my life.[24]

Travis's confession continues when he visits Jane for the last time. This requires an explicit narrative reworking of their story, which is told by Travis within the confines of a phone-sex booth that really operates as a metaphoric confession booth. The subsequent scenes of the film serve as a veritable confession. The parallel with Augustine here is plain: the confessions of Travis, like the confessions of Augustine, serve to usher in a deeper search. Travis is now compelled to confess his sins to his lover—and, eventually, is freed to search for what might heal him.

Travis does not explicitly ask for forgiveness during his confessions to his son and Jane, but there is a clear implication of his needing forgiveness. His work to reconcile his son and Jane is evidence of this need. To do this, Travis must rework the past narrative into a narrative of reconciliation, a narrative that can be altered, mutated: and, so, he begins his story, "Can I tell you something? . . . It's kind of long . . . I knew these people . . .

---

24. Shepard and Wenders, *Paris, Texas*, Twentieth Century Fox, 2004.

They were in love with each other . . ."[25] As intimated earlier, Augustine situates the past in light of alterability, such that

> the past only occurs initially through the supplement of the trace it leaves in the future—a trace which, in *De Musica*, Augustine clearly (like Aristotle) regards as ontological . . . The past, on this understanding, only *is* through memory, and while this does not abolish the ontological inviolability and irreversibility of pastness, it does mean that the event in its very originality is open to alteration and mutation.[26]

Travis can and does re-narrate his story to include his work in the present. As Augustine saw, there cannot be an "entirely discrete past event unaffected by what came later," and, so, the process of forgiveness is, for Travis and for us, a re-narration in light of our continuing story.[27] So, even here, after disclosing the events to Jane, after confessing, the search for forgiveness continues.

At the end of the film, it is clear that Travis needs to continue his search—one apparent metaphor for this is seeing Travis swathed in the (as described at an earlier point in the film commentary by director Wim Wenders) "greenish-poisonish" light of a parking lot, watching Jane and their son. Lastly, we see Travis driving off into the twilight. So the search continues. This time, apparently, hopeful, fruitful—Travis aware of the work that needs to be done, no longer running away from his past. Augustine was aware that his confessions served to "excite the human mind and affection towards God; [and] the act of writing the [*Confessions*] had done that for himself . . ."[28] Similarly, Travis' confession spurs him on to continue his search, to recount the things he has forgotten (to "fill the gap" he has lost), to confess further so that he might "find rest," to "forget [his] evils and embrace [his] one and only good . . ."[29]

25. Ibid.
26. Milbank, *Being Reconciled*, 53.
27. Ibid., 53.
28. Chadwick, "Introduction," xiii.
29. Augustine, *Confessions*, 5.

8

Graphic Theology

Community, Imago Dei, and Temptation in *300*

MEGAN J. ROBINSON

A KING TEMPTED. A fight against overwhelming odds. An outcast's betrayal. These are the basic threads of the film *300*, loosely based on the historical battle of Thermopylae, Greece, in 480 A.D. Critics panned Zack Snyder's 2007 film, calling it homoerotic, right-wing, pro-war propaganda, a paean to gay love, and so on. It is mocked as a bold film lacking nuance and subtlety, leaving little to the imagination; viewers see everything and nothing but what they want to see in it. There appears little else to say. Perhaps the only point of agreement amongst everyone: the film is a wild, hairy, bloody mess of a ride; one carefully based on Frank Miller's 2000 graphic novel of the same name.

Snyder said of the film, vis-à-vis viewers' reactions, that "it's a fun movie experience. Whatever people want to say about it—it's a sword and sandals epic, it's a war movie—all that stuff. The truth is that in the end I really just wanted to make a movie that is a ride."[1] Of the intentionally pared-down, vibrant, dynamic aesthetic in the graphic novel, which

1. Miller, "An Interview with Zack Snyder, Director of *300*," 5.

Snyder incorporated into the superb digital effects of the film, Miller says that he wanted to "lose the sense of this being an old story. It's not an old story; it's an *eternal* story."[2] Snyder again: "Frank took an actual event and turned it into mythology, as opposed to taking a mythological event and turning it into reality. That's the refreshing thing about it. He wanted to get at the essence, as opposed to the reality . . ."[3] Mythology. Eternal. Essence. Odd words to use about a film whose director just wanted to make "a ride."

While we can never fully escape our personal and socio-cultural contexts in interpreting any cultural object, and, recognizing that there are issues of socio-historical verisimilitude which must be left for others interested in such minutiae to address, let us take the film *300*, and its story, at face value. Can we ask of it eternal questions? Is there anything more to it than blood and guts (both spilled and chiseled)? The mythic mode of the story itself encourages us to try. A mythic story is one that is usually simply, even abstractly, told, and rarely depends on the usual narrative attractions such as suspense or surprise. Characters weave a "pattern of movements" that conveys a relevance and significance to our lives, and while it may be a sad or joyful experience to receive the story, it is always "not only grave but awe-inspiring . . . It is as if something of great moment had been communicated to us."[4]

300 satisfies the basic structure of a mythic story, not least of which is the conveyance of something momentous: there is no happy ending, yet we walk away imprinted with thought-provoking images that linger even after the credits finish rolling. It isn't history *per se* (neither was Herodotus, really), but "the story does what no theorem can quite do. It may not be like 'real life' in the superficial sense: but it sets before us an image of what reality may well be like at some more central region."[5] Dare we fall down this rabbit hole? If we do, we may see more in this film than critics and even its makers realized. In asking eternal questions, we cannot help but do so within a given theological framework, which, in this case, will be Christian theology. Let us return to the opening words of this essay: a king

---

2. Movies Central, "*300* Full Production Notes,"

3. Movies Central, "*300* Full Production Notes."

4. Lewis, "On Myth," 41–44.

5. Lewis, "On Stories," 15.

tempted. Early in the film, Leonidas of Sparta is offered "earth and water,"[6] the chance to be warlord of all Greece, gain immense wealth, power, and status, if he will submit to the Persian "god-king" Xerxes. It is Leonidas' choice, his character, on which the entire story hangs.

Leonidas of Sparta: king, warrior, lover, father, friend. Leonidas is trained as a Spartan soldier to peak physical condition, a man whose ultimate end and final glory is to die in battle serving his country. He is also trained as king, to lead, judge, and protect Spartan, and Greek, citizens. Indeed, Leonidas is always surrounded by people. His entire life is spent in the community of others: squabbling politicians, ever-present citizens, loyal warriors, adoring son, loving wife. As we see Leonidas in his world, this variety of roles—king, husband, judge, prophet, lover, warrior, friend, brother—begins to develop for viewers the picture of a man formed in community with his soldiers and family, by community with greater Greek civilization and ideals, for serving and upholding that community so that it can continue. Leonidas is not a king by himself, or for himself.

Human beings always have a choice, toward good or evil, right or wrong, and each test in life provokes a response from an individual that at the same time defines his or her character: "action is character; character is action."[7] Some tests are simple, and others complex, but all of them are formative. The response determines both the individual's capabilities and identity. "But each person is tempted, when he is lured and enticed by his own desire."[8] Temptation is a specific form of testing in which a victim is lured or manipulated by either an external or internal force toward a forbidden or wrong thing; must make the choice whether to resist or succumb; and then, must act on the choice made. Indeed, because character is determined by an individual's responses to tests, we often remember "many . . . characters especially for their heroism or ignominy in isolated moments of specific testing."[9] Xerxes is the obvious agent of temptation in *300*, offering wealth, power, status, and pleasure to Leonidas. But we also see Xerxes making a similar offer to an apparently marginal character, that of Ephialtes, who is in every way the opposite of Leonidas.

6. Snyder et al., *300*, Warner Brothers, 2007.

7. Ryken et al., "Test Motif," 855.

8. Jas 1:14, ESV

9. Ryken et al., "Test Motif," 855.

Ephialtes of nowhere: peasant, loser, loverless, childless, friendless. By contrast, the viewer's first introduction to Ephialtes is partial; we see only misshapen fingers as he stealthily spies on the Spartan squad. When Ephialtes and Leonidas first meet, the Spartan captain wants to attack this strange creature, for he hardly looks human, and must be a threat. Yet Ephialtes desires to be a complete Spartan, fighting alongside the other warriors as his father once did. He shows Leonidas the fighting moves, a strong thrust with the spear as his father taught him. But we never learn the name of this invisible father, nor of Ephialtes' mother either. All we know of these parents is that they fled Sparta, because Ephialtes' mother loved him so much that they chose exile rather than submit to the Spartan rule that mandates death for any flawed or deformed child. Due to his physical deformity and his parents' selfishness (according to Spartan law), Ephialtes is an exile from his country and from the rest of humanity. Yet he still desires glory and fame, some sort of recognition among men.

Xerxes at first presents the image of himself as lordly benefactor to both Leonidas and Ephialtes. His temptation of Leonidas echoes Christ's temptation by Satan in the desert: we see in each story a man alone, thirsty, physically exhausted, ready for sustenance and rest. "Kneel before me," the tempter whispers. "Submit to me, and I will give you kingdoms, wealth, and glory."[10] There is the question of whether those things are Xerxes' to give, but he doesn't concern himself with that, and neither shall we. It is not difficult to further cast Xerxes as the serpentine seducer, but humor me. His temptation of Ephialtes also eerily echoes another biblical story: that of Eve in Eden.[11] There the tempter Satan presents the divine authority of God as cruel and selfish, deliberately withholding freedom and glory from his creation, much as Xerxes presents Leonidas as cruel for not installing Ephialtes as a full Spartan warrior, and the Greek gods for forming his body so pitilessly. In each paralleling scenario, the tempter offers his own vision of glory: complete autonomy and freedom; independence from any authority save one's own desires; self-satisfaction without limits. Christ resists; Eve succumbs. Leonidas resists Xerxes' offer; Ephialtes accepts. Why?

If, as mentioned above, testing evokes a response from an individual that both reveals and determines his or her identity, what theological

10. Matt 4:1–11; Luke 4:1–13, ESV

11. Gen 3:1–6, ESV

insight might we gain by examining the temptation and the choice confronting both Leonidas and Ephialtes? What revelations about ourselves as human beings can we glean from their characters? Identity and being. Profound and complex ideas lying behind simple words. To address them would take a whole book (and lo! the Bible has been written for exactly that), but for now, let us look at Genesis 1:26a and 27: "Then God said, 'Let us make man in our image, after our likeness' . . . So God created man in his own image, in the image of God he created him; male and female he created them." Much ink has been spilled, reams of paper used, and many words spoken in wrestling with these verses, with what has come to be known as the Christian doctrine and symbol of *imago Dei*—the image of God.

Christian theology is, in many ways, concerned with symbols: concrete shapes that point toward and participate in an abstract reality that lies behind, and beyond, the symbol itself. Cross, book, king: we know immediately what we are dealing with, what concrete and implicit meanings are contained within these symbols. What can mean punishment in one context means salvation in another, and the more we interact with a symbol, especially within the context of Christian theology, the more we come to find that there are far greater and deeper significances that we first realized. Let us then view Leonidas as a concrete, contemporary symbol of *imago Dei*: the picture of humanity as it was created by God to be. Understanding *imago Dei*, in part, is seeing that mankind carries a refracted glory as the representative of a heavenly kingdom to an earthly kingdom, with the responsibility of acting as king, judge, priest, friend, spouse, lover, parent.

Any serious wrestling with what it means to be human will encounter questions of meaning, purpose, and function. Of what value is our life? Toward what goal do we progress? How do we achieve that goal and measure success? If humanity, according Genesis 2:18, is created for relationship by and for the God who himself existed in celestial and Trinitarian community before the creation of the world, then we become more fully human as we exist in community with other human beings. As Bonhoeffer points out, we "exist in duality"—being created male and female—and the only freedom or autonomy we have as individual creatures is the freedom to be in relationship with other creatures: "one human being is free for another human being."[12] The ground of this being is love, for the God who created humanity is love incarnate.[13] Human beings thus have three foci for being in relationship: God, other human beings, and the rest of creation. These three foci are inextricably linked: we cannot have relationships in one area to the exclusion of the others, for imaging God affects every area of human life.

Love is not a noun; it is a verb. It is only in "verb-ing"—doing or *giving* love—that we image God. To be *imago Dei*—with all the freedom, royalty, sonship, physicality, and relationality that that implies[14]—means that our identity and vocation in this life is to count others as higher, more significant than ourselves.[15] In recognizing that our freedom exists so that we might serve the other, to take on the weight of our neighbor's glory,[16] is to look after, to care for and cultivate, the *imago Dei* in each person. When this is modeled for and by a community, then glory—a good reputation, the divine accolade—becomes a shared good, not a rare commodity. Leadership in such a community (not, as it is often understood, a grasping after status and power) instead becomes an avenue to greater freedom, that is, greater servanthood. To be a leader, a king, is to display ever-greater love, even to the point of laying down one's life.[17]

We see the difference in communities built around, and against, a loving servanthood, in the scene where Xerxes reiterates his offer to Leonidas: "Have Greece kneel at your feet, if you will but kneel at mine."[18] Leonidas, ever snarky, refuses, his knees being "too stiff" from the morning's battle. Xerxes, furious, now throws all pretense of seduction to the wind, prophesying that there will be no glory in the Spartans' foolish, principled sacrifice, and makes very clear how he feels about his army, his community, such as it is: "I would gladly kill any of my men for victory."[19]

---

12. Bonhoeffer, *Creation and Fall*, 64.

13. 1 John 4:16, ESV

14. For more information on the doctrine of *imago Dei*, see Clines, "The Image of God in Man"; Grudem, *Systematic Theology*; Hall, *Imaging God*; and Kline, *Kingdom Prologue*.

15. Phil 2:3, ESV

16. Lewis, "The Weight of Glory," 45.

17. John 15:13, ESV

18. Snyder et al., *300*, Warner Brothers, 2007.

19. Ibid.

Leonidas fires back, "And I would die for any one of mine."[20] Greater love, indeed. Love celebrates the life of the other, recognizes and insists that it is truly "other," not simply an extension of oneself. Another human being can never truly be "mine" to use and manipulate as a tool. We are free only to be "yours."

As created human beings, we have a limit or a boundary in our very creatureliness.[21] There are some things, some ways of being that we simply cannot do or be. And if love is the ground of our being, we cannot bear that boundary of our creatureliness without both giving and receiving love. To be in community, and specifically in Christian community, is to bear one another's burden—of being human, with all that that entails; not to be subsumed into an undifferentiated collective, but to encourage one another as uniquely gifted members serving together as one body, so that it, "when each part is working properly, makes the body grow so that it builds itself up in love."[22]

The phalanx, the Spartan fighting unit in which each soldier protects with his shield his comrade to the left, is a beautiful image of the members of a community bringing itself together into a body that operates for a common purpose. This illuminates why Leonidas cannot accept Ephialtes into his army as a Spartan warrior, but also, how Ephialtes' understanding of and desire for a certain kind of glory causes him to reject Leonidas' counter-suggestion to be part of the "cleaning crew." The phalanx must have able-bodied members, but neither can it function properly if the battlefield is still littered with dead bodies. Ephialtes does not want this sort of glory; it is too humble, too weighty. He does not understand that the Spartans' greatest strength is "the warrior standing next to us."[23]

If Leonidas, in himself and in his community, is a symbol of *imago Dei*—mankind as the image of God—then we may see Ephialtes as a symbol of the image of Man. The rejection of the symbol of *imago Dei* leaves mankind broken, isolated, and incomplete. Because Leonidas does not lead for himself, but to serve his community and his country, he does not desire the vision of glory offered by Xerxes, nor does he need greater

20. Ibid.

21. Bonhoeffer, *Creation and Fall*, 99.

22. Eph 4:16, ESV

23. Snyder et al., *300*, Warner Brothers, 2007.

power, wealth, or status. This is why he resists Xerxes, though it comes with great cost, and not just for himself, but for others in his community.

In contrast, to withdraw from or reject the community of others, as Ephialtes was forced by birth, and then later chose, to do, is to choose oneself as the highest good, to refuse to see the *imago Dei* in others, and to refuse to love and be loved through serving under the weight of true glory. To be separate from any sort of community, to not see oneself or others as we are created to be, leaves us open to any offer that promises glory, pleasure, satisfaction, and freedom. The tragedy of Ephialtes is that he wants, desperately, to belong to a community, not as he is able, but as he desires. Indeed, the only thing he specifically asks of Xerxes is to have a uniform. He accepts the picture of glory Xerxes paints, though it means losing himself in the process.

As the highest expression of *imago Dei* is that of a conquering victim, a kingly servant, so Leonidas fully participates in the life of his community; there is no joy or sorrow that he does not share with his friends. He grieves with his captain, when the captain's son Astinos is slain on the battlefield; he exhorts his men to "prepare for glory," and he shelters and leads them as a parent leads a child.[24] He suffers with them as friend and father even as he encourages them as king and priest to continue in their mission. When Stelios, pierced through by Persian arrows at the end, crawls to his king's side for a final handclasp, he gasps, "My king, it's an honor to die at your side." Leonidas responds, "It's an honor to have lived at yours."[25] The greater love persists.

Leonidas' sacrificial life and death become the rallying cry and focal point for another community to form and grow; his story, as told by Dilios, spurs the Spartan and Greek army to gather at Plataea the next year to battle the Persian invaders yet again, this time, one presumes, to win victory. For Leonidas and the Spartans, their highest good, their greatest glory, is found in serving the ideal of a free, democratic Greek state, and as warriors, in dying "a good death." Their focus in either case is on something greater than themselves, and in living toward a goal that can only be achieved by creating a community that serves and encourages each other in mutuality, solidarity, and love.

24. Snyder et al., *300*, Warner Brothers, 2007.
25. Ibid.

We circle back to our initial questions: what eternal things can we learn from *300*, from Leonidas? Human beings are located at the very heart of the symbol of the cross in Christian theology, at the intersection of its horizontal and vertical axes. Through the characters of Leonidas and Ephialtes, we gain insight into how the horizontal axis of relationships and community may aid and define us at points of testing in our lives, which is to say, at every point in our lives. For those in Christian community, this contemporary, mythical film may help drive the vertical axis ever more deeply into our lives, so as to "re-enchant" our vision of our family, friends, neighbors, and community. After all, "there are no ordinary people."[26] If Genesis 1:26 is true, then we each display the symbol of *imago Dei*, though it may be obscured, rejected, or even (hopefully) cultivated once again in the course of our testings. What do King Leonidas and the brave three hundred finally, eternally, teach us? Above all, to prepare for glory. If such is our goal and hope, we begin to find that in serving and cultivating the *imago Dei* in others, we may yet see in and through each other to the true *imago Dei*: the Christ who is both the glorifier and the glorified.

---

26. Lewis, "The Weight of Glory," 46.

9

Making Dinner

The Artistry of Communal Meals
in *Babette's Feast* and *Antonia's Line*

JAMES H. THRALL

THROUGH THE VISUAL SHORTHAND of film, images of table fellowship can convey significant meaning powerfully yet economically, even in such gently paced movies as Gabriel Axel's *Babette's Feast* and Marleen Gorris's *Antonia's Line*. With the complexity of fine wine, scenes of people sharing food may carry overtones of other human needs: for companionship or acceptance or sexual connection—or for spiritual communion. As Angel F. Méndez Montoya notes, "food matters," not only as necessary for physical existence but as evocative instigator of "psychological, affective, and even spiritual transformation."[1] What does or does not happen around a filmed dining table can say much about the characters sitting at it.[2]

1. Montoya, *The Theology of Food*, 2.
2. A few revelatory depictions of food and dining in film might include: the inordinately long table separating Charles Foster Kane (Orson Welles) and his second wife Susan (Dorothy Comingore) as their marriage dissolves in *Citizen Kane* (1941); the erotic and communal significance of eating in *Like Water for Chocolate/Como agua*

Perhaps just because of the spiritual *gravitas* of food and table, in fact, images of dining may also be mined, as in these two films, for their subversive power. Simple—and not so simple—meals may suggest unsettling alternatives to the prevailing status quo. Both Axel and Gorris use representations of eating around a table to construct scenes that oppose and at the same time complete the dominant religious cultures of their filmed communities. In each case, what might be called the incarnational or inclusive "Catholicity" of the dining table corrects the perceived deficiencies of normative Christian institutions: a Catholic parish for Gorris; a small Protestant sect for Axel. Yet in both films what I would call the "excess significance" of food and table fellowship ultimately escapes Christian confines altogether to point toward broader and less easily defined intersections of artistry and religion.

Based on a short story by Isak Dinesen, pseudonym for Danish author Karen Blixen, *Babette's Feast* highlights a moment of table fellowship as an extraordinary event—a feast—that opens up new understanding of God's bounty. To describe the plot simply, Babette (Stephane Audran), a refugee from France's nineteenth-century civil unrest, uses all of the proceeds of a lottery winning to prepare one extravagantly sumptuous meal for her benefactors in the bleak Jutland village that has taken her in. Babette, formerly a celebrated chef in Paris, works in the village as a servant for two spinster sisters, Martine (Birgitte Federspiel) and Filippa (Bodil Kjer), who lead the pious but increasingly contentious members of their deceased father's Protestant community. In this instance, the subversive aspect of the meal is all too clear. The richness of the banquet Babette prepares contrasts unmistakably with the congregation's staple and unappetizing diet of split cod and ale-bread. The ascetic disciples, committed to their founder's admonition to eschew worldly things, and fearful that Babette's unfamiliar concoctions constitute a "witches' sabbath," resolve neither to enjoy nor to praise the meal. Babette's culinary achievement, however, aided by her guests' unaccustomed indulgence in champagne, undoes them. Despite themselves, the sect's members discover a new con-

---

para chocolate (1992); the reconciling power of cooking for someone else in *Big Night* (1996); Lester Burnham's (Kevin Spacey) freeing disruption of stifling family dinners in *American Beauty* (1999); and the telling ability or inability of characters to appreciate Vianne Rocher's (Juliette Binoche) magical confections in *Chocolat* (2000).

viviality and willingness to let go of deep-seated grudges as they confess and forgive old wrongs.

Yet, ironically, the subversion is itself a fulfillment of the founder's austere vision. He wrote the hymn about "Jerusalem, my heart's true home" that the congregation sings regularly, expressing trust that God will provide for their physical needs for food and clothing, and will lead them eventually to the New Jerusalem of God's kingdom. He also wrote the regularly intoned prophetic prayer that proclaims God's ways are unknowable and lead along unexpected routes: "God's paths run beyond the seas and the snowy mountain peaks, where the human eye sees no tracks." Precisely in the unexpected path of the worldly lures of physical sensuality—the lures the founder instructed his disciples to avoid—they find the fulfillment for which he and they at least had the wisdom to long. Having "fallen into the sin of ordinariness," Diane Tolomeo Edwards writes, the congregants require "an extraordinary experience to awaken them once more to the mystery of life."[3]

Ingrid Shafer, drawing on Catholic writers as diverse as Thomas Aquinas, David Tracy, and Andrew Greeley, would call this a prime example of "Catholic imagination" at work. Such a sensibility, she argues, by no means limited to Catholics, stresses the sacramental nature of the physical world in which "nature and the whole spectrum of human activities" may be the bearers of grace. It is a "both-and" way of thinking, she maintains, that understands the sacred potential of such profane and fundamental objects of life as food.[4] One approach to understanding the sacred power of Babette's marvelously profane meal is to note the Eucharistic symbolism that evokes both the Last Supper and the Supper's priestly re-enactments. For those she serves, Babette's self-sacrificial act creates a moment of redemption marked by confession and absolution; she is the thirteenth person serving a group of twelve; she is assisted by a young boy as waiter/acolyte; the main course has the biblically resonant name of "quails in sarcophagus." The list goes on.[5] But Babette's consummate skill in feeding hunger—physical and spiritual—resonates as both an avenue of grace and

---

3. Edwards, "*Babette's Feast*," 426.

4. Shafer, "The Catholic Imagination in Popular Film & Television," 52.

5. See Edwards, "*Babette's Feast*," 427. Others who note the Eucharistic associations of the meal include Wright in "*Babette's Feast*," and Marsh in "Did You Say 'Grace'?,"

an exercise of artistry in ways that make the Eucharistic reading only approximate at best.

The first thing to spill out of the specificity of Eucharistic or even Christian symbolism appears, in fact, to be the food. While Babette sincerely wishes to repay the kindness of the two sisters, she admits proudly after the meal that her true motivation has been desire for artistic fulfillment. In Paris, she recalls, "I was able to make them happy when I gave of my very best," but it is unclear whether she expected, understands, or even knows of the spiritual effect her dinner has had on the diners. For the chef that she is, the meal is her work of art, offered ultimately for its own sake and nothing more. Filippa, herself an unfulfilled musician, can still offer a Christian interpretation, murmuring rapturously in the film's final words that Babette's true fulfillment as an artist will be achieved in heaven. Shafer observes as well that "in the Catholic perspective, consciously or unconsciously, artists are sacrament makers, revealers of God-in-the-world, and there is no artistic medium that is excluded from this invitation or opportunity."[6] Still, it seems that in the end Axel, following Blixen, places the theological import of the meal within an artistic framework, rather than the other way around. Even though Babette's grand gesture may function as a self-sacrificial act of thanksgiving, the food and the artistry that produced it take on significance of their own as sheer enjoyment of the meal transports the participants. Christian critics, in fact, may voice some qualms about the extraordinariness of the feast. Clive Marsh, for example, asserts that for all of the banquet's wonder, any meal approached with the right attention to its communal implications could be equally transformative, lest, perhaps, God's grace be seen as dependent on exquisite seasoning.[7]

Although it can only be speculated, possible motivations behind Blixen's original short story might offer at least some sense of the great scope being claimed in the film for art and the various kinds of "food" it produces. Blixen reportedly wrote "Babette's Feast" after a friend suggested a story about food would help her break into the American maga-

6. Shafer, "Catholic Imagination," 52.

7. Marsh, "Did You Say 'Grace'?" 215–17. In the particular instance of Babette's meal, Marsh acknowledges, excellent cooking certainly helped: "[T]hrough their special meal they had more than glimpsed something new and fresh which would affect their future gatherings" (ibid., 217). But as a result, "their bread and fish meals . . . would take on a new quality" (ibid., 218).

zine market.[8] Might her engagement with the topic, however, have been more personal? According to biographer Judith Thurman, Blixen, though not a Christian, likened herself to a Catholic priest, "a wise, celibate and lonely figure," who sacrificed all for the writer's "opportunity to perform a great spiritual service for humanity."[9] It was a sense of vocation that incorporated long-standing issues with food. A conscientious and even extravagant hostess, Blixen herself "ate frugally," Thurman notes.[10] Even in her adolescence, Blixen showed a proclivity to fasting, "undertaken in an effort 'to achieve greatness' through 'hunger and suffering.'"[11] Fasting "became and remained for her, even when she was an old woman dying of emaciation, an ironic, powerful, and essentially feminine act of heroism," Thurman recounts. Starting in 1921, Blixen also suffered from mysterious bouts of severe abdominal pain that further interfered with her ability to eat, and which she, at least, attributed to the syphilis she had contracted from her husband as a young woman.[12] Whatever the cause for the pain and its contribution to the anorexia that marked her later life, by 1949, the year "Babette's Feast" was written, Blixen was already on the road toward the malnutrition that would kill her a little more than a decade later.[13] Her periodic bouts of depression, in connection with her health problems, also led her on occasion to tell friends that she believed she was dying.[14] Might she, of anyone, have had reason to attribute supreme importance

8. Biographer Judith Thurman describes the writing as the result of a wager with friend Geoffrey Gorer who suggested she "write about food . . . Americans are obsessed with food" (Thurman, *Isak Dinesen*, 329).

9. Ibid., 426.

10. Ibid., 328.

11. Ibid., 65.

12. Thurman attributes Blixen's acute health problems, including anorexia, diarrhea, and vomiting, to the continued effects of the syphilis, and specifically to syphilis of the spine or *tabes dorsalis* (ibid., 255). Linda Donelson MD, however, argues that Dinesen's syphilis was effectively cured by 1919, and suggests psychological causes, or poisoning from the arsenic Blixen took as treatment. See Donelson, "Appendix I," 349–57.

13. Donelson and Thurman attribute Blixen's final, fatal loss of weight to a 1956 surgery for a duodenal ulcer that removed a third of her stomach, leaving her unable to eat normal quantities of food (See Donelson, *Out of Isak Dinesen*, 355; and Thurman, *Isak Dinesen*, 387). Thurman, however, includes anorexia among Blixen's chronic health issues in describing her 1931 bout with abdominal pain, and notes that Blixen was hospitalized to gain weight in preparation for the stomach operation (Thurman, *Isak Dinesen*, 256–57)

14. Thurman, *Isak Dinesen*, 330.

to both food and the artistic creativity that had been the *raison d'etre* of her life? Conceivably, it was an importance for which not even Eucharistic symbolism would suffice.

In Axel's film, Babette's skill is described as the ability to "transform a dinner into a kind of love affair."[15] In *Antonia's Line*, sharing food again encapsulates sharing love—communal, filial, and sexual. Gorris presents regular, bucolic shots of the members of a multi-generational community enjoying the edible fruits of their farm around a rough country table set up outdoors. The faces smiling at each other across the hearty repast are linked by kinship in some cases, marriage or non-married partnership (both heterosexual and homosexual) in others, and generous affection in all. Numerous axes of the film converge to define this vision of how Gorris would shape a spiritual community, a vision so lovingly idealized that one critic describes *Antonia's Line* as a feminist's "wish-fulfillment" film.[16] In contrast to Babette's feast, the table here evokes the ordinariness of the relations and routines that sustain life, but in a way that highlights just how extraordinary those ordinary rhythms are.

The film opens at the end of World War II as the widow Antonia (Willeke Van Ammelrooy) returns to her home village in the Netherlands with her teenaged daughter, Danielle (Els Dottermans). She proceeds to create a matriarchal commune, gathering, in particular, the village's misfits and outcasts. Antonia's non-traditional "family" develops for the most part haphazardly though organically, in accordance with the apparent logic of particular moments of human connection. By the end of the film, Antonia's table has brought together the mentally retarded couple of Loony Lips and Deedee, the lesbian couple of Danielle and Lara, the unmarried, but highly reproductive couple of Letta and an ex-Catholic curate (simply called "the Priest"), as well as Antonia's own "line" of granddaughter Therese and great-granddaughter Sarah, both born out of wedlock. Antonia herself is paired in a companionable, unmarried liaison with a neighbor, Farmer Bas. In a way, the table also includes an absent member of the community, Crooked Finger, a nihilistic philosopher who never leaves his house in the village yet serves as mentor to both Therese and Sarah.[17]

15. Edwards, "*Babette's Feast*," 421.
16. Klawans, "Antonia's Line," 36.
17. Cast list: Loony Lips (Jan Steen), Deedee (Marina de Graaf), Lara (Elsie De

With her scenes of ever-burgeoning table fellowship, Gorris celebrates a broad understanding of fecundity that encompasses the more usual sense of reproducing offspring, but also the enjoyment of rich sexual and filial relationships, as well as the farmed land's cyclical blooming with food. Significantly, the other primary scenes in which nearly all the members of the community are present tend to be natural life transitions such as births and deaths, harvests, and a sequence, played for its humor, in which young Therese complains that she can't sleep because of the noise of joyful coitus coming from the farmhouse's different bedrooms. It would be hard to miss the connections drawn throughout the film between the life-generating functions of eating food and making love: Danielle first expresses her desire for Lara, for example, by describing the delicate act of eating of an artichoke. But in this last sequence of simultaneous, boisterous sex, Gorris cuts from Therese sleepily rubbing her eyes to a medium long-shot of the community again gathered at the outdoor table, just to make sure.

As in *Babette's Feast*, the subversive contrast of Antonia's table with the religious status quo is unmistakable. The sterile, celibate realm of the village's Catholic parish, where men and women sit on different sides of the church, is made the foil for the privileged fertile realm of earth mother Antonia. Against Antonia's stolid, self-assured, and independent figure is set the furtive and hypocritical head priest (not the curate who joins Antonia, but his superior), whose enforcement of sexual abstinence does not preclude his abuse of young girls in the confessional. Antonia and Danielle first step off the bus against the backdrop of the village's forbidding church and graveyard, but their future role is made clear as they walk under a banner proclaiming in roughly spelled English: "Welkom to our liberaters."

Antonia's alternative world, however, could be seen to evoke or perhaps perfect the Catholic structure it critiques, as though it were a mirror image that reflects even as it reverses. Specifically because of its ongoing association with the "right" or "richest" way to love, in all its manifestations, Antonia's table seems to echo the Christian parable of gathering society's outcasts into the wedding feast/kingdom of God (Matt 22). In

---

Brauw), Letta (Wimie Wilhelm), the Priest (Leo Hogenboom), Therese at different ages (Carolien Spoor, Esther Vriesendorp, Veerle van Overloop), Sarah (Thyrza Ravesteijn), Farmer Bas (Jan Decleir), Crooked Finger (Mil Seghers).

this earthly and earthy kingdom as Gorris has envisioned it, Antonia could be said to out-Catholic the Catholics, both in the inclusive sense of the word "Catholic" and in terms of Shafer's understanding of an incarnational Catholic imagination. Gorris floats what could be seen as a vision of a Christian community as it should be, if the community could be stripped of the encumbrance of rigid sexual mores, and be left to practice non-judgmental love. Antonia, a skeptical but regularly attending member of the parish, straddles both worlds after all, even as parish membership dwindles and the ranks of her line swell. Gorris also incorporates the church's cyclical and seasonal observances within her celebration of the natural cycles of life, though she makes it clear that the church rituals are at best imperfect vestiges of the annual rhythms that gave them birth. Antonia and Danielle, for example, plot to find a suitable male to father Danielle's baby while walking in a church procession for the officially sanctioned fertility rite of blessing the fields, a rite that invokes the "sacred feminine" through the chanting of female saints' names. That the procession is led by a supposedly celibate male who, despite his own sexual indiscretions, stands as champion of the church's insistence on sexual abstinence, winds the springs of irony even tighter.

At the same time, this is, admittedly, to read against the grain of Gorris's presentation, which will take Christian connotations only so far. She is more apparent in leaving the field clear for a certain pagan "religion of nature" that goes considerably beyond hints at the fertility cults absorbed in Christianity's roots.[18] The representations of church ceremonies, for example, include a funeral, the blessing of the fields just mentioned, and sermons, but no Eucharist to parallel and thus overly define the commune's country table. Instead, Gorris stresses the familiar yet mysterious cycles of birth, reproduction, and death, so much so that the film might better have been called Antonia's Circle than Antonia's Line. "This is the only dance we dance," Antonia says when her great-granddaughter asks whether there is a heaven. But that does not delimit the wonder and hope Gorris attributes to that dance, a hope held as much in the face of Crooked Finger's nihilism as the church's weak-kneed hypocrisy. "Nothing dies forever," Antonia states. "Something always remains from which something

---

18. At one point, Antonia embraces darker elements of that nature religion when she threatens to curse—with graphic specificity—a man who has raped Therese.

new grows." "Why?" asks Sarah. Replies Antonia, "Because life wants to live."

The film's structure itself is a cycle, opening as Antonia wakes on what she knows will be the last day of her life, and ending as she dies at the day's close. In between, her story is rendered as an extended flashback by a nameless narrator, who, it is revealed in the film's final moments, is Sarah, grown into the adult author of her great-grandmother's story. The seam, the point at which that story rejoins the frame of Antonia's final day is, of course, again the outdoor table where the surviving members of the community gather for their last table fellowship with her. With Sarah's vision of dead friends and enemies watching from a perimeter around the table, Gorris seems to be looking both ways, toward what could be taken as a Christian image of the universal and eternal communion of saints, but also toward a more naturalistic understanding of the remarkable interdependence of life and death. At the center of either vision is the connecting power of the table and the food upon it. By now the almost all-knowing skill with which Antonia has shaped her community has shown her to be in touch with a wider, or perhaps it is a deeper, understanding of how that connection can indeed bind a world together. Like Babette, she has had the rare creative skill to bring it about through an artistry that is, in her case, mirrored in the vocations of her descendants: Danielle the painter, Therese the musician, and finally Sarah the writer. And if Antonia's artistry has created a community, Sarah's storytelling conveyed through Gorris's filmmaking has created an audience, or so Gorris may hope, expanding the fellowship to include all who watch the movie, and having watched, feel drawn to sit at the table and eat.

Section III

From the Light, Into the Darkness:
Horror, Sci-Fi, Fantasy, and Apocalypse

10

The Parable of the Poltergeist

Making Righteous Use of the Element of Horror

TRAVIS PRINZI

ONE OF THE FIRST horror movies I ever watched was *Poltergeist*, a 1982 film that has become a classic of the horror genre. I think I was quite young for horror films when I watched it, probably ten or twelve years old. I developed a fascination for Gothic stories and began devouring Stephen King novels and watching the films. Something about the genre intrigued me, drew my imagination, pulled me to want to find out what was hiding around the corner, what was underneath the ground of the cemetery, what was hiding in the closet.

Perhaps much to the surprise of the believers in some theologies, I have never been drawn to the occult, never performed a Satanic ritual, and never been possessed by a demon. Nothing in any of the horror films I watched ever made me want to do that. Quite the opposite, in fact, and this is the point I want to argue in what follows: that horror films are for Christians. And I'm going to use *Poltergeist* (and a few great Christian thinkers) to do it. We'll begin with theoretical foundations for the use of horror in art. We'll give consideration to Gothic imagery in other forms of art, notably architecture and literature. We'll then proceed to apply this to film, with particular reference to *Poltergeist* to illustrate the points.

"Making Righteous Use of the Element of Horror"

Guillermo del Toro is an interesting figure. He was once offered the opportunity to direct the first Narnia movie, *The Lion, the Witch and the Wardrobe*. He turned it down, he told the Associated Press, because he was a "lapsed Catholic" who could not see himself bringing Aslan back to life.[1] Instead, he made *Pan's Labyrinth,* a movie about a young girl (Ofelia) who once belonged to a magical Underworld where she was a princess, and who, upon sacrificing herself for the life of her brother, is finally able to return to that world.

Jeffery Overstreet notes the irony: del Toro turned down a movie that was overtly Christian, but made one that reflects some very Christian themes, most notably the shedding of innocent blood for salvation.[2]

For many Christians, the combination just doesn't work: a "lapsed Catholic" who can't accept the resurrection of Aslan (Christ) makes a horror movie, and some of us think that the horror movie has Christian themes? Impossible. We're warned against horror movies—they involve supernatural fear, sometimes the occult, and we're told to avoid these things, right? When *Sherlock Holmes*—not even a "horror" film—came out, I received emails from some Christians with dire warnings not to see it, because there were occult elements. If *Sherlock Holmes* is dangerous for the Christian mind,[3] surely horror movies must be. Don't they celebrate the grotesque and draw toward the occult?

Not necessarily. There is, in fact, a very appropriate place for horror movies in the life of the discerning Christian. Good art—whether painting, sculpture, story, or film—should tell the truth about the world with imagination and beauty. But what if aspects of the truth are not beautiful? That question is at the heart of the argument that Christians should create and watch films that fit into the genre of Gothic or horror.

---

1. Chattaway, "Del Toro, *Pan's Labyrinth,* and *Narnia* Redux."
2. Overstreet, "Pan's Labyrinth," *Christianity Today.*
3. To be clear, it's not. The "occult" people are the movie's bad guys, and the bad guys are shown to be powerless in the end.

First, let's take a look at the common opposition to horror films, and then we'll progress to the positive argument in favor of them for Christians. Objections to horror films generally focus on a few key points: (1) Satanic or occult elements, (2) gore or grotesque imagery, and (3) guarding the Christian mind against evil.

Concerning the first issue, I find this to be a non-starter. The mere presence of Satanic or occult elements in a story cannot possibly be enough to rule out the genre, because we'd then have to stop reading the Scriptures. Satanic elements, even in horror movies, are generally considered evil; the occult is the significant portion of the horror to be feared, avoided, or defeated. If the movie is actually an all-out celebration of Satanism, then perhaps we have a concern, but I don't think you'll find this often.

Concerning the second, there will be more to say about the grotesque and its appropriate use in Christian art to follow. At present, we should note, once again, that significant portions of the Scriptures would have to be avoided by the same rule. From Ehud's plunging the knife completely into King Eglon's belly, to Ezekiel's having to cook his food on burning dung, to King Herod's being eaten by worms, to the supernatural monsters of Revelation, there is gore and grotesque imagery throughout the Bible.

Concerning the third issue, it is certainly imperative to guard our hearts and minds, but as already argued in response to the first issue, evil is generally considered evil in horror movies. The evil is the element that creates the fear, and the "good guys" of the film are opposed to the horror. Some may regard the feeling of fear itself created by the film to be dangerous for the Christian mind. I find this argument weak. We experience fear regularly in life, and as children do with fairy tales, it may be quite beneficial for us to put symbols to our fears in story form on a screen in order to learn to name them and deal with them. Far from being dangerous, experiencing fear in story form is actually a very good thing.

George MacDonald made this point well. MacDonald was a nineteenth-century pastor, theologian, and writer and critic of fiction, with particular emphasis on imaginative, or fantasy, fiction. He wrote defenses of fairy tales, as well as fairy stories of his own. In a preface to a book called *Letters from Hell,* MacDonald takes up the issue of Christian engagement with horror.

> I would not willingly be misunderstood: when I say the book is full of truth, I do not mean either truth of theory or truth in art, but something far deeper and higher—the realities of our relations to God and man and duty—all, in short, that belongs to the conscience. Prominent among these is the awful verity; that we make our fate in unmaking ourselves; that men, in defacing the image of God in themselves, construct for themselves a world of horror and dismay; that of *the outer darkness* our own deeds and character are the informing or inwardly creating cause; that if a man will not have God, he can never be rid of his weary and hateful self.[4]

MacDonald argues that horror shows us the "awful truth" of dehumanization—what happens to human beings who stray from their created purposes. We see this kind of Gothic imagery in our best monster movies: vampires, goblins, zombies, and werewolves are all humans or former humans. MacDonald argues that we should "make righteous use of the element of horror."[5] Moreover, he warns those who oppose the use of horror in art: "Let him who shuns the horrible as a thing in art unlawful, take heed that it be not a thing in fact by him cherished; that he neither plant or nourish that root of bitterness whose fruit must be horror—the doing of wrong to his neighbor; and least of all, if the indifference in the unlawful there be, that most unmanly of wrongs whose sole defence lies in the cowardly words: 'Am I my sister's keeper!'"[6] In other words, when we fear the use of horror, we dismiss something of great value: an imaginative reminder of the consequences of rebellion against God. In fact, we become cowards ourselves, comfortable in our sin, committing the very evils we say we should not be viewing in a movie. When we throw out the horror genre altogether out of fear of Satanic influence, we give in to fear itself, become cowards, and lose a valuable conduit for truth. This is not to throw discernment out the window in choosing and evaluating films, but we err on the other side when we pharisaically rule out the genre altogether.

Did not Christ himself use terror is his stories and in his encounters with other humans? Gehenna, undying worms, a rich man in the torment of hell, murder, and life after death all play roles in Jesus' stories. He had actual encounters with demons who drove people insane, caused them

4. MacDonald, *Preface to* Letters from Hell, vi–vii.

5. Ibid., viii.

6. MacDonald, Preface to *Letters from Hell*, ix.

to throw themselves into fires, screeched and screamed, and the evangelists did not shy away from these stories when recounting Jesus' life. In a world where horror is real, stories must contain monsters and demons. Evil should not be celebrated, but it should be portrayed in our art, music, and movies.

Many horror films, especially those containing supernatural terror, belong to the symbolist tradition of storytelling. In other words, horror films belong in the fantasy fiction genre. They are fairy tales, in essence, because they use imaginative worlds and creatures to create a myth-like experience that conveys truth. So the Ring Wraiths of Middle Earth are Gothic figures, monsters of horror that fit alongside zombies and vampires as symbols of dehumanization.

Dr. Ann Blaisdell Tracy believes that "the Gothic world is above all the Fallen world, the projection of a post-lapsarian nightmare of fear and alienation."[7] She wrote, "novels with Gothic overtones might best be identified not as those which contain some superficial trapping like a ruined monastery or the rumor of a ghost . . . but as those . . . which contain imagery or action pertinent to the Gothic/Fallen world., i.e., wandering, delusions, temptation."[8] Horror and Gothic films, then, help us put symbols and images onto the many nameless and shapeless fears we experience in this Fallen world. They give us an imaginative context for thinking about what it means to live in a chaotic world that is not as it was created to be.

Poltergeist as Parable

We'll illustrate this now with reference to *Poltergeist*, but we have to back up a little bit and introduce some art criticism that pertains to and serves as a foundation for the subject at hand. This may seem like it's coming out of nowhere, but let's talk about architecture for a bit. Trust me, I'll bring it back around to film; architecture, oddly enough, is key to understanding the true terror of *Poltergeist*. We need to backtrack a few centuries prior to film and learn from John Ruskin. Although he was well known in his day and has had a profound effect on society as we know it, many people have never even heard of John Ruskin. If you've heard of Ruskin at all, it's probably because Oxford's college of English is named after him; or per-

7. Tracy, *Patterns of Fear in the Gothic Novel*, 313.
8. Ibid., 327.

haps you've read his fairy tale, "The King of Golden River," which I highly recommend. But Ruskin was most known for two other things: criticism of art and architecture, and political philosophy.

Ruskin argued that the best and most Christian kind of architecture was Gothic. He wrote at length about this, but here we'll focus on two characteristics of the Gothic that apply to the discussion at hand: "savageness" and "grotesqueness."

Savageness: Our Houses Are Lies

Ruskin argued that Gothic architecture told the truth, because the world that God created is not full of symmetry and perfectly straight lines, but constant change—of landscape, from mountains to valleys to plains, from land to sea, from wild to calm, high to low, straight to jagged, rough to smooth.[9] And no one would say that God is a bad artist or architect. I suspect Ruskin would be rather upset by many of our modern housing developments. Every time we focus on symmetry and perfection in our art and architecture and story, we're hiding the truth.

Housing developments where all houses look symmetrical, pristine, perfect, and exactly alike are attempts by a deceitful human heart to create an illusion of safety and perfection that simply does not exist in a fallen world. That sounds like a pretty strong statement about houses, but it's true. The safety of fences and perfect angles is a created illusion in the wild world we live in. Gothic architecture, with its jagged lines and asymmetry looks more like the world God created. If you find yourself more easily able to worship in an old stone church, especially a Gothic building, you might be tempted to think you're not spiritual enough to worship just anywhere, but you'd be wrong. That architecture tells us something about the world. The spaces we create to focus on God tell us something about what we believe about him and about ourselves. Ruskin said any art that strives toward perfection is bad art. Look at the world, he said. Take a look at the way God himself created. Is any mountain perfectly symmetrical? When God made mountain developments, did he create the same thing over and over? Even things that look the same—daisies, snowflakes,

9. Ruskin, "The Nature of Gothic."

maple trees—have endless variations from one to the other.[10] Hang on to this point about savageness; we will return to it.

Grotesque: Our Houses are Haunted

We know that God's brilliant, changing, wild creation is also fallen. Because of this, the lie of the perfect house is compounded by the fact that not only does it fail to represent God's creativity, but there are ghosts in the closets. It's not as peaceful and perfect as it looks.

We do this not only with our houses, but with our stories. When we want our heroes flawless, or at the very least, when we want to make sure they never get away with any wrongdoing, we lie about reality. This has been a common complaint with the *Harry Potter* stories, for example. Harry, the hero, lies and sometimes gets away with it. That's supposed to be a bad example, but the truth is, it's reality. We're flawed people, and sometimes we lie and get away with it.

It's believed by many that horror stories are not Christian. Now there are some horror stories that simply rejoice in what is disgusting and embrace what Russell Kirk calls the diabolic imagination.[11] But the horror genre itself is the furthest thing from non-Christian. Horror stories tell the truth. Every time we try to clean up a Grimm fairy tale and make it nicer, we begin to cover up scars of the curse and lie to ourselves. When we hide our kids from scary elements of these fairy tales because they might be afraid or have nightmares, we lie to ourselves and our children about the world. Kids (and adults!) are going to have nightmares whether they read the scary story or not. At least in reading the scary story, Maurice Sendak would say, we find an analog for our nightmares somewhere in our waking experience, and we no longer feel that we're alone.[12] This is why it's perfectly fine and even very Christian to read and enjoy Bram Stoker, H. P. Lovecraft, and Stephen King.

As noted above, art should tell the truth with imagination and beauty. But the question still remains: What if the truth is not always beautiful? The truth of the Fall is not beautiful in the least. It's terrifying. But it is

---

10. Ruskin, "The Nature of Gothic."

11. Kirk, "The Moral Imagination," 37–49.

12. Natov, "Harry Potter and the Extraordinariness of the Ordinary," 310–27.

reality, and as creative truth-tellers, Christians should be highly involved in the horror film genre. We dare not neglect to tell the truth. This means that Christians who create and enjoy the art of film should engage in the imaginative and symbolic portrayal of the terrors of our world. Christians have long embraced the Gothic imagination in their artwork, sculptures, and fiction; we should embrace it, with a commitment to truth-telling, in our movies as well.

Poltergeist as Parable

The 1982 classic horror film *Poltergeist* illustrates well the kind of imaginative, horrific truth-telling that can be accomplished in film. *Poltergeist* is a good film for illustrating the points at hand, precisely because it is a *good* film; and by that I mean it is artistically well done. It was met with widespread critical acclaim and continues to be a popular horror film with discussions of remakes in the works.

At the beginning of the film, the stage is set: After an initial scene where five-year-old Carol Anne Freeling hears voices in the television, the film opens with a panning shot across a massive housing development (one Ruskin would have hated), a happy neighborhood on a Sunday afternoon where kids ride their bikes, ice cream trucks make rounds through cul-de-sacs, and the biggest problem the community faces is remote controls on the same frequency, causing neighbors to accidentally change the channels on those next door. It is, perhaps, the kind of American dream environment for which many of us hope—a safe place to raise our kids and enjoy the fruits of our labor.

But even on that peaceful Sunday, Carol Anne has to experience death for the first time—the death of her pet canary. It's handled with a burial, and then it's back to the business of Sunday fun and relaxation. That night, Carol Anne finds herself talking to a fuzzy TV again, and something supernatural makes its way into the house. Carol Anne does not yet know she's about to come a lot closer to death than the corpse of a pet bird.

The next day, we begin to see the difference between the lie being told by the perfect, pristine neighborhood, and the reality of the terror below. The story unfolds with two different story arcs for the day, one mundane, and one supernatural. Steve, Carol Anne's father, happens to be very important as a salesman in this housing development. We see him at work, showing houses, and receiving some very telling feedback from one of his clients: "I can't tell one house from the other."[13] Remember Ruskin's architecture criticism.

Back home, however, weird things have begun to happen. Chairs are moving seemingly of their own accord. If an object or person is placed in a specific spot on the kitchen floor, it will move on its own to the other side of the kitchen. These supernatural phenomena are met with excitement and fascination by Carol Anne and her mother, by fear from Steve when he returns home.

That night, Carol Anne is taken away by a poltergeist, and the rest of the film is spent in an attempt to retrieve her through the use of paranormal experts and a medium. We get a picture of the deception and lure of evil in the explanation given by Tangina, the medium: "A terrible presence is in there with her . . . It keeps Carol Anne very close to it and away from the spectral light. It lies to her, it tells her things only a child could understand. It has been using her to restrain the others. To her, it simply is another child. To us, it is the Beast."[14] Here we have a picture of the deceit of sin. Doesn't sin attract us in much the same way? Didn't the serpent speak to Eve in words she could understand, make itself seem like her friend, her ally, when all the while it was deceiving her? This is the evil that the family in *Poltergeist* (a family referred to in the film, interestingly enough, as "Christians") has to battle. It is also the evil that we have to battle daily.

What is particularly interesting is the cause of the poltergeist invasion. After Carol Anne has been rescued, and peace has ostensibly returned to the house, all hell breaks loose again, as the poltergeist makes one more attempt to get to Carol Anne. Skeletons are unearthed from the ground, and Steve recalls that the housing development is built on an old cemetery that was supposedly moved. Confronting his boss, the development's owner, he shouts: "You moved the cemetery, but you left the bodies, didn't you? . . . you left the bodies and you only moved the headstones! You only moved the headstones! Why? Why?"[15]

Here we've come to the real truth-telling value of the horror genre. We can do everything in our power to mask the Fall, to create an illusion

13. Spielberg et al., *Poltergeist*, Metro-Goldwyn-Mayer, 1982.
14. Ibid.
15. Spielberg et al., *Poltergeist*, Metro-Goldwyn-Mayer, 1982.

of safety and tranquility. But underneath it all, the terror of our rebellion against God and its consequences remains. Nothing symbolizes this better than death, which is why the horror of *Poltergeist* culminates in dead bodies coming up from the ground. As the perfect, pristine house is destroyed in a supernatural explosion, the lies they formerly believed about the world come undone: The world is not predictable. It is not safe. It is not peaceful. Even those who believe in Christ are risen from *the dead.* "You were dead," St. Paul reminds us. And if that weren't enough, our sinful nature still wages war against us (Gal 5). The destruction of the Freelings' house by the supernatural dead tells a much truer story than the image of the tranquil neighborhood that opened the film.

There are plenty of other lessons we could pull from *Poltergeist,* but I think the point is sufficiently established: the film, whether the writers intended it or not, artistically conveys spiritual truth, and there is value in it for the Christian.

Noble Grotesque and Evil Grotesque

None of this means discernment gets thrown out the window. Just as there are edifying and evil action, drama, and romantic films, so there are edifying and evil horror films. Ruskin argued that there was a grotesque that belonged to a moral imagination and that which did little more than celebrate evil. Of course, for the Christian, discernment is necessary.

We do well to note that the response of some people does not implicate the film in evil. In other words, just because someone's depraved imagination receives something grotesque in a movie as "cool," it does not mean the film should not be viewed. The problem might very well be in the response of the individual rather than in the film itself. Continuing with the *Poltergeist* illustration, the scene when the paranormal expert imagines himself tearing his own face off is, indeed, grotesque. But it's certainly not meant for us to respond with delight: "Wasn't it awesome how he tore his own face off?" It's supposed to create in us a response of fear of evil: "Look at the deception wrought by the Beast. Look at the way he used fear to drive them away."

An important question should be raised and answered here: What about horror films that do not have happy endings? What if the bad guy, the demon, the vampire "wins"? Isn't that anti-truth? Consider the classic horror film, *Night of the Living Dead.* The walking dead succeed in killing the main characters. Or Hitchcock's *The Birds*; the terrifying birds are not defeated in the end. How can these films be embraced by Christians? Don't we believe that good wins in the end?

Yes, of course we do. But I submit that a horror film that ends with evil winning is not, by default, a movie that tells a lie. At the end of all things, justice will be done and evil eradicated. In the meantime, however, in this fallen world, many stories end, in the short term, with the victory of evil over good. We should not shy away from this in our storytelling. Even Tolkien, who argued strongly for the importance of the "happy ending" for fairy tales, wrote stories like *The Children of Hurin,* which hardly has what you could call a "happy" ending. If we're committed to the truth in our storytelling, we will probably, at least sometimes, create or view movies where the bad guys win. It will hopefully drive us once again to hope only in Christ for salvation, and not in ourselves.

The Fall and Our Fears In Film

I conclude, then, that there is a very important place for the horror film in the life of the Christian. Horror films provide a symbolic scaffolding for us to frame our thoughts about the fallen state of the world and the fear which accompanies it. Earlier, I referenced Maurice Sendak. Sendak is the author of *Where the Wild Things Are*, which was recently made into a film as well. He's very outspoken, sometimes harshly so, about children being allowed to learn to cope with weighty matters of fear. When asked whether the monsters in his book were too scary for children, he responded: "Most frightening to children is to dream their own figures of fear and find no analogue in anything they hear about or read. Children need to see their feelings, particularly the darkest ones, reflected in their stories. Mitigating the darkness of the fairy tale takes away their power to reassure children that they are not alone in their fearful imaginings; that they are shared and can be addressed."[16] There's wisdom there. I submit that it is not children alone who need this, but adults as well. We adults might be worse at coping with fear than many children, in fact. This fallen world we live in is a terrifying place, and we need some framework to get a handle on it, to think about it, to put symbols and words to nameless fears, to experience

16. Natov, "Harry Potter," 310–27.

it in an atmosphere where we can talk it out with other people on the same journey. Zombies and vampires become pictures of the spiritually dead who feed on the living. Perhaps more important, Jeckyl and Hyde or Frankenstein and his monster become symbols of the evil that dwells within our own hearts. In all of these images, we find the same answer that del Toro found symbolically, even after he rejected Aslan for *Pan's Labyrinth*: we are only saved from it all by the sacrificial death of One on our behalf, One who went through all our terrors and took our death and came out alive, whose perfect love will one day cast out all fear.

11

The Undiscovered Country

Star Trek and the Christian's Human Journey

KEVIN C. NEECE

Who would fardels[1] bear, to grunt and sweat under a weary life, but that the dread of something after death, the undiscovered country, from whose bourn no traveller returns, puzzles the will, and makes us rather bear those ills we have than fly to others that we know not of?
—*HAMLET*, ACT III, SCENE 1[2]

IN ITS ORIGINAL CONTEXT in Shakespeare's *Hamlet*, the phrase "undis-covered country" refers to the afterlife and its terrifying potential to consist of either damnation or oblivion. In Hamlet's view, humankind's only motivation for bearing life's burdens may well be nothing more than the fear that death will lead us to something worse. However, in *Star Trek*, a universe replete with references to Shakespeare, this phrase is re-contextualized. In the 1994 film, *Star Trek VI: The Undiscovered Country*,

1. Burdens
2. Shakespeare, *Hamlet*, 75.

the Klingon Chancellor Gorkon uses the term "undiscovered country" to refer to the future and the possibility of peace at the end of the sometimes frightening road of reconciliation. By the film's end, Captain Kirk again uses this phrase to describe the future voyages and discoveries of the starship *Enterprise*, a nod to the then current series, *Star Trek: The Next Generation*.[3]

Call it "the undiscovered country," "the final frontier," "new worlds," or "where no man has gone before,"[4] but Star Trek[5] has always been about the pursuit of something beyond our earthbound human grasp. From its inception as a television series in 1966, through five additional series and eleven (soon to be twelve) feature films, Star Trek has remained, if nothing else, the story of a quest. For the Christian pop culture scholar, then, the question becomes, "What is Star Trek's quest ultimately seeking and how does it relate to my journey and teleological aim as a follower of Christ?" Or, put more simply, "What can Christians learn from Star Trek?"

Let me be clear. I am not seeking here to propose a secretly Christian agenda in Star Trek, though I do find God strangely ever-present in its supposedly atheistic universe. Rather, as it has so thoroughly captured the hearts and imaginations of an ever-widening fanbase over the past forty-six years, I seek instead to ask what it is that Star Trek is hitting upon that so many are seeking. More specifically, I am concerned with what *Star Trek* has found that perhaps our modern Christianity has failed to find or, more properly, has lost.

This may seem odd to anyone with a basic knowledge of Star Trek. One might wonder what a Christian is to find that is of value in this particular science fiction franchise. After all, the Trek universe is hardly a Christian allegory. In fact, in all its incarnations, Star Trek's worldview

---

3. Meyer, *Star Trek VI*, Paramount Pictures, 1991.

4. These three quoted phrases are derived from the opening monologue of the original *Star Trek* TV series. The phrase "where no man has gone before" also appears in the films *Star Trek II: The Wrath of Khan* and *Star Trek V: The Final Frontier*. *Star Trek VI*, *Star Trek: The Next Generation*, and the 2009 film *Star Trek* all use the phrase "where no *one* has gone before," while *Star Trek: Enterprise* opted for "where no *human* has gone before."

5. Throughout this chapter, I will italicize the words "Star Trek" only when referring to a specific Star Trek series or film title. When de-italicized, the words refer to the franchise and/or philosophy of Star Trek as a whole. This is in keeping with convention and to avoid confusion with specific references to the original TV series or the 2009 film, *Star Trek*.

has consistently and firmly rested on the philosophical foundation of a thorough-going humanism. However, it is precisely that humanism that is of interest here. While Star Trek is certainly concerned with the future, technology, exploration, and how humans might advance as a species, the journey of the *Enterprise* (and that of her sister ships and space stations) has always been a metaphorical one. Though the ship's crew may encounter strange alien species, these species merely stand in for different types of humans. Through its fictitious peoples and their imagined struggles, *Star Trek* has always been able to address relevant cultural issues, sometimes in ways that would never have been directly discussed on television. Over the years, its stories have been thinly veiled discussions of such topics as racism, war, religion, gender and sexuality, terrorism, bigotry, and euthanasia, to name a few.

Hiding within a science fiction adventure show has always been a philosophical inquest. Thus, the true journey of Star Trek has never been simply a journey outward, but also a journey inward. Like characters in Chaucer, the characters of Star Trek reveal and explore the human condition in the process of their quest.

For many modern Christians, such a focus on humanity is uncomfortable. The notoriously dualistic nature of much of Western Christian thought sees a strong divide between the spirit and the flesh. Seeking to avoid the messy, complicated, sinful world of the here and now, this view focuses instead on what might be called a "there and then" ideal, where spiritual purity lies waiting on the other side of an escape from the prison of a human body. To those with such a perspective, being human is a waiting game until "the Lord calls us home." So repugnant to many of us is our human nature that we live in a state of constantly denying its needs, its beauty, and its purpose. Indeed, if there is an undiscovered country in modern Christianity, it is perhaps our own humanity.

A deeper, more holistic view, however, recognizes that we are human for a reason. God created us as humans to be humans and not anything else. It then becomes clear that an understanding of who we are as human beings is intrinsic to our understanding of who we are as children of God. If we can deeply explore what it means to be human, then and only then can we discover what it means to be human to the glory of God.

It would seem, though, that Star Trek, as a standard-bearer of antireligious, atheistic humanism, would be far too empty a story to contain fuel for such a fire. However, there are caveats to Star Trek's humanistic philosophy that are essential to understanding its Christian application. *Star Trek*'s humanism rests upon, among other things, two basic beliefs about humanity. The first is the continuing forward progress of the human race. The founding concept of the Star Trek universe is that its stories take place in a future time when mankind has evolved enough and has achieved sufficient technological advancement to eradicate many diseases, end war and conflict, abandon religion and superstition, end hunger and unite as one world to reach out into the stars.

This supposed utopia of creator Gene Rodenberry's imagination, however, is mentioned but never fully realized onscreen. The simple reason for this is that Star Trek's writers have always understood that story thrives on conflict; without conflict there is—in general—no story. In other words, in a perfect world, nothing interesting ever happens. In fact, one of the central tenants of Star Trek ultimately seems to be the human need for challenge and growth through struggle in order to advance as a species. Ironically, Roddenberry's over-zealous optimism left little room for such a struggle and he never seemed completely comfortable with the contrast between his stated vision of the future and the one actually portrayed in the Star Trek TV series and films. "Mr. Roddenberry really believed in the perfectability of man, of humans," *Star Trek VI* director Nicholas Meyer said. "In fact, in his original *Star Trek* concept, there wasn't any conflict, so he always had problems with writers who were trying to write conflict, 'cause that's what drama is."[6]

This juxtaposition of ideal and reality does, however, result in a possible, if underlying, philosophical motivation for Star Trek's characters as they venture out into the galaxy. If what Roddenberry says is true and life on his imagined 23rd-century Earth is as idyllic as he makes it sound, then perhaps the men and women of Starfleet are—however unconsciously—actually seeking out the conflicts they often find in space. Since human beings intrinsically need conflict and struggle to grow, an Earth that no longer included these obstacles might compel humans to look for challenges elsewhere.

Whatever the case, Star Trek does succeed in portraying a vision of the future that is decidedly more hopeful than that of its contemporaries in the sci-fi genre. In the 1950s and '60s, science fiction was consumed

6. Meyer, "Nick Meyer on His Gene Roddenberry Regret."

with stories of alien invaders coming to Earth to destroy or enslave humans. Reflecting the pervasive paranoia of the burgeoning nuclear age, these films and television shows brought for their audiences both excitement and a cathartic expression of the fears and anxieties that plagued the country and the world. At the same time, conflicts over racial segregation in the United States were at a boiling point and the fear of infiltration by Cold War spies was prevalent. These sci-fi stories, then, reflected a growing fear of the "other," be they Russians across the sea or people of another race living down the street.

By contrast, on *Star Trek*, humans of different races worked side-by-side as equals and even alongside alien species. Additionally, it is not insignificant that the *Enterprise*'s impulse engines are fueled by a nuclear reaction, transforming a widely feared weapon of war into the fuel for a vessel of peace. In these ways and others, the series offered hope that, as Roddenberry stated, "there is a tomorrow. It's not all gonna be over with a big flash and a bomb,"[7] and that the human race, which presently seemed poised to destroy itself, was improving and advancing toward a more peaceful future.

Such optimism is necessary for a humanist who does not wish to also be a nihilist. The fact of existing as human beings is that we deteriorate, die, and decay. It is therefore particularly important for a humanist that the human race advance, progress, and grow. There is something about improving ourselves as human beings that seems to counteract the nagging approach of death. If we are a part of something that is greater than ourselves, then we can have a purpose. If all we are ends in dust and nothing ever changes, then there is, as Hamlet observes, no point in living beyond a fear of death.

An optimism about the human race and indeed a conviction about its nobility, beauty and excellence emerges in an episode of *Star Trek: The Next Generation* in a conversation between Captain Picard and Q, a powerful being who has a penchant for forcing the crew of the *Enterprise* to participate in bizarrely constructed games—often with life and death stakes.

> PICARD: Listen to me, Q. You seem to have some need for humans.
>
> Q: Hmm . . . concern regarding them.

7. Beck, *Star Trek 25th Anniversary Special*, Paramount Pictures, 1991.

PICARD: Well, whatever it is, why do you demonstrate it through this confrontation? Why not a simple, direct explanation, a statement of what you seek? Why these games?

Q: Why these games? Well, the play's the thing. And I'm surprised you have to ask when your human Shakespeare explained it all so well.

PICARD: So he did, but don't depend too much on any one single viewpoint . . .

Q: It's a pity you don't know the content of your own library. Hear this, Picard, and reflect: "All the galaxy's a stage . . ."

PICARD: World, not galaxy. All the *world*'s a stage.

Q: Oh, you know that one. Well, if he were living now he would have said "galaxy." How about this? "Life is but a walking shadow, a poor player that struts and frets his hour upon the stage and then is heard no more. It is a tale told by an idiot, full of sound and fury, signifying nothing."

PICARD: I see. So how we respond to a game tells you more about us than our real life, this tale told by an idiot. Interesting, Q.

Q: Oh, thank you very much. I'm glad you enjoyed it. Perhaps maybe a little *Hamlet*?

PICARD: Oh no, I know Hamlet. And what he might say with irony, I say with conviction: "What a piece of work is a man, how noble in reason, how infinite in faculty, in form and moving, how express and admirable. In action, how like an angel, in apprehension, how like a god!"

Q: Surely you don't see your species like that, do you?

PICARD: I see us one day becoming that, Q. Is it that which concerns you?[8]

The scene ends with an infuriated Q hurling a book of Shakespeare at Picard's chest and vanishing from the captain's ready room, clearly threatened by how close Picard is getting to the truth about his motivations and possible insecurities. Q is drawn to humans in part because he is threatened by their current level of development and their achievement of reaching out into the stars. But it is their potential—their future—that most clearly unsettles him. It is not what they have achieved, but what they are on the path toward achieving that he finds most irksome—and

8. Bole, "Hide and Q," *Star Trek: The Next Generation*, Paramount Pictures, 1987.

most dangerous. Ironically, his very annoyance with human advancement and his attempts at poking holes in the achievements of the human race are themselves evidence that the people of Earth may indeed be heading in the right direction.

As Q goes out of his way to mock and deride human history and the progress of the species, it seems that although he can explain away their past, he cannot divert them from their future. Unlike other adversaries the *Enterprise* has faced, Q is not bested by phasers and photon torpedoes. He is not overcome by human technology. Instead, as this scene demonstrates, Q is most threatened by the human *spirit*, something intrinsic within the species that has the potential to undermine the godlike arrogance of Q and his Continuum.[9] It is at the line "how like a god!" that Q finds himself unable to contain his anger, bolting from his reclined posture in Picard's chair to a defensive, standing position. He himself wishes to be seen as a god and cannot bear that another—far more limited—species would have such aspirations.

Because these are indeed portrayed as human aspirations and not as a present state of perfection, this scene is also an excellent example of a somewhat tempered version of Roddenberry's aforementioned utopian ideal. "I see us one day becoming that," Picard says, suggesting that *The Next Generation*'s thematic core is perhaps focused more on a vision of humankind in progress toward perfection, rather than having already arrived at that goal. More than an image of a totally perfected version of humanity, the hope of the future, it seems, hangs on the notion of an ever-improving human condition.

In this context, the question then becomes, "Is the human race truly advancing?" Are humans becoming what Picard envisions in his duel of Shakespeare quotes with Q? This question is, in fact, the impetus for Q's first appearance in *Star Trek: The Next Generation*'s pilot episode, "Encounter at Farpoint," as he seeks to put all of humanity on trial. Have humans truly put aside their barbarism and violence for higher, more civilized ways? Or does the appearance of advancement actually mask baser interests? Ultimately, such a question can likely never be answered for humankind as a whole. Indeed, Q's continued occasional presence in the rest of the series is a result of his decision to defer judgment on the matter of the maturity of the human race.

9. Q is a member of the Q Continuum, a race of apparent super-beings with seemingly divine abilities.

Though here couched in the terminology of a quest for godlike status, for Christians the idea of a human race that continues to improve may be seen as a gospel-centric goal of bringing hope from despair and life from death. Indeed, these are ways in which we are intended to become like God. This is our essential calling. Christians ought to be a force in the world that inspires others to seek to become the best versions of themselves. God is glorified when human beings live as the best humans they can be. Like an artist who is known as great because of the greatness of his works, so God the artist of all creation is known as great when his works (humans) reflect the great things he has made us to be. In this way, Christians should understand that living deeply engaged, fully human lives and reaching the potential intended for us by God brings glory to him, even when our efforts are not seeking his glory, because we still demonstrate the power of what he has created.

This brings us to the second, somewhat surprising basic belief about humanity upon which Star Trek's humanistic philosophy is based: the spark of the Divine in all human beings. This may seem unbelievable as a tenant of the life's work of an atheist—and it is. But Gene Roddenberry was not, as so many believe, an atheist. Neither was he a Christian, nor even a monotheist, but at least by his latter years, he did not embrace atheism. Having been raised in a Southern Baptist church, Roddenberry rejected religion in his teens. It would appear, however, that he retained what might be called an indelible Christian imagination,[10] whether he spent some time as an atheist or not.[11] It seems that, while he rejected Christian religion and what might be called a propositional gospel, he still embraced the idea of a greater dimension to human existence and sought a philosophy of life that was in harmony with what might be called an incarnational gospel—that is, a living out of a better human ideal. Whatever his journey, Roddenberry ultimately owned a kind of theistic humanism that blended his humanistic convictions with a pantheistic theology. Regarding faith in God, Roddenberry said, "As nearly as I can concentrate on the question

10. This phrase is a nod to the book, *Afterimage: The Indelible Catholic Imagination of Six American Filmmakers* by Richard A. Blake.

11. Given Roddenberry's reputation as an atheist, I have to concede that he may have been one at some time in his life. However, I have no evidence of this and it appears from my research that his atheist reputation is the result of assumptions made based on his opposition to religion and the actions of a number of atheist organizations and websites, who have quoted him or misattributed quotes to him over the years.

today, I believe I am God; certainly you are, I think we intelligent beings on this planet are all a piece of God, are becoming God."[12]

Roddenberry noticed in human beings something transcendent, which transcendence often makes its way prominently into Star Trek. In an episode of *Star Trek: The Next Generation*, Lt. Commander Data brings to light the scientifically observable nature of a greater dimension to human existence. He does this through a discussion of unusual phenomena known as emergent properties, which essentially occur in systems that are more than the sum of their parts. "Complex systems can sometimes behave in ways that are entirely unpredictable," he explains. "The human brain, for example, might be described in terms of cellular functions and neurochemical interactions. But that description does not explain human consciousness, a capacity that far exceeds simple neural functions. Consciousness is an emergent property."[13] Data may as well be (and essentially is) describing the human soul. He is referring to an added dimension of humanity, the observance of which helped lead Roddenberry to his pantheistic beliefs. However, those emergent properties in human beings that Roddenberry saw as parts of God, Christians recognize as the fingerprints of our Creator on his "very good" creation.[14] These "fingerprints" are a strong and essential element of Star Trek's worldview, in part because they are universally compelling.

We, like Roddenberry, are drawn to human excellence in any form. We watch the Olympic games to see athletes push themselves to the limits of human capacities. As they stretch themselves to seemingly superhuman levels of strength, speed, and endurance, we nonetheless intrinsically recognize that they are, while totally exceptional, like *us*. Watching the Olympic games gives us hope that the human potential to achieve amazing things is not just limited to people who get to be on TV, but that it is in all of us. In these moments of powerful, compelling achievement, the flags on the uniforms disappear and we see, not a foreign country vying for a prize, but a human person like us reaching inside themselves to pull out the best of their capabilities. We are moved, not by patriotism or a competitive spirit, but by another human being who, for at least a moment, we can relate to in ways that we might not normally find within ourselves.

12. Sweeney, *God &*, 11.

13. Bole, "Emergence," *Star Trek: The Next Generation*, Paramount Pictures, 1994.

14. Genesis 1:31.

In these moments, we experience a glimpse of what Roddenberry envisioned for the future of humanity—and, I would contend, what Christ envisioned for his followers. The reason for this just might be that in seeing the highest possible achievements of God's crowning creation, we see something of the God who imagined such beings into existence and why Christ came to seek and save the same. It reminds us that we have value as human persons because we are made in the image of God and that the image of God is an impressive thing. "[Star Trek] speaks to some basic human needs," Roddenberry said, "We have things to be proud of as humans. No, ancient [alien] astronauts did not build the pyramids. Human beings built them—because they're clever and they work hard. And *Star Trek* is about those things."[15]

This Divine spark and penchant for amazing achievement may well be why the god-like Q is driven, whether he admits it or not, by a fascination with humans. Similarly, Data displays intense curiosity about what it means to be human. Himself an android, Data seeks to become as near to being human as possible. In reflecting on this goal, he says, "If being human is more than simply a matter of being born flesh and blood, if it is instead a way of thinking, acting and feeling, then I am hopeful that I will one day discover my own humanity. Until then . . . I will continue learning, changing, growing and trying to become more than what I am."[16]

What Data does not seem to realize is that, by engaging in those very actions, he is already participating in the project of being human. As his desires fuel his quest to learn, change, grow and advance, so each of us is fueled by our loves to become the best version of ourselves we can be. We may not believe we have it in us to become a more complete image of God. But Data also reminds us that faith is an important, even essential part of being human. As he tells Lieutenant Worf,

> DATA: I once had what could be considered a crisis of the spirit.
>
> WORF: You?
>
> DATA: Yes. The Starfleet officers who first activated me on Omicron Theta told me I was an android, nothing more than a sophisticated machine with human form. However, I realized that if I were simply a machine, I could never be anything else. I could never grow beyond my programming. I found that difficult to ac-

15. Beck, *Star Trek 25th Anniversary Special*. Paramount Pictures, 1991.

16. Wiemer, "Data's Day," *Star Trek: The Next Generation*, Paramount Pictures, 1991.

cept. So I chose to believe that I was a person, that I had the potential to be more than a collection of circuits and sub-processors. It is a belief which I still hold.

WORF: How did you come to your decision?

DATA: I made . . . a leap of faith.[17]

A faith in the unseen—both a hope for what lies "out there" and an unconfirmed, yet stalwart belief about one's own nature and indeed the nature of humankind—is at the heart of what it means to be human in Star Trek. Mystery here exists constantly alongside the known and it is the pull of that mystery as much as the power of warp engines that propels us forward. Such mystery is also intrinsic to our quest for the Divine. We may ask why this is—why God doesn't blatantly show himself in empirically measurable ways, with the kind of "simple, direct explanation" that Picard demands from Q. I would contend that God is mysterious in part because he operates according to an aspect of human nature that he created and that Star Trek understands deeply: curiosity.

It is one thing to have the answer handed to us in a perfunctory fashion. But, as Roddenberry notes, humans are clever. As such, we distrust things that ask us not to be. Instead, we are drawn by our innate curiosity to things on the outer edges of our perception. As fantasy author Obert Skye notes, "There are many kinds of secrets, but all secrets are much more interesting if whispered. And if that whispered secret is a haunting, life-altering one that has to hunt you down, then all the better."[18]

Perhaps God remains a mystery to be sought after so that, in our curiosity, we may desire to seek him—so that we are not forced irrefutably, but drawn irresistibly. As Star Trek reminds us, our human curiosity is insatiable. It is compelling enough a force to drive us to the very stars. For that reason, we value both the journey we embark upon and the things we discover along the way far more than if they had simply been dropped into our laps. We treasure these things. We have earned them and we will not let them go.

---

17. Kolbe, "Rightful Heir," *Star Trek: The Next Generation*, Paramount Pictures, 1993.

18. Skye, *Leven Thumps and the Whispered Secret*, 444.

12

Theological Reflections and Philosophical Themes in the New DC Comic Films

Faith and Spirituality, Self-Identity, and Worldview through Comic Book Cartoon Movie Adaptations

SCOTT SHIFFER

Introduction

IN 2007 DC COMICS began releasing a series of PG to PG-13 straight to video super hero films. Each film runs about 75 minutes in length, and each explores a number of philosophical and theological issues. The films began with *Superman: Doomsday*, in which the *Death of Superman* comic series from the 1990s is transformed into an animated cohesive story. This film was followed by *Justice League: The New Frontier* in 2008. This DVD is based on the graphic novel by Darwyn Cooke, which is a dark take on the formation of the Justice League set in the 1950s. The film clearly paints a more sinister world than the one found in most 1950s television sitcoms that are remembered today.[1]

1. The Justice League is the superhero team made up of Batman, Superman, Green

Following this film, *Wonder Woman* and *Green Lantern: First Flight* were released in 2009. Both of these films serve as movies to share the origin of these characters with a new audience. *Superman/Batman: Public Enemies* was also released in 2009 as the film version of the first several issues of the *Superman/Batman* comic book from the early 2000s. This film is based on the election of Lex Luthor, Superman's arch nemesis, as President of the United States. It finds Superman and Batman as outlaws racing against time to keep a giant meteorite from destroying the earth.

In 2010, three more full length films were released: *Justice League: Crisis on Two Earths*, *Batman: Under the Red Hood*, and *Superman/ Batman: Apocalypse*. *Crisis on Two Earths* tells the story of a parallel world where the heroes and villains find their roles reversed. As the movie begins, all but two of the unlikely heroes on this earth have been killed. One of these, the Jester (a hero version of the Joker) is quickly put to death while helping the other hero, Lex Luthor, transport to new earth to seek the aid of the Justice League.[2] In *Under the Red Hood*, Batman must deal with the death of his second sidekick, Robin II, Jason Todd. Jason is murdered by the Joker, but resurrected by Ra's al Ghul.[3] These issues are presented within the framework of stories taken directly from the comic books. The film, *Apocalypse*, picks up where *Public Enemies* leaves off, without missing a beat it continues the story by introducing Supergirl back into the DC universe.[4] As she is discovered by Superman and Batman, she is also discovered by Darkseid, the evil ruler of the planet Apocalypse. His intentions are to steal the Kryptonian girl away from Superman and brainwash her into serving in his own army.

These films are much more intense than anything a teenager would view on Saturday Morning Cartoons. They are also steeped with contro-

---

Lantern, Wonder Woman, Flash, Martian Manhunter, and others. The comic team has been around in some form since 1960, and since 1940 appearing as the Justice Society of America in DC's *All Star Comics*.

2. New earth is the home planet to the main storybook characters of the DC Universe.

3. Ra's al Ghul is a long time enemy of Batman who has lived for centuries, preserving his youth by dipping into "The Lazarus Pits." These pits are said to be able to return the dead to the world of the living. Ra's al Ghul tests this theory on the young Jason Todd, but only to find that he returns as a much more vigilant person who will attempt to control evil as opposed to stopping it.

4. Supergirl was killed in the 1980s *Crisis on Infinite Earths* event. Her character had been missing from the comics for over a decade until she was re-introduced in 2003 in the Batman/Superman comic series. She now has her own title.

versial issues, confrontational worldviews, spiritual questions (and some-times statements), and philosophical ideologies. The comic books of the DC Universe are written for older readers and as such they contain more poignant and often more thought provoking messages. The writers do not always make statements, but frequently raise awareness of cultural is-sues and look at political controversies from multiple perspectives. These kinds of ideas are translated well into the films of the DC Universe. The films provide a plethora of situations where viewers must ask themselves how to rightly interpret someone's actions or views on justice. It is to these issues that attention may now be focused.

Faith and Spirituality

It has been said that superheroes are akin to Greek Mythology in today's culture. This is no truer than when the Greek Myths of old are brought back to life in the telling of the story of Wonder Woman. Wonder Woman is created from the earth, just as God created man from the earth in Genesis 1. She is formed from the dirt and sculpted into a princess, the daughter of the Queen of Themyscira. She is called Diana and is to live on her mystical island, Themyscira, her entire life. However, this island is made up entirely of women. It is a world uncorrupted by man. Apart from certain Greek deities who are imprisoned there, no men are even to step foot on the island. The Greek deities who have been imprisoned are to have no real communication with the Amazon women of the island. One deity imprisoned there is Ares, the ancient God of war.

As the movie unfolds, Ares cons his way out of the prison by deceiv-ing a young prison guard, and he escapes from the mystical island to wreak havoc on the modern world. The Amazonian women of Themyscira com-pete to see which one will venture after this fallen god and bring him to justice. The women compete through gladiatorial games and the masked gladiator who wins the prize is none other than Diana. As she leaves the island, the film finds Diana learning to adjust to modern culture; a world with men; a world that is full of religious skeptics; and a world where evil is purely evil. Not only must Diana come to terms living in a world with men, she must learn to deal with women who are willing to view themselves as weaker, and who are willing to accept it when men objectify them. Diana will not allow herself to be objectified, but despite her display of strength, will, and power, she remains beautifully feminine. Throughout the film, Wonder Woman must ask herself if the humans are really worth saving and she must find the inner strength to stop Ares before he destroys the world. As Wonder Woman comes to love humans, despite their faults, she also comes to a deeper self-understanding of who and what she is meant to be. Wonder Woman is a strong character and an icon of virtue. She is a woman who will not be forced into any mold by society, not even her own, and she is a devout woman of faith. She continually prays and seeks "the gods" strength as she strives to bring order back to the earth.

The issue of faith is also breached when watching this movie by calling viewers to ask, "Exactly what is a god?" Does God exist? If so, what God? The movie treats Greek Mythology as reality, but only as one reality in a universe of multiple realities. In the DC comic universe, there is actually a place for Yahweh as well as the ancient myths. This is an interesting take because it places the whole comic book universe on the side of faith as opposed to science. Perhaps this is an intrinsic quality of fantasy; after all, superheroes are fantastical creations in the same right as characters from Narnia or Middle Earth.[5] However, by assuming that greater beings exist, these films and this comic book universe give readers and viewers the inclination to ask questions about God without subliminally encouraging them to rule out his existence.

In addition to Wonder Woman being a spiritual character, comic readers and casual fans of Superman cannot help but to see the Messianic characteristics in the "Man of Steel." Superman was created by Jerry Siegel and Joe Schuster, during World War II. Superman was the only son, sent to earth to help the people on our planet. He is virtuous, self-sacrificing, and always inclined to do what is right. Over time his character has been known to make mistakes and he has been transformed over the years to be less messianic, but some basic qualities still exist.[6]

In *Superman: Doomsday*, the Man of Steel makes the final sacrifice, giving his life to save the planet from doom. He crushes the monster (Doomsday), but is fatally wounded in the process. Lex Luthor, the arch villain of Superman, states, "There comes a time when even Gods must die," and for a lengthy portion of the film, everyone asks what they will

5. Narnia and Middle Earth are places in fantasy worlds created by C. S. Lewis and J. R. R. Tolkien, respectively.

6. Even in the 2006 film, *Superman Returns*, the man in blue proclaims that the people need a savior, and that he hears all of their prayers.

do in a world without Superman. Lex Luthor finally resorts to creating a clone to protect the city. But the clone proves to be more concerned with keeping people safe than doing what is right. His power goes to his head and he begins to see vengeance as something he himself can exact on others. After a period of time, the real Superman is resurrected, just as Christ was resurrected after dying for humanity on the Cross. Then Superman returns to Metropolis, his home, and finds that he must deal with the imposter who has come in his absence.

As one watches this film, the viewer is reminded that Christ said many would come claiming to be the resurrected Christ. But these that come claiming to be Christ are not the genuine thing, just as the Superman imposter is not the true Man of Steel. There are many spiritual elements within the Superman character, but there are also many spiritual issues surrounding his story in this film. When Superman dies, one wonders about the subject of life after death. Is death the end? Is there a resurrection? Is life worth saving? Does life have a point? Is there meaning in life or in death?

When one wonders about whether or not life is worth saving, the films *The New Frontier* and *Under the Red Hood* are quickly brought to mind. In *The New Frontier*, actual events from the 1950s are portrayed as part of reality in the film, including the Korean War. The Green Lantern is shown killing a young soldier, probably a teenager, and all because he is afraid of losing his own life. The scene reminds viewers that Augustine once stated that greater love for one's own life is what causes someone to take another as an act of self-defense. While the Green Lantern, Hal Jordan, is shown fighting in the war, Wonder Woman has allowed a group of female refugees in Indo-China to massacre the very people who would have pillaged and killed them. Superman confronts her for allowing such horrific retaliation, and she replies that she gave the women freedom. This spawns conversation about the fact that normal humans will always fear those with super powers. The world of the *New Frontier* is dark and only when it concludes are there glimpses of brighter days, but those days are a long way away as the cold war is now beginning. This film does much to explore the darker side of humanity. It calls into question the justification of war, the manipulation of data by the media, human prejudice, and humanities inhumanity. It also raises questions about human selfishness, greed, and manipulation.

Under the Red Hood paints a brighter picture of humanity, but a darker picture of Gotham. As the movie opens, the Joker is beating Robin, Jason Todd, to death with a crow-bar. After puncturing his lung, he leaves him handcuffed in a building with no way to escape. As Robin looks around with what little vision and strength he has left, he sees that he was given another present by the Joker, a bomb. The bomb explodes minutes before Batman arrives killing the boy. Five years after this event, a new vigilante drug lord, the Red Hood, moves into Gotham with the intention of either killing Batman or forcing Batman to kill the Joker. As it turns out, this drug lord is Jason Todd, returned from the dead by the healing waters of the Lazarus Pit.[7] The resurrection experience has left Robin's moral compass somewhat altered. He cannot understand why Batman did not kill the Joker for murdering him.

After organizing a chain of events that leaves the Red Hood facing off with Batman while the Joker is tied to a chair, the Red Hood tosses a gun to Batman. He demands that Batman pull the trigger on the Joker or that he will do it himself.[8] Throughout the film, the Joker kills numerous people and attempts to kill many more. The Red Hood also murders a number of drug dealers and at least one assassin. Batman never takes a life. He does not kill, because that is not what heroes do. Heroes like Batman bring villains to justice, but they never resort to the inhumane acts that the villains will perform without batting an eye. For a villain to take a life it means nothing, for a hero to take a life it means everything.[9]

In the climactic scene, the Red Hood looks at Batman and in regards to the Joker exclaims: "Ignoring what he's done in the past. Blindly, stupid, disregarding the entire graveyards he's filled, the thousands who have suffered, the friends he's crippled. You know, I thought . . . I thought I'd be

7. The Lazarus Pit is a fountain of youth. There are multiple pits found around the world. They were used by Ra's al Ghul, one of Batman's enemies, on many occasions to prolong his life. His life was prolonged for hundreds of years as a result of these mystical waters.

8. While very early comics sometimes portray Batman using a gun, over time it has become accepted that a gun is the one weapon that he will never use. When Batman, Bruce Wayne, was ten years old, a man shot and killed both of his parents in front of his eyes in a dark alley behind a theatre. The alley became known as Crime Alley. Batman chose never to use the weapon that murdered his family.

9. Wonder Woman has been known to kill her enemies on occasion, but she is generally looked down upon by other heroes for doing what they will not do. In some cases, she is even told that she does not truly understand humanity.

the last person you'd ever let him hurt. If it had been you that he beat to a bloody pulp, if he had taken you from this world, I would've done nothing but search the planet for this pathetic pile of evil death-worshiping garbage and sent him off to hell."[10] Batman replies that the Red Hood has never understood that if Batman allows himself to cross the line and take a life, which would be easy, it would be too hard for him to ever turn back. In other words, Batman cannot kill, because it would turn him into a killer. In Batman's eyes, allowing himself to kill the Joker would make him the same filth as the Joker.

This may be one of the most profound statements in the entire film. The message is that killing is something that, even when done in the name of justice, makes the killer no better than the nihilistic evil filth that is being taken out of the equation if the superhero does kill him. Even when heroes want to exact revenge, it is not their place. In this regard, this and the other films speak to the sanctity of life. In the Universe of DC Comics, the heroes do all they can to stop the villains without taking their lives. There are very few exceptions to this rule. Life is sacred; it is not to be taken. Christians understand that humans are created in the image of God and that even in our fallen state; humans remain God's image bearers— broken images, but image bearers nonetheless. By refusing to take life, one moral message that these films and comic books teach is that we should hold all life as sacred. Humans can and must put a stop to evil in their lives, but they must never do so by accomplishing a greater evil. Killing is always an evil, because life is not ours to take.

In our own lives, it is too easy to seek revenge on others. Once a person finds him/herself exacting revenge on another person, it leads to a downward spiral of events where before long, the person who was originally seeking justice, can no longer see the light. While humanity is dark, Batman believes it is worth saving. Life is too valuable to be taken from someone else, even someone who clearly deserves to forfeit his own.

Self-Identity

In *Green Lantern: First Flight*, pilot Hal Jordan shows a tremendous amount of courage . . . well maybe pride. He has no problem talking to

10. Jason Todd, aka the Red Hood, from Vietti, *Batman: Under the Red Hood*, Warner Brothers, 2010.

women, he knows what to say, how to say it, and thinks he can conquer the world. The problem is that he also has a knack for crashing aircrafts. When an alien spacecraft crash lands on earth mortally wounding its pilot, Green Lantern Abin Sur, his ring seeks a fearless person to succeed him in the Green Lantern Corps—an intergalactic police force. The ring locates Hal Jordan and calls him into the Corps. Throughout the film, Hal Jordan must deal with the prejudice and discrimination which comes with being the first and only human ever chosen to be in the corps. He must also learn that life is bigger than himself and that there is value in sacrificing for others. There is also value in being forced to prove yourself to those around you. It is characters like Hal Jordan who teach young men that being "a man" is about more than driving a nice car, wearing expensive clothes, and seeking pleasure as a good hedonist. It is about sacrifice, giving, leading, and working to do whatever one has been chosen to do. It is about doing what is right, not simply doing what is convenient. When people are scared of the changes that occur in the teenage years leading to manhood, super heroes like the Green Lantern are there to help boys learn how to build confidence and see the big picture.[11]

As it turns out, in our culture today, Superheroes are not just role models for boys. Supergirl has become an icon in our culture as well, and she is a very real teenage girl intended to be a positive influence on any females who become familiar with her story. That story begins in the movie, *Superman/Batman: Apocalypse*. A young alien crashes to earth unaware of where she is, what powers she will possess there, or how to communicate with humans. It turns out that she is the cousin of Superman, and that she is from his home planet. As the movie unfolds, one sees Kara Zor-El, as a teenage girl who deals with all of the normal issues that teenager girls face, from insecurity and femininity, to aggression and equality. She is faster that Superman, she heals more quickly, she is perhaps stronger, and she has a lot more attitude. She is also drawn in such a way that she is both an extremely powerful character and a physically attractive young woman.

The way she is drawn is nothing new; comic book characters have been drawn as ideal images for many decades now. Comic book heroes

11. In his article, "Violent Media is Good for Kids," Gerard Jones states that it was the Incredible Hulk who made him feel like he could go to a new place without being afraid, and it was Tarzan who helped his son conquer the fear of climbing trees. Even when violent characters and stories are written constructively and positively, they can have positive effects on readers and viewers (Jones, "Violent Media is Good for Kids.").

frequently have a massive amount of muscle. The muscles are "over-exag-gerated" in the male characters.[12] This is done because comic books are in-tended to be a visually striking. Writers attempt to draw idealized images of the characters, knowing that boys wish they could look like Superman or Batman. This is also true for the female characters. Most young women wish they could look like Supergirl or Wonder Woman or any other num-ber of female heroines. The key is to make the images ideal but to also keep the characters real enough that they are accessible by readers. Comic book characters reflect the idealized culture within which they are drawn. Supergirl may be "super-sexy," but she reflects our culture's view of beauty. This author is not suggesting that our culture rightly views beauty. Clearly beauty is more than skin deep, but because of where and when we live, what we see in the mirror clearly shapes who we are. When female readers see Supergirl asking the same questions they ask, then they can relate to her and see her as a real role-model in her own right.

In *Apocalypse*, Supergirl must discover who she is and who she wants to be. She disdains the idea of being kept a secret, but she also fails to real-ize what kind of power she possesses. By the end of the film, she knows who she is, and she is not about to let Batman or Superman forget it.

When it comes to discovering self-identity, Batman is an interest-ing superhero because the guise of Bruce Wayne is how he hides his true self—the Batman. Most heroes wear a mask because they wish to protect their families. They are real people and the hero they become is the se-cret. Batman is "The Dark Knight," he is not Bruce Wayne. Sometimes in discovering who we are, we must also come to realize who or what we are not. Batman is a creature of the night. He is a vigilante. He lives to war on criminals, but makes appearances in society as a means of keeping his operation running. As teenagers work to discover who they are, they must also come to grips with who they are not. Teenagers often want to portray

12. See, for example, *Supergirl: The Last Daughter of Krypton* (2008). It was con-cerning to this author how female heroes were drawn until this Supergirl documentary was released and Gail Simone, author of *The Secret Six, Birds of Prey*, and now *Wonder Woman*, made some of the same claims for female heroes. It was not that they were trying to exuberate sexy for men, but rather that they were trying to produce positive role models who were strong characters that girls could relate to, who also happened to be idealized images of young girls today. Sometimes images of female superheroes still make this author uncomfortable, and one wonders how ideal a character must be drawn. However, through this documentary, one does at least have a wider perspective on the nature of female heroes.

a certain image, but they may attempt to define themselves through several different images until they finally discover the heart of who they are. In discovering who we are, we must also answer a number of fundamental questions about philosophy.

Worldview/Philosophy: Reality

Justice League: Crisis on Two Earths, presents the idea that there are multiple earths all stemming from "Earth Prime." On each earth, there are similar yet different versions of the main earth, also known as "New Earth." The movie raises serious questions about the fundamental nature of reality. Are there multiple dimensions of creation? Could there be another earth where I exist but live a completely different life? An earth where my parents never meet and where I am never born? This film finds itself in the intersection between possibility, reality, and potentiality. The focus of the film is placed on Owl-Man, the evil version of Batman on the alternate earth, who devises a plan to destroy earth prime. His theory is that if he is able to destroy the original earth, then all the other earths should also cease to exist. In his warped mind, this is the only way to cure humanity of its problem—namely itself.

All Owl-Man can see in humanity is pain, suffering, and evil. To make these things go away, he must make all humans "go away." In his solution to evil, he believes that even he must cease to exist. He is a nihilist who, even as he dies, exclaims that it doesn't matter. In addition to dealing with philosophical questions about reality and existence, one also finds the strong film making statements about the political realm.

Just as power is shown to corrupt when Lex Luthor becomes President in *Superman/Batman: Public Enemies*, *Crisis on Two Earths* shows that when evil people come into power, they do exceedingly wicked things. The villains in *Two Earths* hold a totalitarian view of might makes right, where they believe that anything they have the capacity to do is within their power to do. They can tax citizens unlawfully, they can make governments grovel at their feet, and they can take whatever they want on earth and make it their own. It causes viewers to question whether or not actions are permissible just because one is capable of taking such actions. In our culture, there is often an idea of might makes right whenever people are deciding for themselves whether or not their actions are permissible.

It is only when someone else follows the same principle to take something from these people that they realize someone is being wronged.

One final issue that arises in the *Superman/Batman* films is the philosophy of the mind. Frequently one sees Superman as the hero who thinks with his fist, while Batman questions everything, analyzes every detail, and constructs a finely-tuned plan for solving the threat. Even when Superman is absent, as is the case with *The Red Hood*, one still sees Batman using his mind as his greatest weapon. In philosophy, one is taught to think—to question everything. It is only by questioning, that one comes to know the self. Batman knows himself better than anyone else because he is the kind of philosopher who asks questions. Batman also knows his enemies and his friends better than they know themselves. This is the power of observation that aids in producing wisdom. The mind is a great tool. When it is used to analyze and dissect reality, the thinker will always be better for having used his or her mind.

Conclusion

Each of these films makes numerous statements and raises thought pro-voking issues. Whether the messages cause you to question your beliefs or discover them, the films certainly encourage viewers to use their minds. In all the new DC movies, one finds statements about the consequences of seeking revenge or misguided justice. One discovers the challenge to understanding and upholding moral absolutes. One is challenged by these cartoon role models to make choices about what kind of person someone will be. Viewers are asked to explain what it means for a being to be a god, and what that kind of being's powers say about the frailty of humans without godlike capabilities. Viewers are presented with spiritual and philosophical quandaries and they must make decisions about who they will be in light of what they see.

The world of superheroes is fraught with fantasy, but somewhere in the midst of these stories, viewers are able to grapple with questions about reality, philosophy, and theology. It is in this world of fantasy where the informed individual can watch a film grounded in fiction and walk away with new ideas about reality and with new beliefs about how to live.

13

C. S. Lewis Contra Cinema

BRUCE L. EDWARDS

I read *Don Camillo* some years ago, but can't imagine how it could be made into a film. I suppose they drag some love story into it? (But then I'm, as you know, rather allergic to the films).

—C. S. LEWIS, *Letter to Mary Willis Shelburne, August 3, 1956*[1]

Introduction

"ALLERGIC" IS A RATHER tame, understated way for C. S. Lewis to describe his decidedly negative assessment of cinema and its value for assisting Christians in enriching or sharing their faith. But his confession that he "can't imagine how it could be made into a film" is likely intended as literally true. From his earliest exposure to the cinema to his middle-aged reflections, Lewis had struggled to decipher what we might call the "grammar" of film, finding its component elements and their collective effects on audience most unsatisfying, especially when a film attempted to adapt a work of literature he happened to hold dear. Though by the late 1950s

---

1. Lewis, *Letters to an American Lady*, 59.

Lewis had mellowed a bit in his view of the cinema, softening his often pointed observations to friends about film as a medium of cultural transmittal, he remained firmly opposed to its formidable rise and its unwarranted rivalry with prose and poetic narrative as a means of storytelling.

When it came to the possibility of allowing his own work to be produced as film or video, in particular, the Narnian chronicles, Lewis was consistent in his adamant opposition. Jane Douglas, a sympathetic American playwright who admired his "fairy tales," corresponded with Lewis in the middle of 1954, proposing she share a television script for his review for *The Lion, the Witch, and the Wardrobe*; Lewis replied to her initial inquiry with skepticism: "I am sure you understand that Aslan is a divine figure, and anything remotely approaching the comic (above all anything in the Disney line) would be to me simple blasphemy. But how are you going to manage any of the animals?"[2]

Undaunted, Douglass worked several years on a script and eventually offered it to Lewis for response; Lewis again politely declined:

> I am sorry to have been so long returning your script. I can't judge it myself (I think I told you how un-film-minded I was). There are, to be frank, things I don't like about it. I don't think there's any point in Lucy's feeling "creepy" in the study: it was the long, empty passages upstairs that did that. And I don't like committing myself to exact ages for the children. But all these objections may only show my ignorance of the medium. A friend, better qualified than I to judge, read it and pronounced it "un-cinematic": said there was too much static dialogue.[3]

One wonders whether the posthumous Lewis would have rewarded the big-budget productions of his first three Narnian Chronicles with any greater respect. However, in this essay, I wish mainly to explore the sources of Lewis's dismissal of cinema as a viable means for exploring the mythopoeic imagination, a genre of literature both loved and championed by Lewis and Oxford friend J. R. R. Tolkien, and one practiced amidst their illustrious, supportive community of writers, the Inklings. It is surprising that Lewis should have found film so unsuitable a medium or form to house the depiction of the stories he had loved as a child and wrote as an adult—given his openness to, appreciation for, and defense of the popular

2. Lewis, *The Collected Letters of C. S. Lewis*, vol. 3, 491.

3. Ibid., 937.

genres of science fiction, fairy tales, and "dressed animal stories." But this is just one of several paradoxes and incongruities to unpack in a consideration of Lewis and his relationship to cinema. I will begin first with his relationship to genre fiction.

Genre Baiting

C. S. Lewis once told Sister Penelope, a winsome, lifelong correspondent of his, who had written to him about the provenance of his first space travel adventure, *Out of the Silent Planet:* "Any amount of theology can now be smuggled into people's minds under cover of romance without their knowing it."[4] "Romance" was Lewis's catch-all term for the genre most congenial to the science fiction and fairy tale genre he and J. R. R. Tolkien hoped to reinvent and restart for a twentieth-century audience— an audience they felt was too easily subverted by rampant literary naturalism and modernism. In a famous anecdote, Lewis remarked to Tolkien at one point early in their friendship, "Tollers, people don't write the books we want, so we have to do it for ourselves."[5]

What kind of books *did* Lewis and Tolkien want? Simply put: stories of derring-do, daunting quests, vistas populated by fantastic yet credible characters traversing mysterious landscapes that intrigue and delight through repeated encounters. Such tales would feature a central theme that simultaneously uplifts our spirits while challenging the conventional wisdom, our "disenchantment," of the present age, pushing us toward the true reality now made visible. *Mythopoeia* was the label for this reinvigorated art of re-enchantment—"the sub-creation" of secondary, alternate worlds that could host readers' escapes, not *from* reality, but *to* reality, a return to the story of civilization and a destiny hidden from them. In other words, they coveted books that provided a literary portal to another world, an authentic Neverland where justice reigns and the good, the true, and the beautiful are honored and celebrated.

Mythopoeia, this act of modern missionary myth-making, inspired freshly invented mythographies of time, place, and character: Tolkien's Middle-Earth is nostalgic England, England now and forever; Charles Williams, a fellow Inkling, contributed Arthur's lost Logres; Lewis's

4. Lewis, *The Collected Letters of C. S. Lewis*, vol. 2, 262–63.

5. Carpenter, *Tolkien*, 190.

Perelandra emerges as Eden unveiled, unspoiled, unfallen, unexplored, now reintroduced.[6] They treated the category of myth as one irreducible to legendary tales told with dubious authority; instead it is a medium for restoring mythopoeia as a means of authoring grand overarching narratives that create the reason to be, and to become, for all members of the village, polis, nation touched by its encompassing themes, images, characters, and plot lines.

Neither anti-historical, nor a-historical, myth evokes awe, wonder, passion, and, what's more, *pursuit*—a culture's myth is the story that has the power to explain the origin and destiny of a people, the text that orients them in history, guides them in the present, and points them to a future in which they and their offspring will live and move and have their being. It places them in the presence of their Creator and Benefactor, Judge or Advocate, and answers the questions when, how, who, and why. A "true myth" has the power to explain where we came from, shape our identity and purpose, instill hope, promote justice, sustain order. This, anyway, is how Lewis sought to rehabilitate both Christianity and myth.

When Lewis speaks to Sister Penelope of "smuggling" theology into the minds of an audience, deceitful as it sounds, he is not confessing a breach of ethics, but, rather, revealing a strategy for embedding important content that would otherwise be ignored. In his vocation as a science fiction novelist and Christian apologist, Lewis preferred, with utmost integrity, a more straightforward approach, preparing his readers, announcing, narrating his premises as much as possible, so that they could follow, if they wished, his reasoning. Lewis was not trying to trick his readers, but to reach them, even at the popular level where he was writing, albeit suffused with deeper-level meaning.

But, what if, as Lewis had observed in the first third of the twentieth-century, and certainly in wartime, too many citizens, too many readers had been unwittingly drained of the motivation for considering Christian revelation for what it was; indeed, had perhaps lost the capacity for hearing "good news" in the typically prosaic and moribund terms in which it was usually presented by churchmen. Perhaps if they saw and heard the

---

6. Swashbuckling British actor, Ronald Colman, star of *Lost Horizon* (1939), is said by his daughter to have wanted to adapt Lewis's space novels for film, playing protagonist Edwin Ransom: "He was interested in making Lewis's Perelandra trilogy into films" (Colman, *Colman*, 169).

message, meeting the grand narrative in a different setting, within a different *genre,* like science fiction or the fairy tale, they could be "surprised by joy" in the same way Lewis himself was when he returned to faith as an adult.

This is, in fact, how Lewis helps explain how he found his own way back: reading such pre-twentieth-century stories and tales and poems that presented faith in a way disarming the unsuspecting reader; Lewis's own "conversion" (actually a species of *reconversion,* given his baptism as an infant and upbringing in an ostensibly Christian home in Belfast) is eventuated in large part through his "dangerous" readings of poet George Herbert, fantasist George Macdonald, and paradox-monger G. K. Chesterton, and certainly by his friendship with Tolkien. Everyone on this list is a writer and a dreamer who found ways to explore and express transcendent truth within the boundaries—or exceeding them—of *genre.* And they were open both to classical and popular genres, which is to say, at an ultimate level, new or refurbished *media.*

Science fiction. Fairy tales. New myths. This sub-creation of imaginary worlds to serve as hosts for serious contemplation of human nature and its future—these are commonplace enough now, even omnipresent, in books and television and motion pictures, but once upon a time they were neither objects of serious study, nor deemed worthy of emulation. A stigma was attached as a tax on those who would presume "genre equivalency" for such subject matters and forms. In 1930s Oxford, it was not thought a proper predilection for a respectable medievalist and literary historian to be associated with such tawdry popular genres, and Lewis's colleagues let him know they believed it cheapened and diluted his authority as a scholar, and, by extension, theirs. By 1938, when his first science fiction novel, *Out of the Silent Planet,* was published, Lewis was already credentialed as the author of a well-respected, well-reviewed magnum scholarly opus, *The Allegory of Love,* yet he was undaunted in his celebration and open affection for fairy tales and science fiction, the staple reading of his youth and adulthood.

These two vocational pursuits—venerable literary historian and genre-busting contrarian—did not seem mutually exclusive to him, nor to his diverse tastes in literary study. But his detractors' decided opinion that Lewis gave too much credibility to clearly inferior popular texts grew even more fierce with Lewis's open affirmation of Christianity in very public forums, such as his BBC broadcasts during WWII. Lewis himself had discovered in "romance" a worthy vehicle for reinvigorating and reinserting relevant discussion of Christian ideals and the biblical worldview into popular discourse. Such was simply not done. Later in his letter to Sister Penelope, Lewis underscored the inability of hail-fellow, well-met literary reviewers of *Out of the Silent Planet,* even to recognize the biblical source of his themes: "You will be both grieved and amused to learn that out of about 60 reviews, only 2 showed any knowledge that my idea of a fall of the bent One was anything but a private invention of my own?"[7]

Lewis had selfishly adopted this emerging popular genre as a means for defeating what he called, via Owen Barfield, the "chronological snobbery" of his age, the presumption that truth was a function of the calendar: the old is passé, and the new is, *de rigueur,* valid.[8] He would add in his response to Sister Penelope that it was an essential genre to combat what he saw as a growing menace among the intelligentsia of his time who were taking the "dream of interplanetary colonization quite seriously, and the realization that thousands of people, in one form or another depend on some hope of perpetuating and improving the human species for the whole meaning of the universe—that a 'scientific' hope of defeating death is a real rival to Christianity."[9]

While Lewis's *Out of the Silent Planet* depicted space exploration as an endeavor that would yield the discovery of superior species of sentient beings who could teach earthlings how to live more abundantly and morally in the cosmos, and *Perelandra* presented an unfallen Eve and Adam in New Eden (Venus) choosing to thwart an attack on their primordial innocence, the third volume of Lewis's trilogy, *That Hideous Strength,* offered the warning to humankind that science practiced without ethical and historical context, untouched by revelation, becomes mere *scientism,* individual personhood sacrificed on the altar of preservation of the species, and a threat not just to Earth but to the cosmos at large.

Thus Lewis and Tolkien sought, though each in his own way, to create new myths that could serve as an "alternate histories," winsome, redemptive, inclusive tales whose worldview would restore personal dignity and a promised destiny to those with ears to hear, and eyes to see.

7. Lewis, *Collected Letters,* vol. 2, 262.

8. Lewis, *Surprised by Joy,* 207–8.

9. Lewis, *Collected Letters,* vol. 2, 262.

A history alternate to what? Simply put, alternatives to the false history written in the rise of a dehumanizing and disenchanting determinism that reduces men, women, children, even whole civilizations to instincts, impulses, genetics, environment: "cosmic accidents" whose dreams and visions nevertheless point them to longings they cannot account for in starkly "scientific" terms.

Now we twenty-first-century inhabitants know this well enough, and we link this phenomenon of mythopoeia not only to the now rehabilitated and well-honored genres of science fiction and fantasy *literature,* but also, in large measure, we link its incarnation to celluloid *film,* to digital *movie-making,* to narratives that are truly "grand" because of the enormity of the budgets assembled to bring these stories to (green) screens and sound-stages, and to the large numbers of audiences willing to consume them. And what is more, we understand that the these same audiences now have the means to create "user-generated" media of their own, to use them to comment, to imitate, to distribute their wares and wherefores, as widely, if not more widely, than the printing press ever could, to millions on the internet. The tools of genre are no longer in the eyes of the beholder; they are in the hands of the moviegoing, consumer public.

Genre Bashing

Lewis, however, would have trouble seeing this denouement. Having established his anachronistic openness to popular genres in which to convey his mythopoeic themes, it is shocking to discover that Lewis regarded "movies" as an unredeemable popular form that could only misdirect, exhaust, and/or deceive the imagination, an imagination that is better exercised, perhaps exclusively exercised, in the consumption of written prose and poetry: "Nothing can be more disastrous than the view that the cinema can and should replace popular written fiction. The elements which it excludes are precisely those which give the untrained mind its only access to the imaginative world. There is death in camera."[10]

It is not clear who was advocating the replacement of "popular written fiction" through the agency of the cinema, but Lewis keenly felt the implied threat. And the power he attributes to the unidentified "elements which it (cinema) excludes" is an odd provocation that deserves further

10. Lewis, "On Stories," 16–17.

analysis below, but this much is clear: because Lewis had no access to the tools of the cinema, its dynamics, its logistics, and its unique schema for storytelling, he regarded its entire creative process with profound suspicion, detrimental to the individual imagination of the consumer.

It is, of course, the case that the vast majority of twentieth-century moviegoers shared Lewis's dilemma, indeed had no analogy to and no grasp of the mysteriously collaborative production process that comprised the cinema. They did not care as much as Lewis whether this new art form was organically salutary to viewer's souls. They had only the results to consult, and the visceral effects to chart. Because the images moved, and the characters (eventually) spoke, and the soundtrack mirrored the intended emotional discharge of the script, it was the closest art form to rendering "real life" since the invention of dramaturgy—but one that could package the "same" performance over and over for repeated viewings. This new "mediated life" had a "life of its own" that exceeded even the boundaries of the stage, its technology making possible a mass audience.

Cinema also represented something else that triggered Lewis's reservations: a process that, unlike individual authorship, distributed responsibilities among many technologies and "trades," and inevitably diffused authorial intention, perhaps even theme itself, to a madding crowd. From Lewis's point of view, cinema, as an emerging art form, succeeded in freezing for the viewer one, singular version of the story through its flickering images; its unilateral perspicacity of its vision threatened to rob an audience member of any truly imaginative participatory function. Unlike mythopoeia, it did everything for the audience; this new "narrative" seemed to derive its meaning from a univocal whole despite its disparate parts. But this was an illusion; unlike a book, film delivered a totalistic experience with no room for the exercise of the imagination, there was nothing for the viewer to provide: the screen "filled in" all the dreamscapes with detail. Thus, for Lewis, film could only arrest imaginative development, could only be disruptive. In short, it could neither join nor enjoin the experience of Story itself. It could only displace it.

Lewis's disarming antipathy to cinema masks its promise for extending the literary experience into a new dimension. He is seldom so careless or categorical in assessing something he clearly has no affinity for, and Lewis warns others that they should not offer criticism of things that they neither understand nor value near the close of his essay defending science fiction: "Do not criticize what you have no taste for without great caution. And above all, do not ever criticize what you simply can't stand . . ."[11] Because Lewis has no touchstone for the creative process behind cinema he has no grasp of how it might have become simply an equally/differently able art form within which to project one's Christian-themed narratives stealthily against the tide of the scholarly demurral practiced by his Oxford colleagues—a demurral in which Lewis found himself entrapped. Considering cinema as an alternative or complementary medium, albeit with dependence on a different "grammar," and a different technology for storytelling, was a pathway blocked to Lewis.

While this is inconsistent with the devil-may-care Lewis who flaunts his magnanimity in accepting the value of the popular literary genres of science fiction and fantasy, it is of a piece with his lifelong suspicion of technology, of the Machine, and its detrimental effects on culture. For Lewis, the rise of technology of all kinds separates us from our past and disconnects us from our future. Lewis seems not to have been aware of motion pictures such as Fritz Lang's *Metropolis* (1927) or Charlie Chaplin's *Modern Times* (1936), dystopias that pointedly share Lewis's skepticism of the modern world's fixation on technology as savior. He is oblivious to the place cinema might have in rectifying this state of affairs.

In his 1954 inaugural address, accepting the Chair of Medieval and Renaissance Literature at Cambridge University, Lewis offered a sweeping historiographical tour of the West's decline, its crescendo decrying the epoch-dividing nature of "birth of the Machines":

> Lastly, I play my trump card. Between Jane Austen and us, but not between her and Shakespeare, Chaucer, Alfred, Virgil, Homer, or the Pharaohs, comes the birth of the machines. This lifts us at once into a region of change far above all that we have hitherto considered. For this is parallel to the great changes by which we divide epochs of pre-history. This is on a level with the change from stone to bronze, or from a pastoral to an agricultural economy. It alters Man's place in nature. The theme has been celebrated till we are all sick of it, so I will here say nothing about its economic and social consequences, immeasurable though they are. What concerns us more is its psychological effect . . . [I] submit that what has imposed this climate of opinion so firmly on the human mind is a new archetypal image. It is the image of old machines being

---

11. Lewis, "On Science Fiction," 72.

superseded by new and better ones. For in the world of machines the new most often really is better and the primitive really is the clumsy. And this image, potent in all our minds, reigns almost without rival in the minds of the uneducated. For to them, after their marriage and the births of their children, the very milestones of life are technical advances. From the old push-bike to the mo-tor-bike and thence to the little car; from gramophone to radio and from radio to television; from the range to the stove; these are the very stages of their pilgrimage. But whether from this cause or from some other, assuredly that approach to life which has left these footprints on our language is the thing that separates us most sharply from our ancestors and whose absence would strike us as most alien if we could return to their world. Conversely, our assumption that everything is provisional and soon to be super-seded, that the attainment of goods we have never yet had, rather than the defence and conservation of those we have already, is the cardinal business of life, would most shock and bewilder them if they could visit ours.[12]

The Western world that Lewis chronicles here is waning, and its celebration of and newly minted dependence upon technology inevitably creates a cultural amnesia culminating in an abandonment of permanence and enduring values. We have come to live, Lewis avers, in a culture of planned obsolescence—of expected succession by newer, better machines to replace the just replaced older ones. To Lewis, cinema looms as just an-other "machine," standing for the entire process of the creation of movies as whole, and the consumption of movies as the product of an impersonal technology, rather than a deliberate communication from an "author."

And it is against this canvass that the critical views of Lewis regarding the medium of film must be considered. When we confront this counter-intuitive fact that Lewis himself treated cinema as an unworthy, unforgiv-ing, and, indeed, death-dealing medium, not only incapable of being an analogue to prose and poetry as a viable medium for story-telling and mythmaking, but as hellish rival to the human imagination, it gives one pause—and sends us searching for a reason for more explicit reasons to account for his extreme reaction.

12. Lewis, "De Descriptione Temporum," 10–11.

Seeing Pictures

Ironically, this threat assessment of cinema by Lewis is contrary to his own testimony to how he himself composed. His muse was imagistic, if not cinematic. Lewis explained the provenance of his Narnian tales as putting into stories those images that animated his daydreams and dreams alike:

> Some people seem to think that I began by asking myself how I could say something about Christianity to children; then fixed on fairy tales as the instrument; then collected information about child-psychology and decided what age-group I'd write for; then drew up a list of basic Christian truths and hammered out "allegories" to embody them. This is all pure moonshine. I couldn't write that way at all. Everything began with images; a faun carrying an umbrella, a queen on a sledge, a magnificent lion. At first there wasn't even anything Christian about them; that element pushed in of its own accord. It was part of the bubbling.
>
> Then came the Form. As these images sorted themselves into events (i.e., became a story) they seemed to demand no love interest and no close psychology. But the Form which excludes these things is the fairy tale. And the moment I thought of that I fell in love with the Form itself: its brevity, its severe restraints on description, its flexible traditionalism, its inflexible hostility to all analysis, digression, reflections and "gas." I was now enamoured of it. Its very limitations of vocabulary became an attraction; as the hardness of the stone pleases the sculptor or the difficulty of the sonnet delights the sonneteer. On that side (as Author) I wrote fairy tales because the Fairy Tale seemed the ideal Form for the stuff I had to say.[13]

Lewis's description certainly sounds like a kind of informal storyboarding, events shaped from images:

> All my seven Narnian books . . . began with seeing pictures in my head. At first they were not a story, just pictures. *The Lion* all began with a picture of a Faun carrying an umbrella and parcels in a snowy wood. This picture had been in my mind since I was sixteen. Then one day, when I was about forty, I said to myself: "Let's try to make a story about it."[14]

13. Lewis, "Sometimes Fairy Stories May Say Best What's to Be Said," 36.
14. Lewis, "It All Began With a Picture," 42.

Lewis testifies that in transporting these images explicitly in the form he had chosen taught him

> how stories of this kind could steal past certain inhibitions which had paralyzed much of my own religion in childhood. Why did one find it so hard to feel as one was told one ought to feel about God or about the sufferings of Christ? I thought the chief reason was that one was told one ought to. An obligation to feel can freeze feelings. And reverence itself did harm. The whole subject was associated with lowered voices, almost as if it were something medical.
>
> But supposing that by casting all these things into an imaginary world, stripping them of their stained-glass and Sunday School associations, One could make them for the first time appear in their real potency? Could one not thus steal past those watchful dragons? I thought one could.[15]

By lifting these images out of their commonplace venues and relocating them amidst different confines and contexts, they regain life and poignancy—analogues to the way filmmakers conceive and construct their movies. Given Lewis's quite vivid recollection of the power of image to be a catalyst for mythopoeia, one must ask, what prevented Lewis from making the connection to or awarding value to cinematic composition and consumption? Simply put, why couldn't cinema help Lewis steal past those watchful dragons too? The answer lay in early and bitter disappointments in Lewis's moviegoing.

There are a number of references in Lewis's letters and journal entries that shed some light on this, but a few stand out for their fierce poignancy that provide a window onto Lewis's detection of film's core weaknesses when compared with literature. For instance, writing in 1933 to childhood friend, Arthur Greeves, about Noel Coward's *Cavalcade,* which he had just seen, Lewis wrote,

> [I] have actually been to the films today!—to see *Cavalcade!* This is one of the most disgraceful confessions I have ever made to you. I thought it would be interesting historically, and so I suppose it was: and certainly very clever. But there is not an idea in the whole thing from beginning to end; it is mere brutal assault on one's emotions, using material which one can't help feeling intensely. It appeals entirely to that part of you which lives in the throat and

---

15. Lewis, "Sometimes Fairy Stories May Say Best What's to Be Said," 37.

chest, leaving the spirit untouched. I have come away feeling as if
I had been at a debauch.[16]

Lewis here focuses his analysis on the visceral effects of viewing a movie
in and of itself, rather than reflecting on the suitability of the medium for
artistry. But he is clearly made uneasy by the experience and considers
this at best what we would now refer to as a "guilty pleasure," since it is
lacking "an idea . . . from beginning to end," it is merely "a brutal assault
on one one's emotions."[17] Its ultimate failure is declared in this telling sentence that Lewis considers axiomatic: "It appeals entirely to that part of
you which lives in the throat and the chest, leaving the spirit untouched."[18]
Perhaps it is an indication of the power he sensed beneath the surface of
the movie "event," and his inability to articulate fully its impact, that com-
pels this less "disgraceful" confession less than a month later, to Greeves:
"You will be surprised to hear that I have been at the Cinema again! Don't
be alarmed, it will not become a habit. I was persuaded into going to *King
Kong* because it sounded the sort of Rider Haggardish thing that has always exercised a spell over me."[19]

In a 1939 letter to a former undergraduate friend, A. K. Hamilton
Jenkin, Lewis asks his assessment of *Snow White and the Seven Dwarves*,
Walt Disney's first full-length animated film, and then proceeds to offer
his own caustic review:

> What did you think of Snow-White and the vii Dwarfs? I saw it
> at Malvern last week on that holiday . . . Leaving out the tiresome
> question of whether it is suitable for children (which I don't know
> and don't care) I thought it almost inconceivably good and bad—I
> mean, I didn't know one human being could be so good and bad.
> The worst thing of all was the vulgarity of the winking dove at
> the beginning, and the next worst the faces of the dwarfs. Dwarfs
> ought to be ugly of course, but not in that way. And the dwarfs'
> jazz party was pretty bad. I suppose it never occurred to the poor
> boob that you *could* give them any other kind of music. But all the
> terrifying bits were good, and the animals really most moving: and
> the use of shadows (of dwarfs and vultures) was real genius. What

16. Lewis, *They Stand Together*, 455.
17. Ibid., 455.
18. Ibid., 455.
19. Ibid., 461.

might not have come of it if this man had been educated—or even brought up in a decent society?[20]

Here Lewis is fearlessly intemperate in his ad hominem debunking of the genius of Walt Disney, the animator and storyteller behind *Snow White*. (Ironic, given Lewis's relative contempt for Disney, that Walt Disney Studios were the distributors of the first two Narnian movies from the Lewis canon.) He finds the filmmaker essentially guilty of lacking imagination, ahem, an imagination (i.e., the kind Disney would deploy had he been "brought up in a decent society") that would have been informed by the grammar of fairy tales, the code that would have enabled him to avoid the "vulgarity" in his depiction of dwarves. The intensity of his response may be traced to a staple in mythopoeia to which he is especially attuned, namely, his lifelong affection for dwarves, which is captured in this throwaway line from his autobiography, *Surprised by Joy*: "I fell deeply under the spell of Dwarfs—the old bright-hooded, snowy-bearded dwarfs we had in those days before Arthur Rackham sublimed or Walt Disney vulgarized, the earthmen. I visualized them so intensely, that I came to the very frontiers of hallucination; once, walking in the garden, I was for a second not quite sure that a little man had not run past me into the shrubbery. I was faintly alarmed."[21] It seems this exposure to Disney was seminal in determining his movie-going experience and confirmed his severe judgment of the limitations of cinematic art as well as its dangers of overwhelming mythopoeia itself: the medium erasing the message. Lewis reasserted this assessment in a later, scholarly volume on John Milton.

In *A Preface to Paradise Lost*, Lewis is concerned with defending genre once more, in this case, the validity of the classical epic poem as a worthy host for Milton's reimagining of the Fall of Man. In nineteen sprightly written chapters, Lewis propounds the essential notion that Milton was constructing his narrative in such a way as to reach a popular audience, and deliberately chose the form of the epic poem, even though it might have been considered an anachronistic choice. In one chapter, Lewis pauses to articulate the "rules" of what he labels Milton's "rhetorical poetry," a variation of the epic poem chosen deliberately for its persuasive power to convince its audience of the historical reality of the Fall. The primary convention of this form, Lewis observes, is, above all, to eschew

20. Lewis, *Collected Letters*, vol. 2, 242.

21. Lewis, *Surprised by Joy*, 55.

novelty. Then, to illustrate this, he surprisingly returns once more to Disney's *Snow White* to underscore its failure to stay "grammatical" within the contours of genre:

> That strange blend of genius and vulgarity, the film of *Snow-White*, will illustrate the point. There was good unoriginality in the drawing of the queen. She was the very archetype of all beautiful, cruel queens: the thing one expected to see, save that it was truer to type than one had dared to hope for. There was bad originality in the bloated, drunken, low comedy farce of the dwarfs. Neither the wisdom, the avarice, not the earthiness of true dwarfs were there, but an imbecility of arbitrary invention. But in the scene where Snow-White wakes in the woods both the right originality and the right unoriginality were used together. The good unoriginality lay in the use of small, delicate animals as comforters, in the true märchen style. The good originality lay in letting us first mistake their eyes for the eyes of monsters. The whole art consists not in evoking the unexpected, but in evoking with a perfection and accuracy beyond expectation the very image that has haunted us all our lives.[22]

Lewis has matured a bit in his assessment of cinema, and has nuanced his objections to the film that he had originally dismissed offhandedly in his letter to Jenkin; Lewis can now praise certain elements ("the right originality" and "the right unoriginality" are kept in proper tension in certain scenes). But the overall syntax of movie-making fails the test of a "whole art" that can evoke with a "perfection and accuracy beyond expectation the very image that has haunted us all our lives." That is, for Lewis to consider film as a viable art, it must be able to achieve this transcendent evocation of a secondary world in collaboration with the viewer, and steadfastly refuse to substitute a different meaning or symbol unrelated to its original source.

What is really irksome to Lewis is that the film medium itself encourages, even demands "the imbecility of arbitrary invention," e.g., in its depiction of the dwarves it ignores centuries of storytelling tradition and consistently and thoroughly fills in narrative gaps that should be supplied by the audience's own organic wonder with the stock, manufactured experience supplied by a responsible filmmaker. Cinema, for Lewis, lacks the very authorial tenacity and imagistic resiliency needed to sustain those elements that poetry (and prose) can handle, presumably with aplomb,

22. Lewis, *A Preface to Paradise Lost,* 58.

as the rest of his analysis of Milton's command of the art of epic poetry attempts to adduce.

Lewis's *coup de grâce* in arguing the inferiority of film to text is found in an essay written roughly five years after the publication of *A Preface to Paradise Lost*. Lewis takes up the topic of Story itself, beginning with an aside on how "astonishing how little attention critics have paid to Story considered in itself . . . [as a] series of imagined events."[23] Lewis finds it remarkable that little to no attention has been paid to its unique and compelling characteristics; therefore, his goal in the essay is to delineate those elements once and for all that set "story" apart as an art form, and the obligations upon those who would recite, rework, or invent their own stories. Storytelling is for Lewis a distinctively human act and is peculiarly reflective of our journey through this life to the next; an eventual subtext in the essay is the deficiency of cinema in accomplishing what the oral and written story does effortlessly: the creation of a "net" for temporarily capturing the ineffable, i.e., those "successive moments" that are not, in "real life" really successive, but rather simultaneous.

The plots and themes of stories resemble but do not do justice to how lives actually unfold; they are wily simulacrums, nets, that hold, only for an instant, moments, gestures, dialogues, that permit denotation and reflection, but, nonetheless are a kind of grand misdirection. Art is not life, though it may tolerably imitate it. Film is problematic for it presents the illusion that it can do more than just imitate life; it may substitute for it, or create the desire that it do so. In the midst of this exposition, Lewis pauses to articulate the unsatisfactory nature of film in this regard. In an extended exposition, Lewis explains what one of his favorite authors, H. Rider Haggard, can deliver in a narrative like *King Solomon's Mines* that is ultimately diminished and compromised in a film version (in this case, the 1937 version, directed by Robert Stevenson).[24] Here Lewis keeps the offending principle of "the imbecility of arbitrary invention" front and center:

> I was once taken to see a film version of *King Solomon's Mines*. Of its many sins—not least the introduction of a totally irrelevant young woman in shorts who accompanied the three adventurers wherever they went—only one here concerns us. At the end of

23. Lewis, "On Stories," 3.

24. Bennett, *King Solomon's Mines*, Warner Brothers, 2005.

Haggard's book, as everyone remembers, the heroes are awaiting death entombed in a rock chamber and surrounded by the mummified kings of the land. The maker of the film version, however, apparently thought this tame. He substituted a subterranean volcanic eruption, and then went one better by adding an earthquake. Perhaps the scene in the original was not "cinematic" and the man was right, by the canons of his own art, in altering it. But it would have been better not to have chosen in the first place a story which could be adapted to the screen only by being ruined. Ruined, at least, for me. No doubt if sheer excitement is all you want from a story, and if increase of dangers increases excitement, then a rapidly changing series of two risks (that of being burned alive and that of being crushed to bits) would be better than a single prolonged danger of starving to death in a cave. But that is just the point. There must be a pleasure in such stories distinct from mere excitement or I should not feel that I had been cheated in being given the earthquake instead of Haggard's actual scene. What I lose is the whole sense of the deathly (quite a different thing from simple danger of death)—the cold, the silence, and the surrounding faces of the ancient, the crowned and sceptred, dead. You may, if you please, say that Rider Haggard's effect is quite as "crude" or "vulgar" or "sensational" as that which the film substituted for it. I am not at present discussing that. The point is that it is extremely different. The one lays a hushing spell on the imagination; the other excites a rapid flutter of the nerves. In reading that chapter of the book curiosity or suspense about the escape of the heroes from their death-trap makes a very minor part of one's experience. The trap I remember forever: how they got out I have long since forgotten.[25]

Now, in one sense, the gist of this lengthy diatribe is that Lewis is saying the quite common thing that he prefers the experience of reading Haggard's "original" story to watching the screenplay's re-plotted and misbegotten shenanigans guiding the film's director and crew; how many of us say, leaving a theatre having watched an adaptation, "the book was better"? But in another way, he is offering an even more radical critique, expressing his exasperation at the director's native inability to use even his chosen medium (cinema) to convey the experience evoked by the original author in his medium (romance). In calling one scene "not 'cinematic,'" (perhaps, not cinematic *enough*) Lewis is wryly suggesting something

25. Lewis, "On Stories," 5–6.

about the "canons" of the director's "own art," indicting his abandoned commitment to the original subject matter, story, character, et al., invented by Haggard. In other words, one tenet of Lewis's campaign against cinema is that as a medium it forces other choices that are neither coherent in themselves nor congruent with the original source, choices Lewis believes are *arbitrary*. Cinema becomes lodged in his mind as the art of "arbitrary invention": choices that compel other arbitrary choices so that eventually the story, no story, is any longer "itself." There is an experience in reading Haggard that the movie does not (and for Lewis, cannot) deliver. He takes this point further later in the essay:

> In the example of *King Solomon's Mines* the producer of the film substituted at the climax one kind of danger for another and thereby, for me, ruined the story. But where excitement is the only thing that matters kinds of danger must be irrelevant. Only degrees of danger will matter. The greater the danger and the narrower the hero's escape from it, the more exciting the story will be. But when we are concerned with the "something else" this is not so. Different kinds of danger strike different chords from the imagination . . . Consider, again, the enormous difference between being shut out and being shut in: if you like, between agoraphobia and claustrophobia. In *King Solomon's Mines* the heroes were shut in: so, more terribly, the narrator imagined himself to be in Poe's *Premature Burial*. Your breath shortens while you read it.[26]

The "something else" here is none other than the deeper human experience of fear and of impending doom, all experienced within the context of an unfolding story, a quality that is not merely the willful insertion of "excitement" for its own sake. The fear and doom must occur *in* a character, and don't exist apart from that relationship. A movie that captures a series of disconnected scenes of escapes from danger, "excitement" artificially attached to no one in particular, excerpted for the degree of intensity in the hair-breath escapes, bore viewers and trivialize human calamity, at least for viewers like Lewis.

For Lewis, Haggard is as capable a mythopoeic author as any he ever encountered, specifically because he believes Haggard understood how to evoke elemental human traits and predicaments, certainly provoking the kind of responses that extend from the "the throat and the chest," but also those that can go further to "touch the spirit." Near the essay's cli-

26. Lewis, "On Stories," 7–8.

max, Lewis cites Roger Lancelyn Green, a friend and writer notable for his retelling of the Camelot and Knights of the Roundtable legends, who offers the opinion Haggard is capable of delivering exploits through his protagonist, Allan Quartermain, that approaches "religious experience." Lewis approves but qualifies his statement by suggesting it is "safer to say that such people had first met in Haggard's romances elements which they would meet again in religious experience if they ever came to have any."[27]

Conclusion

Lewis's embrace of genre fiction as a way to reach audiences who otherwise may be closed to the experiences and worldviews an author may wish to convey makes his blindness to the merits of film as a way to replicate these achievements puzzling and unnerving. But we can reconstruct this instance of reverse chronological snobbery. First, it is clear that Lewis's grasp of the technologies of the film industry always escaped him; as someone who instinctively distrusted machinery (he owned, but did not use a typewriter; his brother Warnie transferred his handwritten texts to the keyboard), the additional mechanisms (lights, special effects, music, projection units, etc.) that allowed films to come into being struck him as being dismayingly sterile to the art of storytelling. He did not understand how he or anyone could tell a story with this medium. Its diffuse and democratic nature confused him, precisely because it defied any sense of authorship with which he was familiar or comfortable.

Secondly, the experience of movie-going itself as he perceived and experienced it was overwhelming, and he presumed it be so for any audience; film's bracing, life-simulating concomitant effects on an audience deprived them of an active role in exercising the imagination. Movies monopolized the imagination in such a way that novelty and originality (two words that Lewis had no fondness for as a literary historian and critic) were its signal traits, creating the pressures for screenwriting and directing to succumb to "the imbecility of arbitrary invention." How could a story not become chaotic considering all the factors that must be coordinated to achieve even modest coherence?

Thirdly, Lewis could only see cinema as corrosive to the future of literature and the act of reading, displacing the role that they would have

27. Lewis, "On Stories," 16.

in cultural preservation and the transmittal of civilized values. Lewis evidently could not conceive of the possibility that cinema, as it matured, could make possible new stories, new orders of all kinds of stories, that would be especially suited to this unique combination of sound and image. It did not occur to him, indeed it did not occur to any of the Inklings, that literature and cinema could share an audience; that cinema-lovers and bibliophiles could be found in one and the same person, that movies provoked readership, and readership promoted movies. He only saw, and lamented, the effects of cinema on stories he knew well and loved, but he appeared never to have experienced a film that expanded or embodied the calibre of transcendent storytelling he endeavored to practice and celebrate. He did not live long enough to see the marvels of the CGI age emerge, of digital media, that would have assuaged his fear of comic or pantomimed versions of Aslan and other talking animals in the land of Narnia, nor the new mythopoeic achievements of Steven Spielberg, George Lucas, or Peter Jackson.

While it is dangerous to speculate on what kind of movie may have ever won over C. S. Lewis and rehabilitated the genre as a whole for him, I have thought recently that it would likely be a movie like Joss Whedon's 2005 movie, *Serenity,* based upon his ill-fated *Firefly* series for Fox Television. Hardly anyone at mid-century had read science fiction more widely, treated it more critically, or reviewed its canon more appreciatively than Lewis. Plotwise, as suggested earlier, Lewis despised stories that championed any form of human colonization in outer space, even at its most benign, since it threatened to spread the shame and sin of humankind to other planets—rejecting any kind of scheme that placed survival of the human species above all, even to the extent of "conquering" other worlds. He took human fallenness seriously and would not revel in a story whose plot allowed vain and vicious men to achieve in space what they could not do on Earth.

At the same time, he was not fond of depicting aliens as voracious invaders, either, intent on taking over Planet Earth; after all, he called Terra "the silent planet," quarantined by our rebellion against our Maker. While it is an exaggeration to call his an "optimistic" view of space creatures and interplanetary travel—it is clear that Lewis thought we were the problem, not other planets or creatures God may have made elsewhere. Other universes? Other beings? To paraphrase Narnia's Prof. Kirke, "Nothing is more probable"—to Lewis.

I believe Lewis would find Whedon's speculative universe in *Serenity* very congenial to his own thematic temperaments, because *Serenity* is that rare space movie that truly cares more about its characters than its special-effects, more about what human greed and sin do to the soul than whether or not everyone will live happily ever after. There is in *Serenity* what Lewis prized most about really good fiction of any sort: realism of presentation. There is, he said, a modern penchant for prizing realism of content over realism of presentation; that is, fantasy and science-fiction tended to be dismissed out of hand as inferior "popular" genres—since, obviously, they lacked "realism of content." But, Lewis averred, realism of presentation can redeem a narrative focused on the fantastic—if it plays by a consistent set of rules, and stays within the genre to produce its own kind of realism. Even genre fiction, Lewis argued, brings its own realism to its storytelling as long as it does not pretend to be something else. Lewis's favorite example of this was Tolkien's Middle-Earth.

That's a good description of the twenty-sixth-century, post-Terra world that Whedon has created in *Serenity*. It's a fully realized "neo-Western" landscape, with horses and guns, villains and conspiracies, bad guys and good guys, as well as ragged, intrepid communities of faith and fellowship, holding out for goodness on the good ship Serenity, boasting even an explicitly spiritual character known as Shepherd—but most importantly, a Ransom-like ship captain who, if he doesn't know exactly what the source of true goodness is, he does know what is right. This character, Mal(colm) (Mal-content?) Reynolds, played by Nathan Fillion, is a brilliantly rendered tortured man of action, always on the run, and intent on keeping the universe, the part he's in anyway, free of oppression and avarice. Yes, he is an outlaw of sorts—but one who understands like Robin Hood that robbing from the greedy-rich is not the same as stealing from the poor and downtrodden. His character and the unusual River Tam, a young woman prematurely, precociously wise, and unable to cope with the knowledge she has of high level nefariousness, provide viewers with two of the most stimulating and stirring characterizations in an sf setting.

Would Lewis come to appreciate *Serenity*? Indeed, I believe he would, embracing its realistic depiction of where utopian schemes lead in crushing the human spirit and ending the search for joy and true serenity that only God ultimately can give. Mal once was a believer, and may be so again. *Serenity* shows once again that allegiance to what Lewis called the "conditioners" of society in *The Abolition of Man* (and depicted uncompromisingly in his third sf novel, *That Hideous Strength* among the N.I.C.E.) leads inevitably to ruin. At the center of both works—Whedon's and Lewis's—is the concept of the Tao, a universal tableaux of traits and standards that are inviolate.

Each artist articulates and thematizes it differently, but arrive at the same conclusion: neither humanity nor its government alliances can build a "world without sin," as Capt. Reynolds admonishes near *Serenity's* last scenes.[28] To try to do so is catastrophic. Humanity cannot be reengineered; it can only be redeemed. One cannot change human nature. And not from the inside out; the remedy comes from outside, from "far, far away," and in the person of the Rescuer, riding on a white horse, or commanding a spaceship. Perhaps having viewed *Serenity*, Lewis could have learned to trust a medium that had so well captured in film what he had labored so diligently to convey in his vocation as apologist and storyteller, a new medium, worth defending, to assist viewers in stealing past watchful dragons of those who would rob them of their humanity.

28. Whedon, *Serenity*, 118.

14

Fantasy, Escapism, and Narrative in *Pan's Labyrinth*

JEFF SELLARS

THE FILM *PAN'S LABYRINTH* is a beautiful and disturbing two-fold portrayal of post-civil war Spain in 1944 and a timeless fairytale world. Our young heroine, Ofelia, is brought, along with her pregnant mother, to war-torn Spain to live with her vicious and cruel step-father, Captain Vidal, who is rooting out Maquis soldiers in the mountains. The movie's center, however, is revealed in the opening scene: the movie begins by telling us about Ofelia's larger story; she is a princess (Princess Moanna) from the Underground Realm who escaped to Earth. She has forgotten her former life, and her father, the King, hopes for her return.[1] With a rich narrative

1. Here follows a brief synopsis of the film: The story unfolds as Ofelia discovers an insect that she believes to be a fairy. The insect (now revealed as a fairy) leads her to a labyrinth where she meets a faun. The faun recounts her story and gives her three tasks to complete before the full moon. Only after she has proven herself worthy can she return to the Underground Realm. Her first task is to retrieve a key from a toad that is hiding in a fig tree. She is dressed up in her new dress and shoes for a dinner being held by the Captain. She crawls into the tree through a hole and tricks the toad into eating magic stones given to her by the faun. The toad vomits up the key. Her new dress and shoes are ruined through the process and she is sent to her room without dinner. Ofelia's pregnant mother has a serious incident of bleeding and is put on bed rest. Captain Vidal is only

and haunting visuals, there is much one could examine in *Pan's Labyrinth*: for example, the connections between the Underground Realm, Ofelia's forgetting and subsequent *anamnesis*, and its relation to Plato's allegory of the cave (as well as the inverted imagery of this metaphor in the film); the borrowing of mythic and fairytale tropes and themes; the political ramifications of the story; the use of violence and war in the film; the very Catholic structure of the film.[2] What I want to focus on in this essay, however, are a few broader elements. I want to examine these elements, where appropriate, and loosely, through the film *Pan's Labyrinth*. First, I

---

concerned for the baby boy he supposes Carmen is carrying. The faun gives Ofelia a way to cure her mother: she must place a mandrake root in a bowl of milk under her bed. Ofelia must also feed the mandrake root by giving it two drops of blood each day. Ofelia is given the second task, which is to use the key to obtain a dagger. She must get this dagger out of a grotesque monster's home. The monster is particularly dangerous to children it appears (for pictures adorn his walls that show him killing and eating children). The monster presides over a large feast. Ofelia has been instructed by the faun not to eat anything at his table, but she disobeys and awakens the monster. The monster kills two of her fairy companions, but she escapes by drawing a door with a magical piece of chalk. The faun is so upset at her disobedience that he refuses to give her the third task. As the fighting rages on in the mountains of Spain, Ofelia is eventually caught feeding the mandrake root. The Captain's anger with Ofelia is stopped only by Ofelia's mother asking the Captain if she can deal with Ofelia alone. Ofelia's mother tells her that fairytales are not real. She burns the mandrake to make the point to Ofelia. However, once she does this, she goes into labor and dies while giving birth to her son. Ofelia is eventually locked in her room but finds a way to escape. The faun gives Ofelia one last chance to prove herself. He instructs her to take her younger brother to the labyrinth. She finds her way into the center of the labyrinth and sees the faun waiting for her with the dagger she retrieved from the Pale Man. The faun tells her that only innocent blood will open the portal to the Underground Realm and asks for her brother. Ofelia refuses to hand over her brother and the faun becomes angry with Ofelia for her disobedience. The faun asks if Ofelia is willing to give up her chance at being a princess in the Underground realm for her brother. Ofelia nods yes; the faun says "As you wish," and disappears. Captain Vidal appears and tries to take the baby from Ofelia. He does so and shoots her in the process. Ofelia falls to the ground, bleeding onto the altar, thus opening the portal to the Underground Realm. Ofelia is then seen in this realm with her father, the King. She sees her mother resurrected as the Queen of the realm. The faun is also there with her fairy friends. Ofelia learns that by sacrificing herself and not her brother that she has passed the final, true test.

2. Del Toro himself noted the very Catholic structure of the film—specifically when he showed the film to his friend, Alejandro González Iñárritu: "When I showed Pan's Labyrinth to my friend Alejandro González Iñárritu, he said: 'That's a truly Catholic film.' And there was me thinking that it was a truly profane film, a layman's riff on Catholic dogma. It's true what they say: once a Catholic, always a Catholic" (del Torro, "Pan's People").

want to consider the way in which fantasy can get us to look at our world differently—to find something unexpected and mysterious—and open us up the possibility that the world contains more than what we might normally assume. Second, I will explore the charge of escapism that is leveled against fantasy—namely, that fantasy is a retreat into wish-fulfillment or simply nonsensical play. Third, I will examine the notion of knowledge and its relation to narrative—by looking at what we encounter in and through narrative.

"Imagining the World Otherwise"

In James K. A. Smith's book *Thinking in Tongues: Pentecostal Contributions to Christian Philosophy,* he notes that film gives us "an opportunity to re-narrate the world . . ."[3] We get a chance to see the world as other than "what it is"—the common notion of what counts as real or rational in the modern mind. As Smith observes, "imagination is a mode of intending the world that retains a high degree of freedom vis-à-vis the 'reality principle' of modernist instrumental rationality. In fact, it is phantasy or imagination that subverts the regnant paradigms of 'rationality' . . . that would consign our hoped-for world to the impossible realm of 'utopia.'"[4] Imagining the world as otherwise might also lead to 'new' knowledge—it may not be exact, straightforward or propositional but at the very least imagining the world as otherwise may allow an opening up of other 'rationalities,' to see another way other than our own as a means to knowing the world differently, to see reasons that we might never have considered, to see a way to knowledge that may have been inaccessible to us. The world of fantasy opens us up to possibilities; it demands of us a reevaluation of what is real and what is possible—one that flies in the face of our conceptions of 'normal' reality; it, then, can break us out of *alltaglichkeit,* out of 'everydayness.' In *Pan's Labyrinth,* this is just what we get. We are put into a world of magical wonder and at the same time are in a world of 'mundane' (often brutal) immediacy. The fantasy world is presented to us as real, as a place that Ofelia actually inhabits—just as real (in fact more real) than the one she inhabits in the war-torn countryside of Spain. To signal our entrance into this reality, the film begins with an iteration of the

3. Smith, *Thinking in Tongues,* 84.

4. Ibid., 84–85.

famous line, "Once upon a time"—in this case, it is "A long time ago . . ." The phrase is a narrative magical spell. As Helen Pilinovsky notes,

> *Once upon a time* . . . these words are an incantation, signaling the beginning of a spell of enchantment—a magical spell, or a spell in the sense of a timeless period, or often some combination of the two. They describe a *then* that could have occurred at any time, in any place, a *then* which hovers in a delicious void of possibility. However, the thing that we—the modern readers, lovers, enchanted connoisseurs of fairy tales—can sometimes forget is that the prospects of the *then* can be equally relevant in the *now*.[5]

The "now" of Ofelia's time connects in an intimate way with the "then" of the Underground Realm—Ofelia's other reality. The things that happen to Ofelia in Spain are shaped by the things that happen in the Underground Realm: they are permeable realities, intertwined. This "now" that Pilinovsky writes about is also our "now"—the world of the viewer. The narrative can inform our own times, our own lives.[6] Furthermore, we, as viewers, are left to decipher these realities. Will we ascribe to one reality the "truth"—that one is, in fact, the "true world" in which she and we live—and will we ascribe to the fantastic world the moniker of "false"— the world in which Ofelia "retreats" in order to deal with her brutal reality? This is a move we make, in some way, on our own. But if the components of the film—the story, music, characters, setting, etc.—are done well, this so called "false" reality will be presented in such a way as to make us question our assumptions of its falseness. It will demand that we, at least for the time we behold it, imagine the world as otherwise. These two realities are not separate. They ask us to expand our notions of the real. They ask us to expand our notions of the rational to include the imagination. If the rational is more than the merely material, the merely rationalistic—if Ofelia's phantasmagorical existence is the continuation of her "real world" experience, the true depth that fills out the meaning of her "normality"—and if the imaginative is more than mere fantasy, then how might we encounter and learn about this expanded reality? Might one way we do so be through the explicitly image-full manner of story, myth, and fairytale? And if there is more to reality than the merely mate-

---

5. Pilinovsky, "Spells of Enchantment," 1.

6. This theme will shortly be picked up on again in the section dealing with escapism.

rial, might the emplotting[7] of our world into this "more than" lead us to this expanded reality and not merely to escapism, wish-fulfillment and false-fanciful-inventedness?

Escapism

The common push against fantasy comes in the following form: fantasy causes one to leave behind reality in favor of some created fancy; it is little more than an escape from the world, from reality. Even Ofelia's mother, Carmen, warns her against fairytales, telling her that they are "nonsense" and that she need not fill her head with such things. The counter-push against this is to admit that fantasy does in fact cause an escape, but it is not (or does not have to be) merely *escapism*; it is, hopefully, an escape to a world where the "mundane" is renewed—where one can come back to "reality," to the so-called "mundane" world, with a deeper, enchanted sense of reality. The reality we see then becomes more than the "mundane." The world is infused with a renewed meaning. Of course, fantasy can lead one into mere escapism—where the "mundane" world is left

---

7. Additionally, we might also note that there is a discordance (in the Augustinian sense) in our view of time (which Paul Ricoeur contrasts with the Aristotelian idea of emplotment), which could be seen as a reiteration of longing for the divine, the experiencing of divine longing as a pang of discordance—which we will pick up again in this essay under the guise of a 'strange' epiphenomenon of (in this particular instance) the storied arts. As an example of this distinction, Paul Ricoeur noted, "I found in [Aristotle's] concept of emplotment (*muthos*) the opposite reply to Augustine's *distentio animi*. Augustine groaned under the existential burden of discordance. Aristotle discerns in the poetic act par excellence—the composing of the tragic poem—the triumph of concordance over discordance" (Ricoeur, *Time and Narrative*, 31). In his book *Paul's Way of Knowing*, Ian W. Scott also uses this term in describing St. Paul's epistemology. For example, when describing Paul's self understanding, Scott notes that in Romans 15:29 Paul situates his 'little story' in terms of a 'bigger story'—so that when "Paul says he knows . . . that when he comes to Rome it will be 'in the fullness of the blessing of Christ.' In other words, when he disembarks at the wharf in Ostia, makes his way up to Rome, and is greeted on the Romans' own thresholds, he will be doing so (in terms of the story) as one who is endorsed by God, one in whom God's benevolent power is at work, one who is experiencing the dawning of the eschatological fulfillment . . . Paul is claiming that anyone who can interpret his life properly will understand his very ordinary acts of thinking and writing to be the actions of God's representative . . . [T]his knowledge is a matter of discerning that Paul occupies a certain role in the theological narrative, a matter of 'emplotting' him correctly within that story" (Scott, *Paul's Way of Knowing*, 123–24).

behind in favor of a self-centered fancy. This is one such way to guard against the merely self-serving fantasy—to recognize it as such. If the story does not bring one into a focus of meaning (and a pointing to or renewing of a larger *telos*), and it is merely a focus of self-centeredness or wish-fulfillment, then it is to be suspected on just such an account. The fruits of the narrative must be examined carefully. However, this is clearly no easy task. As Gabriel Marcel also noted, "The virtue proper to dramatic creation, where the creation is authentic, consists in the exorcizing of the ego-centric spirit."[8] We must be careful of the blindness that occurs by focusing merely on ourselves: "In so far as I am obsessed by an ego-centric preoccupation, that preoccupation acts as a barrier between me and others; and by others must be understood in this connection the life and the experience of others."[9] However, even if this barrier between ourselves and others is broken down there is still a concern for us; knowledge of the self and knowledge of the other are interconnected:

> The paradox is that at the same time it is also my own personal experience that I rediscover in some way, for in reality my experience is in a real communication with other experiences . . . It is because the egoist confines his thought to himself that he is fundamentally in the dark about himself . . . A complete and concrete knowledge of oneself cannot be heauto-centric . . . The fact is that we can understand ourselves by starting from the other, or from others, and only by starting from them . . . [10]

As mentioned above, in these common conceptions of "escape as retreat" there is a remainder left over, one that is essential to the fantasy experience: namely, the notion of recovery. What can we gain by visiting fairyland? The well constructed narrative gives us not just escape or entertainment (through it certainly does both of those things); it also gives us a sense of something beyond our grasp. This sense is also to be found in Plato's allegory of the cave—the prisoners are not escaping *from* reality but escaping *to* more of it. The prisoner, having escaped the cave into reality, then realizes the shape of the world.

In *Pan's Labyrinth* the enchanted world of Ofelia serves just this purpose. It re-orients Ofelia to the world, gives her meaning and strength to

8. Marcel, *The Mystery of Being*, 7.

9. Ibid., 7.

10. Ibid., 7–8.

cope with her harsh reality—indeed gives her reality a new depth. Ofelia takes with her something from the fairy world (physically—as in the key or the dagger—but also in spirit) that furthers her story and adds meaning to her surroundings. The viewer of this narrative can also take something with him or her from this shared trip into fairyland. Through emersion into the narrative, one can find a way to re-orient oneself to the world, to learn to act (or not to act), to learn to emulate (or not to emulate) what is seen, heard, felt, understood through the narrative. What might we come to know through narrative? We might come to know a kind of vicarious or sympathetic knowledge: knowledge of things through storied experience; that is, experiencing, in some way, "what it is like" to do a particular thing by watching it, which may or may not be exactly the same as "first hand" knowledge or experience (e.g., if we take sky diving as an example, it could be that we get something of what it is like to do such a thing while watching it on screen—if it is done well and conveys the proper feelings—but until we experience it in actuality many would claim that we are missing a vital part of the experience). We might also get more "traditional" knowledge—such as propositional truths: for example, if an argument is presented in an explicit way through the narrative or through a character in a film. We also get an argument through implicit means, by the narrative itself conveying (through image, sound and the like) a case for appropriate action and emotion. *Pan's Labyrinth* provides us with a clue here as well. In a scene with the Doctor and Pedro, we see argument presented in an explicit way. The Doctor and Pedro are arguing about how to proceed in their attack of the Captain. The Doctor argues that even if they defeat the Captain another one will be sent in after him (and another, and another). He thinks it is a lost cause to fight. Pedro thinks there is no choice but to fight. We can certainly discuss and analyze both of these conclusions, teasing out the implications and the arguments on both sides—and even the narrative itself makes a push towards one conclusion over the other. There can also be "practical knowledge" communicated as well—i.e., how to do certain things that could be gleaned from such scenes—but, of course, we may not know if these sorts of "practical" things will work out until we try them.

We might also gain moral knowledge, e.g., we could look to the screen and see exemplars (as well as anti-exemplars) we might emulate (or not emulate as the case may be)—in addition to examples of situations, events, actions, beliefs. In *Pan's Labyrinth*, we can certainly see exemplars, for example, in the guise of our heroine and her helper Mercedes: we see compassion displayed, sacrifice, caring, courage and much more. Their actions speak to us through their presentations in the film: they can awaken in us a sense of the good, the true and the beautiful—so that if we come to the film we might learn (or learn anew). The emotional aspect present in these types of knowing are extremely important to highlight.[11] As J. David Velleman notes, "A story . . . enables its audience to assimilate events, not to familiar patterns of *how things happen,* but rather to familiar patterns of *how things feel.* These patterns are not themselves stored in discursive form, as scenarios or stories: they are stored rather in experiential, proprioceptive, and kinesthetic memory—as we might say, in the musclememory of the heart."[12] Of course, these ideas and examples are not exhaustive but are a mere grasp at a beginning.

Narrative Knowledge

Furthermore, these aforementioned approaches to narrative knowledge[13] are certainly not uncontroversial.[14] For example, in his essay "The

11. For an excellent account of emotion and its relation to film, one would might want to look at Plantinga's *Moving Viewers* or his co-edited volume, Plantinga and Smith, *Passionate Views*.

12. Velleman, "Narrative Explanation," 25.

13. We might also want to follow James K. A. Smith's distinction here: "Normally I would want to make a (Heideggerian) distinction between 'understanding' (*Verstehen*) and 'knowledge' (*Wissen*) . . . I will speak of 'narrative knowledge' as distinguished from something like 'propositional knowledge.' If we were to map this onto the Heideggerian distinction, '*narrative* knowledge' would be that sort of 'knowledge' characteristic of 'understanding'" (Smith, *Thinking in Tongues*, n. 35, 64). This might be seen chiefly when I am talking about 'vicarious knowledge' and a *quality* of knowledge, but also, generally, when writing of narrative knowledge containing other things as well (e.g., 'propositional knowledge,' 'practical knowledge'). Smith also acknowledges this inclusion when he notes, "Narrative knowledge is not *opposed to* propositional or quantifiable or "codeable" knowledge . . ." (Smith, *Thinking in Tongues*, n. 37, 64).

14. I certainly do not want to give the impression that I am advocating the idea that films are merely "literary" narratives set forth in the guise of images. I do believe that in film there is an integral combination of story, sound, and image that cannot be reduced. In this essay, however, I am focusing on narrative for the sake of clarification of what a particular aspect of film can do for us. As Robert K. Johnston notes, "Some have criticized the discipline of theology and film for its heavy concentration on narrative. But this is to misunderstand the nature of the problem . . . It is not story per se but the reduction

Ends of Narrative," Richard Eldridge succinctly summarizes a survey, in *Truth, Fiction, and Literature,* done by Peter Lamarque and Stein Haugon Olsen.[15] This summary and its conclusions will be helpful for us to turn to now—as a simple means to explore some ideas and themes. In Lamarque and Olsen's study, they examine the intersection between literature and knowledge. This examination is of literary narratives, but it can apply generally to narratives of all kinds—and it certainly applies to what we have discussed above as *one* of the things that a film does, though, obviously, not the only thing; clearly film is a unique art form with its own grammar. But there are general ideas that can be gleaned from through this approach.

Lamarque and Olsen consider three suggestions. The first is as follows:

> (1) Literary works might help us to know "what it is like" to be or to be in the situation of a certain character, in the sense of "subjective knowledge" that has been broached by Thomas Nagel and worked out with regard to literature by Dorothy Walsh. Against this, Lamarque and Olsen object first that while we have experiences while reading, we mostly have our own experiences, not the experiences of Leda or Leopold Bloom, Yeats or Joyce. In particular, we mostly observe or imagine characters having experiences. And while we take an interest in this observation, we are not learning the felt qualia of, say, fried kidney for Leopold Bloom. Second, even if we did get some sense of what things are like for characters from reading literary fiction, it is strained . . . to describe what we get as learning something. There are no methods in view for ac-

---

of film interpretation to literary techniques that is the problem. After all, the vast majority of commercial film is narrative in structure, rooted in storytelling. But how that story is to be understood needs redefinition and expansion in many of the present descriptions of movies by theology and film critics. For movies are both 'pictured' and 'heard,' not just described. Thus, there needs to be an expansion of method to include the visual and the aural, if theology and film is to escape its literary captivity" (Johnston, *Reframing Theology and Film,* 19). I am certainly sympathetic to this critique. The aural and visual aspects of film cannot be ignored: films show us a story and tell us a story—there is a storied element within the sound scapes and editing and camera placement, etc.; and films are an integrated combination of image, sound and narrative—an irreducible combination. I believe my focus on narrative here is inclusive enough to account for these aural and visual aspects: the meaning of the narrative and the experience of it beyond the mere recounting and rationalizations of "story" to include the images and sounds is something I am attempting to "get at" in this analysis.

15. See bibliography, Lamarque and Olsen, *Truth, Fiction, and Literature.*

crediting or testing any knowledge claims, such as there are in the sciences, and much of what we might think we learn, we must in fact already have known in order to understand what is going on: for example, that rape is a violent, terrifying, and world-altering experience.[16]

I think that Lamarque and Olsen do have a serious and important point— it is nearly impossible to imagine arguing that the reading or viewing of, say, a rape is the same as actually experiencing it. But I do think that the reading or viewing of such a horrific episode can give the reader or viewer knowledge, understanding. These limits are apparent in narrative structures, but they are also present in our everyday lives: how do we communicate to others that which they have not experienced? We commonly do so analogously. If I have experienced a tooth ache and my friend has not, how do I tell him about how it feels? I may use an analogy. For example, I may try to compare the pain of a tooth ache to some other pain that he has experienced. I may say, "Well, it is like X, only with a combination of Y." I must try to convey my experience through some other experience he has had. With a narrative a similar thing can be seen. One presents an experience, the characters act through the emotions of such an experience—and in film the visual cues and musical cues are also part of this—trying to give the audience an intimation of what is happening. In *Pan's Labyrinth*, we get numerous scenes which attempt just this. The fantasy scenes in particular are revealing for their sense of wonder, mystery, danger and horror—and the communication of longing is clearly present. But the scenes that feature the Maquis fighting are effective in their communication of this idea of "what it could be like." For example, in the attacking of Captain Vidal and the subsequent fighting, we may not be able to experience the horrors of a war in actuality, but we might still learn something of those horrors and experiences—the chaos, the adrenaline, the fear, the horror, the danger, the courage, the sacrifice. In another, earlier scene, we see this displayed as well. We may not have direct experience of what it is like to be lined up by a brutal man like Captain Vidal in the middle of the night (and the absolute fear that accompanies such a thing) but we do get a sense of it—even if vaguely—through the presentation in the film. The absolute brutality shown by Captain Vidal to the old man and his son is startling and deeply affective. Something is conveyed about this

16. Eldridge, "The Ends of Narrative," 139.

experience, and while it may not be direct experience and it may not be propositional, it is a quality of experience. There may be "no methods in view for accrediting or testing any knowledge claims, such as there are in the sciences," but there are methods outside of the sciences for this process, such is the way of affective and embodied knowledge.[17] Narrative knowledge works through the logic of the heart (not a deductive, syllogistic, propositional logic). The logic of narrative tells us things that we could not know in any other way: and a good narrative does this very well. One might see the difference more clearly if one thinks about a straightforward telling of a brutal rape or murder as conveyed in a formalistic-journalistic manner (a mere "factual" account) and the recounting of the event in a storied manner (which, of course, the best journalists accomplish)—the emotions elicited and the imagination required to evoke such thoughts and feelings from the latter method conveys the sense of what we are getting at here; the mere "facts" don't do justice to the brutality of the actions and the emotional impact of what has happened. Narrative or story is then not just a (bad, inferior) means to get across "propositional knowledge" or "direct knowledge or experience." In other words, the story becomes not just the means of communicating the knowledge but it is itself the knowledge.

The second suggestion is as follows:

> (2) literary works might enable us to enrich our store of concepts, or they might modify our sense of the application conditions of concepts we already have . . . Against this suggestion, Lamarque and Olsen object that while some literary works might help us to deploy new concepts or to widen the application conditions of concepts we already have, this is by no means necessary for a work to have literary value. Second, and more sharply, they suggest that some authors sometimes explore the same concepts and conditions of application in different works, so that when one reads a second work, for example, a later play by Ibsen, one may not learn anything new. But the later work nonetheless has literary value, so that learning about concepts and their application conditions is not necessary for literary value.[18]

It may be true that artists do present the same or similar concepts and conditions of application in different works, but does this preclude learn-

17. Eldridge, "The Ends of Narrative," 139.
18. Eldridge, "The Ends of Narrative," 139–40.

ing or gathering (more or different) knowledge? One may read about alienation, angst and longing in Walker Percy's *The Moviegoer* as well as in *The Second Coming*, but the concepts cannot be so easily ripped from their place in the narrative; one must be in some way emplotted in the story, in some sense inhabit Binx Bolling or Will Barrett, to work through these particular instantiations of the concepts and feelings. The presentation of fear and anxiety in *Pan's Labyrinth* and, say, *Hell Boy 2* (another of Guillermo del Toro's films) is not exactly the same precisely because of the stories (the plot, characters, music, images, etc.) involved. If the narrative becomes not just the means of communicating a message but is the message itself, how do we see other narratives (even if dealt with by the same person) in light of this? It is rightly noted that this becomes a problem for multiple readings or viewings of the same work: If we have already "learned" the concept(s) on our first go around, what more is there to learn with a second reading or viewing? But this is precisely the kind of learning that is so profound in narratives: that we can come back to them and discover ever "new" things with multiple viewings or readings. This places the whole of the narrative in an awkward position for affective knowledge: if the story is the knowledge, then the new narrative that uses "old" concepts is still conveying something that the other narrative is not—it is a separate story with its own life. There can also be something else happening to us when we really experience a narrative—the experience of the "other," of a quality that cannot be hemmed in by common conceptual categories. A work of art can open us up to a normally veiled phenomenon: as Hans Urs von Balthasar noted, "In the experiences of extraordinary beauty—whether in nature or in art—we are able to grasp a phenomenon in its distinctiveness that otherwise remains veiled. What we encounter in such an experience is as overwhelming as a miracle . . ."[19] And we can also examine the experience in a way that we may not be able to while we are experiencing it (or even possibly after the fact) in the "actual" world: we can pause, leave it, ruminate, come back to it multiple times, experience it from different angles, be detached from it, or be attached to it. There can be something else happening to us when we experience a narrative that enthralls us: the epiphenomenon of the work is just this quality knowledge. The various forms of fantasy narratives may just be the best way in which to get this quality knowledge across.

19. Balthasar, *Love Alone is Credible*, 52.

The third and last suggestion of Eldridge's summary is as follows:

> (3) it might be that literary works help us to become better per-
> ceivers of the moral lives of persons and so better reasoners about
> what it is good or right to do . . . Against this suggestion, Lamarque
> and Olsen object first, that improvement in moral reasoning is by
> no means brought about by successful literary works, and second,
> that having or furthering the correct valuational stance is not a
> necessary condition for literary value: we can and do value as suc-
> cessful literature works with whose stances and points of view we
> disagree.[20]

Of course, improvement in moral reasoning both can and cannot be
brought about by successful literary works—the perception of the reader
and authorial intent surely must be considered here, too. The certainty
of that thesis seems easy to dispute on just such an account of what
numerous critics, authors, readers or viewers have and have not found
(and put) in "successful" narrative works of all kinds. It seems a rather
uncontroversial idea for many modern people that a "correct valuational
stance" (whose valuational stance are we talking about?) is not a necessary
condition for literary value—the form of a work and its presentation, for
example, can vault a piece to the heights of "success" and "literary value."
Mere didacticism is certainly not the "successful" literary mode—but
aren't the narratives implicitly giving us a valuational stance? Even when
(or if) supposedly leaving one out? And we may find a piece of art beautiful because it follows a proper form, but isn't this beauty precisely some of
the mystery of which we are speaking? The beauty of the form somehow
alerts us to transcendence. Is the beauty and truth we find in these narratives evidence of *something*? As St. Thomas noted, "Every form, by which
a thing has being, is a participation in the divine brilliance . . . 'individual
things' are 'beautiful according to a character of their own,' that is, in accord with a proper form. Hence it is clear that the being of all things is
derived from the divine Beauty."[21] Form and splendor cannot be so easily
separated. But leaving this very large issue aside, when we see a moral
situation presented in a narrative, can we never watch the consequences,
see the ramifications of such actions and responses that the characters
make to it? Does this never give us some idea of the possibilities of what

20. Eldridge, "The Ends of Narrative," 140.
21. Aquinas, *The Pocket Aquinas*, 272.

can happen in certain situations? Does this never make us think about these situations in new ways? This certainly does not mean that narratives all share the same moral *telos*. We can and are influenced in other directions than our own. This is just one thing that a narrative does and does well—it can present to us moral narratives that can get us to rethink positions once held with certainty. The narrative can, in a very subtle way, go where propositional or formal logical methods cannot. If one can be *affected* by a narrative one may be more likely to change his or her heart and mind. The presentation of a formal argument is more often than not an invitation to change premises (e.g., to account for objections or misinterpretations) rather than conclusions. The affective nature of narrative can help one to suspend disbelief—at least to consider the possibility that the world may be other than what we conceive it to be. We do not reduce the human being to a disembodied thinking thing, but rather acknowledge our embodiedness and start to realize the Pascalian maxim that the heart has reasons which reason does not understand.

It could be stated that the above critiques have an unfair advantage by separating out, arbitrarily, these three ideas (of subjective knowledge, conceptual knowledge, and moral knowledge). And Richard Eldridge notes just this when he calls it a "'divide and dismiss' strategy."[22] It could be that what we get through narrative "is some mixture of subjective knowledge, improvement of our conceptual capacities, and moral insight."[23] And it may be a misunderstanding or limitation of the notions of reason and knowledge that lead to this dividing and dismissing. There does appear to be a cutting off of what can be considered knowledge, so that the merely rationalistic and propositional is what is rational, real and true. This is just what we see happen in *Pan's Labyrinth* with the Captain. His refusal to see reality more deeply is precisely his short coming (and the source of his brutality) and down fall. This presentation is also a challenge to the audience viewing the film. There is an implicit "reality check" question proposed for us: Is this all?

Could there be more to reality than this conceptualization envisions? Is there an Augustinian conceptuality that can be employed here? The certainty of rationalism is replaced, hopefully, by a humbleness attuned to wisdom. We often, instead, search for rationalistic certainty, for "surely

22. Eldridge, "The Ends of Narrative," 140.
23. Ibid.

this beauty should be self-evident to all who are of sound mind," but it is not the case:

> Then why does it not speak to everyone in the same way? Animals both small and large see it, but they cannot put a question about it. In them reason does not sit in judgment upon deliverances of the senses. But human beings can put a question so that "the invisible things of God are understood and seen through the things which are made" (Rom 1:20). Yet by love of created things they are subdued by them, and being thus made subject become incapable of exercising judgment. Moreover, created things do not answer those who question them if power to judge is lost. There is no alteration in the voice which is their beauty. If one person sees while another sees and questions, it is not that they appear one way to the first and another way to the second. It is rather that the created order speaks to all, but is understood by those who hear its outward voice and compare it with the truth within themselves.[24]

The understanding comes to those whose mind is attuned to this wisdom; for those who are not attuned, no amount of "rational certainty" is going to convince and enlighten.[25] There is, instead, recognition of a

---

24. Augustine, *Confessions*, 184.

25. Augustine noted, too, that Scripture, when speaking of God, "Both used words taken from things corporeal, as when it says, *Hide me under the shadow of Your wings*; and it has borrowed many things from the spiritual creature, whereby to signify that which indeed is not so, but must needs be so said: as, for instance, *I the Lord your God am a jealous God*; and, *It repents me that I have made man.* But it has drawn no words whatever, whereby to frame either figures of speech or enigmatic sayings, from things which do not exist at all. And hence it is that they who are shut out from the truth by that third kind of error are more mischievously and emptily vain than their fellows; in that they surmise respecting God, what can neither be found in Himself nor in any creature. For divine Scripture is wont to frame, as it were, allurements for children from the things which are found in the creature; whereby, according to their measure, and as it were by steps, the affections of the weak may be moved to seek those things that are above, and to leave those things that are below. But the same Scripture rarely employs those things which are spoken properly of God, and are not found in any creature; as, for instance, that which was said to Moses, *I am that I am*; and, *I Am has sent me to you.* For since both body and soul also are said in some sense to *be*, Holy Scripture certainly would not so express itself unless it meant to be understood in some special sense of the term. So, too, that which the Apostle says, *Who only has immortality.* Since the soul also both is said to be, and is, in a certain manner immortal, Scripture would not say only has, unless because true immortality is unchangeableness; which no creature can possess, since it belongs to the creator alone. So also James says, *Every good gift and every perfect gift is from above, and comes down from the Father of Lights, with whom is no variableness, neither shadow of turning.* So also David, *You shall change them, and they shall be changed;*

faith seeking understanding: we come to the table with a viewpoint and what we find will often be dictated to us by what we are looking for—our imagination precedes our reasoning in this way. Additionally, this is an epistemology that recognizes that the "higher" things must be communicated through the "lower" things. Is it not possible that narrative has a role in this? For then the human mind might draw "nourishment" from these gifts, and "our understanding might rise gradually to things divine and transcendent."[26]

---

but You are the same" (Augustine, *On the Trinity* I.1.2).

26. Augustine, *On the Trinity* I.1.2.

15

Apocalyptic Images and Prophetic Function in Zombie Films[1]

KIM PAFFENROTH

THIS ESSAY WILL EXAMINE how current zombie films—although they depict the apocalypse in outwardly secular terms as a mass plague, usually with no explicit mention of God—nonetheless frequently use that apocalypse to pass judgment on current American society and sinfulness, often sounding much like Old Testament prophets in their decrying of sins and announcement of judgment. The essay will focus on the films of George Romero, whose *Night of the Living Dead* (1968) defined the current zombie genre, taking the monster from its roots in magic and transforming it into a peculiarly modern scourge. As will be shown, the resulting films are recognizably biblical in their apocalyptic imagery, and in their prophetic denunciation of the society in which their creator and audience lives.

First, one should probably note the sheer ubiquity of the humble zombie today. Until Stephenie Meyer's *Twilight* series (2006 and follow-

1. This essay originally appeared in *Reel Revelations: Apocalypse and Film*, edited by John Walliss and Lee Quinby. Sheffield, UK: Sheffield Academic Press, 2010; it is reprinted with kind permission of the editors and publisher. The discussion is taken with some revisions and expansion from my book, *Gospel of the Living Dead: George Romero's Visions of Hell on Earth*. Waco: Baylor University Press, 2006.

ing), it was as though vampires had disappeared from popular culture, and only the zombie remained as the chief representative of the undead. The zombie had always appeared in films, at least as far back as *White Zombie* (1932), but the new millennium saw many more of these than previous decades. It also saw a diversification among the various films, from the straightforwardly horrific depictions of George Romero (*Land of the Dead* [2005] and *Diary of the Dead* [2007]) and his followers like Zack Snyder (*Dawn of the Dead* [2004]) and Danny Boyle (*28 Days Later* [2002]), to comedies like *Shaun of the Dead* (2004), *Fido* (2006), and *Zombie Strippers* (2008). Zombies are favorite targets in video games, led by the *Resident Evil* franchise, which spun off into films (2002, 2004, and 2007). They have also increasingly shambled on to the printed page, either in comic book or graphic novel form, as with the immensely popular *Walking Dead* series (2003 and following), or in novels and short stories, most notably with the hugely successful *World War Z* (2006) by Max Brooks. Though Brooks is the best known author in this genre, many other writers now exploit the narrative possibilities of the zombie, including Brian Keene (e.g., *The Rising* [2003] and *City of the Dead* [2005]), David Wellington (the *Monster Island* trilogy [2004–2006]), and even the author of this essay (*Dying to Live* [2007] and *Dying to Live: Life Sentence* [2008]). As with the films, the literary world of zombies has expanded and diversified, and now includes such highbrow parody as Seth Grahame-Smith's *Pride and Prejudice and Zombies* (2009), and the romantic comedy of S. G. Browne's *Breathers* (2009).

The "rules" of zombies have been fairly consistent throughout all these works, building on the depiction first put forward by Romero in his movie *Night of the Living Dead* (1968).[2] These are not Haitian or voodoo zombies, animated by magic and under the control of a summoner's will.[3] Instead, they are a recognizably modern monster, their magical or super-

---

2. Romero's depiction of zombies or "ghouls" has some precedent in the vampires of Richard Matheson's novel, *I Am Legend*, adapted several times into films: "But by far the most important antecedent for *Night of the Living Dead* is *I Am Legend*. On various occasions Romero has acknowledged that the original idea for his film was 'inspired' by Richard Matheson's novel, and the resemblance between the two works is striking" (Waller, *The Living and the* Undead, 275). Pirie's *The Vampire Cinema*, also notes *I Am Legend* as the inspiration for Romero.

3 Though these too may have a "rational" explanation: see Davis, *The Serpent and the Rainbow* and *Passage of Darkness*.

natural elements rationalized to fit contemporary sensibilities. Zombies in these current depictions are either living people infected with some virus (*28 Days Later*), or people killed by a virus that then causes their bodies to reanimate (Romero's more "traditional" zombie). They are not afraid of garlic, holy water, crucifixes, or any other talisman. They can not be killed by running water or sunlight or a stake through the heart, but only with the very brutal act of destroying their brains, usually with a spectacular head-shot or decapitation. They cannot fly or turn into a bat; they have average strength and way below-average intelligence, speed, and coordination. When pursuing live humans, they are as likely to stumble off a cliff or stagger into a whirling blade or electrified fence, as they are to succumb to the counterattacks of the living. So weak are they, zombies only pose a threat when attacking as a mob. Zombies are overwhelmingly ordinary, which is to say, they are terribly and fully human. This ultimately, I think, is their appeal, for they seem so much more "real" to us than the more superhuman monsters like vampires and werewolves.

It should be noted, however, that the "scientific" explanation is so mysterious as to function almost as "magic": the disease works with a speed unknown among any terrestrial disease ever before seen, killing in seconds in some films, and it is not only 100 percent fatal, but also has the power to reanimate a human body with at least limited motor skills and memory, and apparently, to also keep the body from noticeably decaying way past its normal "shelf life," as some of the stories take place years or even decades after the initial devastation. The virus is pretty clearly functioning to serve the narrative needs of the story, which is to fill the world with walking corpses, and watch how the characters react.[4] The characters themselves seem to strain against the "scientific" framework that is imposed on them, and sometimes give what almost seems the more plausible explanation—that this is a curse or judgment from an angry God (*Dawn of the Dead* [both 1978 and 2004]), something akin to many of God's statements in the book of Ezekiel: "Thus says the Lord

---

4. On the uselessness of explanations, cf. Waller, *Living and the Undead*, 275–76: "To assert that 'mysterious radiation' in some unexplained way causes the dead to roam the land in search of human flesh is finally little better than no explanation at all (especially since this is a quasi-official explanation and therefore likely in *Night of the Living Dead* to be a lie, distortion, or cover-up) . . . Ben and the other people trapped in the isolated house do not have the time to search for explanations, which would make little difference in any case."

God: Disaster after disaster! See, it comes. An end has come, the end has come . . . My eye will not spare; I will have no pity . . . The sword is outside, pestilence and famine are inside; those in the field die by the sword; those in the city—famine and pestilence devour them."[5]

However the process got started, zombies rapidly increase their numbers by attacking and killing uninfected people, who then die and become zombies themselves. The particularly horrible addition made by Romero is that zombies partially eat their victims. This not only enables the filmmaker or author to create scenes of grotesque cannibalism and dismemberment, but it also raises the symbolic stakes of the zombie. Unlike the seductive vampire, who bites his/her victim on the neck in a very sexualized gesture, the zombie tears other people limb from limb and flings their intestines into a steaming pile on the ground. There is nothing attractive or sensual about a zombie attack—it is animalistic and sickening. But since zombies look exactly like living human beings, their cannibalism also brings out the image of humanity preying on itself—the self-destructive and sadistic elements of all people, which have been seen on killing fields all across the "real" world even without a zombie virus to excuse the behavior. One of the more artful uses of this parallelism is perhaps to note the framing in *Land of the Dead*, which begins with a brutal massacre of zombies by gleefully laughing humans, and ends with a zombie feeding frenzy on the human population. Human violence reaps what it sows; the fiction of zombies just makes this more graphic.

Because the zombie hordes multiply so rapidly, the outcome in most all zombie fiction and films is an apocalypse, an end of the world as we know it—an end of "civilized" life and the ushering in of an indeterminately long age of barbarism, terror, and violence. Also, in the original meaning of "apocalyptic," the cataclysm of murderous corpses also "reveals" terrible truths about human nature, existence, and sin, since the zombies are themselves only human. This apocalyptic aspect of zombies is made perhaps the most explicit in the *Dawn of the Dead* (2004) remake, which uses the haunting, apocalyptic Johnny Cash song, "The Man Comes Around," for the opening credits.[6] On the one hand, it is the most brutally and universally hopeless song imaginable: it ends with death and

---

5. Ezek 7:5, 9, 15, NRSV.

6. In an otherwise negative evaluation of the film, J. Russell notes the aptness of this choice of music (see Russell, *Book of the Dead*, 185).

hellfire engulfing the entire earth at God's instigation. In that sense, it is the perfect choice for the movie, as ultimately all the characters are horribly killed. But in apocalyptic—whether it is the Bible's or Cash's or *Dawn of the Dead*'s interpretation of it—there is always some sense that choices still matter, that how we live our lives is important, even if the same horrible, inevitable, and equalizing death awaits each of us. In the song this is expressed in several lines, especially in the assurance that, "Everybody won't be treated all the same." Such reestablishment of righteousness is seriously undermined in much current horror, which is often nihilistic, and depicts everything as ultimately meaningless and random. Such a dismal evaluation is seen in Romero's earlier films, especially *Night of the Living Dead*, but here in the *Dawn* remake a sense of justice reappears, not just in the song, but in how the characters behave and how they die.[7] The ignoble characters die without any pity from us, even with a sense of our approval. And though the noble characters are also dead by the end, they die with our compassion and admiration. Exactly as in Revelation, where many of the elect die, this film shows that biological death (or life) should not be our only focus and is not the source of value in our lives.

Whether or not zombie films have a full sense of apocalypse –both as end of the world and as vindication of the just—and despite their eschewing a supernatural cause for the outbreak, one way in which they consistently resemble the biblical prophets is the strong sense of moral outrage and condemnation of the society in which the filmmaker or prophet lives. This has been a visible, even blatant component of Romero's work throughout his career; it is what distinguishes his work from many of the lesser luminaries working in the horror genre.[8] The Hebrew prophets are known for railing against the moral deficiencies and sinful excesses they saw in contemporary Israel and Judah. The prophet Amos is particu-

---

7. In this sense, the film returns to a more classical, pre-Romero vision of horror movies, as described by J. Fraser: "And once the possibility of splatter effects had been opened up, an interesting tension was established wherein one partly *wanted* horrible things to happen, for their shock effect, and yet at the same time did not want them to happen to everyone. So that one stayed alert for possible clues as to who in some sense 'deserved' to become victims" (Fraser, "Watching Horror Movies," 47).

8. This may be true of "great" horror movies in general: "The great American horror movies . . . seem to me to be characterized not so much by ambivalence—a phenomenon discernible in such eminently mediocre and objectionable works as *The Texas Chainsaw Massacre*—as by the use of the monster as the focus, or the catalyst, for the critical analysis of everything that 'normality' represents" (Britton, "The Devil, Probably," 41).

larly well-known for his denunciation of the economic disparity between rich and poor: "Therefore because you trample on the poor and take from them levies of grain, you have built houses of hewn stone, but you shall not live in them; you have planted pleasant vineyards, but you shall not drink their wine."[9] Another favorite target of the prophets' ire was the smug complacency and reliance on the people's "chosenness" as somehow insulating them from possible misfortune, rather than demanding a higher level of ethical commitment and devotion to justice: "Its [Israel's] rulers give judgment for a bribe, its priests teach for a price, its prophets give oracles for money; yet they lean upon the Lord and say 'Surely the Lord is with us! No harm shall come upon us.'"[10] Romero repeatedly returns to the current versions of those sins in modern America,[11] usually presented as consumerism (not just the hoarding of wealth, but the definition and valuation of oneself as a consumer of goods), and racism (which may well include nationalism, similar to Israel's discounting of other peoples in God's eyes, but with the added animosity and oppression of racial minorities within the United States). I will consider these two elements of social criticism in three of the five Romero zombie films, produced between 1968 and 2005.[12]

Romero's first zombie film, *Night of the Living Dead* (1968), which has virtually defined the depiction of the undead since, also established—albeit in a muted and indirect manner—the films' tradition of critiquing a society they depict as lost and unfaithful to its calling as a force

9. Amos 5:11, NRSV.

10. Micah 3:11, NRSV; cf. Matt 3:9; Luke 3:8.

11. On American society in zombie movies, cf. Waller, *Living and the Undead*, 280: "Perhaps the monstrous creatures in *Night of the Living Dead*, the 'things' that are somehow still men, are the projection of our desire to destroy, to challenge the fundamental values of America, and to bring the institutions of our modern society to a halt."

12. *Day of the Dead* (1985) takes quite a different approach than the other films, returning us to the claustrophobia of the first film, but not making the sweeping social criticism of the second, focusing instead on more general observations of human nature, rather than society. And though I was not as disappointed with *Diary of the Dead* (2007) as some fans, the main target of its satire is our media culture (a self-referential target already at the periphery in *Night* and *Dawn*). While certainly timely in a world where the apocalypse will not just be televised, but will be blogged and tweeted and podcast every moment, it is harder to tie it in to broader critiques in the other films, or to the biblical critiques of similarly bad habits. As for non-Romero zombie films, they have tended to dilute his message (as with Snyder's remake, though it is an exciting action film), or simply take over the brains and intestines for shock value.

for justice in the world. Romero's critique is perhaps most similar to that of the prophet Jeremiah, who depicted his people as faithlessly turning from the higher purposes they had been given by God: "How can you say, 'We are wise, and the law of the Lord is with us,' when, in fact, the false pen of the scribes has made it into a lie? The wise shall be put to shame, they shall be dismayed and taken; since they have rejected the word of the Lord, what wisdom is in them?"[13] Given its time, the appearance of a black protagonist in the film could not help but be remarked on by many viewers and critics, even though the race of the protagonist, Ben, is never noted or mentioned by the characters in the movie.[14] It is hard for viewers sometimes not to "read" back into the film a reaction that is not there, and even critics have asserted that the antagonist, Harry Cooper, is a racist or bigot,[15] but there is no real hint of this in the film itself. But even though the posse that kills Ben at the end makes no remark about his race (they may not even be able to tell it in the dark window at that distance), Romero seems to go out of his way to surround the posse with imagery that makes it nearly impossible to overlook their similarity to an American lynch mob—a crowd of exclusively white men, only loosely governed by governmental authorities, with guns and barking dogs, killing everything in their path.[16] Moreover, in their role as protectors and re-establishers of societal order—which is to say, white, American, capitalist order—against the zombie's chaos, the posse's killing of a black man may be meant to connect him to the zombies as a perceived threat to that order.[17] If racism

13. Jer 8:8–9, NRSV.

14. See Hutchings, *The Horror Film*, 112: "the hero's racial identity is never referred to by any of the characters in the film"; Wood, "Apocalypse Now," 93: "The film has often been praised for never making an issue of its black hero's colour (it is nowhere alluded to, even implicitly)." Dillard, "*Night of the Living Dead*," 14–29, gives an optimistic interpretation of this, esp. p. 19: "Perhaps the only unusual thing about them is that no one of them ever comments about one of their numbers being black, especially in the light of his assuming a natural leadership. But even that lack of race prejudice in a tight situation may be more ordinarily American than we might suspect."

15. E.g., Pirie, *Vampire Cinema*, 143, calls Cooper a "bigot."

16. Cf. Hutchings, *Horror Film*, 112: "More than one critic has seen references here to lynching"; Waller, *Living and the Undead*, 295, who to some extent must rely on the second film: "Though the posse cannot see that Ben is a black man, this murder evokes American racism at its deadliest and most virulent, a topic Romero will return to in the opening sequences of *Dawn of the Dead*."

17. The analysis of Wood, "Apocalypse Now," 93: "It is the function of the posse to restore the social order that has been destroyed; the zombies represent the suppressed

is not explicitly raised by the film, many of the trappings of it are used as background, subtly hinting at its presence in contemporary American society—and with the film's violent, nihilistic ending, hinting at racism's catastrophic results to the health of our country.

Romero's second zombie film, *Dawn of the Dead* (1978), begins with a much more blatant and explicit depiction of racism in the United States. At the very beginning of the film, a SWAT team storms a zombie-infested apartment building, inhabited by blacks and Latinos. Before the siege begins, one police officer expresses the stereotypical, white American rant against government aid to minorities, by claiming that the housing project is an unfair handout and waste: "Shit, man, this is better than I got!" He then begins gleefully and indiscriminately shooting both living and undead people in the head. The transition from a fairly commonly-heard rant against government assistance, immediately into a murderous rampage, seems a pretty pointed criticism of those who use such rhetoric: if societal rules and restraints were to break down, Romero implies, some in the United States would quickly escalate from racist rhetoric to racist violence. Comments made by a United States congressman after hurricane Katrina would tend to make one believe Romero's cynicism was not misplaced or overstated: the congressman joked that the storm—whose official death toll was 1844—had "finally cleaned up public housing in New Orleans."[18] In this sense, the congressman is following what seems one of the less helpful tendencies of apocalyptic—its tendency toward sectarianism and an "us versus them" mentality (in this case, "us" as the wealthy, white, and in power; "them" as the unruly minorities and poor),[19] while Romero's vision is closer to Old Testament prophecy with its warnings against self-righteousness and a feeling of moral or ethnic superiority.

---

tensions and conflicts—the legacy of the past, of the patriarchal structuring of relationships, 'dead' yet automatically continuing—which that order creates and on which it precariously rests."

18. Source for the death toll is the website of the National Weather Service (see bibliography). The comments were made by Representative Richard Baker (R-La.), as reported in the *Washington Post* (Babington, "Some GOP Legislators Hit Jarring Notes in Addressing Katrina").

19. The sectarianism of Jewish apocalypticism reaches a highpoint with the Qumran community: see Regev, "Sectarianism in Qumran," which also includes consideration of later movements such as the Anabaptists and the Shakers.

But *Dawn of the Dead* moves on to consider more positive relations between the races. The most endearing and frequent image is that of a deep friendship between Roger (white) and Peter (African-American).[20] Their rapport begins under fire, highlighting how the shared experience of suffering and horror brings people together and transcends their differences. Like other famous film and literary couples or trios, they are complementary, completing each other's thoughts and actions.[21] Roger spends a good deal of the movie on his deathbed after a zombie attack; the scenes between them are touching, as two very macho and laconic characters try not to express their feelings. Peter is also entrusted with shooting his friend before he can return as a zombie. Again, enacting what rites seem appropriate to his macho demeanor, Peter drinks a toast at his friend's grave. The whole relationship seems quite believable, and their differing races are never mentioned: they are simply and sincerely friends, because fate has brought them together under the horrible circumstances that it has.

Dawn of the Dead goes further, however, than the relatively safe subject of an interracial friendship, daring to tread into what is still mostly taboo in mainstream films—an interracial, heterosexual couple of Peter, a black man, and Fran, a white woman. The film's end is utterly ambiguous as to the couple's ultimate fate, but what is clear is that the future of humanity—whether it is measured in minutes of centuries—will be based on this interracial couple.[22] Whether their life together will be happy—leaving aside the problems of the undead for a moment—is unknown, but how they might relate to each other with a new and better respect, overcoming

---

20. See Wood, "Apocalypse Now," 96, for the possible homosexual overtones of the friendship.

21. On their relationship, cf. Waller, *Living and the Undead*, 304: "Peter and Roger are a confident, effective team who speak the same language, share ideas, and perfectly complement each other."

22. On the failure of traditional relationships and the formation of new ones, see Wood, "Apocalypse Now," 96: "In place of *Night*'s dissection of the family, *Dawn* explores (and explodes) the two dominant couple-relationships of our culture and its cinema: the heterosexual couple (moving inevitably towards marriage and its traditional male/female roles) and the male 'buddy' relationship with its evasive denial of sexuality"; and Waller, *Living and the Undead*, 321: "The couple that survives in *Dawn of the Dead*—a black man and a pregnant white woman—is not the traditional heterosexual couple (Fran and Stephen come closest to filling the role of the new Adam and Eve) or the pair of male buddies (like the team of Roger and Peter), but potentially a new type of partnership."

racial and sexual tensions and expectations, is hinted at earlier in the film. Of all the male characters, Peter is the most polite and respectful towards Fran. He expresses this at their first meeting, even though Fran has just insulted him by objecting to his escaping with them in a helicopter. This is made more awkward, with the two sitting next to each other, but Peter effectively defuses it in the following exchange.

> Peter (nodding toward Steve): "He your man?"
>
> Fran (laughing nervously): "Most of the time."
>
> Peter (smiling): "I just like to know who everybody is."
>
> Fran (smiling): "Me too."

Besides doing the socially graceful thing of overlooking her rudeness and "breaking the ice," Peter also phrases the relationship between Fran and Steve in a revealing way. He seems to show her respect, by implying that Steve might belong to Fran, rather than her belonging to him. Fran welcomes this rapport, just as Roger had responded to Peter's friendly camaraderie earlier. Fran and Peter show here and throughout the film that they have better skills in dealing with people and relationships than do Roger or Steve—Roger being stubborn and headstrong, Steve being envious and insecure. It may not be too farfetched to posit that such a rapport between Peter and Fran stems in part from their similar experiences of being belittled and pushed aside in a racist, sexist America.

Peter subsequently is the first one to agree with Fran that she should have a say in their plans, and should be armed and able to protect herself from now on.[23] Peter is also the only one who welcomes and encourages Fran to learn to fly the helicopter, and her newly acquired skill is the only thing that saves them at the end of the film. When they fly off, he is much more beholden to her and reliant on her than she on him. She has saved Peter from Steve's foolish attempt to defend the mall, and she is now literally in the driver's seat. Given their personalities, we have some reason to think that Peter is more comfortable with this situation vis-à-vis a woman, than Steve could have been.[24] Perhaps even more importantly, we have

---

23. Cf. Wood, "Apocalypse Now," 96: "But in the course of the film she progressively assumes a genuine autonomy, asserting herself against the men, insisting on possession of a gun, demanding to learn to pilot the machine."

24. On their possible future relationship, see Wood, "Apocalypse Now," 96: "Instead of the restoration of conventional relationship-patterns, we have the woman piloting

to remember that Fran is pregnant with Steve's (white) child, not Peter's. Whatever their relationship may develop into, Peter's first role will be as a stepfather to another man's child, the very un-stereotypical situation of a child of one race, born to an interracial couple. It is a strange permutation of the Adam and Eve roles that we might expect at the end of such a movie, but oddly hopeful in its own way. Given Peter's kind, generous, and respectful attitude throughout the story, we have some confidence that he will fulfill such an awkward and demanding role better than most men. It also presents us with a potential future in which the significance of race is seriously undermined, if not totally abolished. But Romero implies that more hopeful future will only be realized when the mindless zombie hordes devour the old, corrupt, racist regime under which we now live.

Besides continuing and making more explicit the theme of American racism, the second film adds what would become perhaps Romero's best-known image: zombies stampeding through a mall as a parody of rampant, American consumer culture. The image has become so much a part of the modern definition of the zombie that there are now mass zombie walks in malls all over, often to gather blood for blood drives, or food for local charities, and usually staged around Halloween or (more blasphemously) Easter.[25] The final image in *Dawn of the Dead*—in which zombies stagger around the mall, mesmerized by the products there, while an absurd tune called "The Gonk" plays on the Muzak system—is perhaps its most iconic, and later films can evoke and pay homage to the whole Romero corpus just by playing Muzak as their characters flee the living dead.[26] Romero's prophetic use of the image is to show that it is not the zombie's bite that turns us into monsters, but materialism and consumerism that turn us into zombies, addicted to things that satisfy only the basest, most animal

---

the helicopter as the man relinquishes his rifle to the zombies"; and Waller, *Living and the Undead*, 321–22: "Fran—carrying within her the prospect of new life—has been the most perceptive of the group, and Peter has been the most skillful and the most inclined to regard her as an equal . . . Perhaps since Fran is piloting the helicopter and Peter has left behind his rifle, this couple is also escaping from the limiting roles fostered by a racist and sexist society that has now been destroyed."

25. "Zombie walk" now has its own Wikipedia page, as well as a website at zombiewalk.com, which offers a forum for enthusiasts to keep informed of upcoming events. Though most are in the USA, the site lists walks in Canada, the UK, Europe, and South America.

26. Romero does this himself in *Day of the Dead*. It is also done in the *Dawn of the Dead* remake and in *Shaun of the Dead*.

or mechanical urges of our being.[27] This is repeatedly shown throughout *Dawn of the Dead* in the behavior of both the zombies and the human characters.

With the zombies, it is shown by their monomaniacal obsession with getting into the mall, even if it means their destruction. Sheer, unthinking tenacity or the search for prey cannot explain why the zombies pick *this* place as the one they feel they must occupy, over any other, and at any cost or risk. Though we will never know for sure, one can reasonably infer, based on Romero's depiction, that in a zombie-infested world, the former churches, libraries, and classrooms are not nearly as crowded with the undead as are the malls. (Even, one could reasonably suspect, conventionally sinful places like casinos, bars, and brothels would not be as crowded with the eager undead as the shopping malls, for materialism and constant, mindless consumption are not just tolerated, but enthusiastically encouraged in our society, while these other sinful behaviors are still regarded as slightly embarrassing and furtive.) Steve interprets the zombies' behavior very accurately when they first land on the roof of the mall: to Fran's question of, "Why do they come here?" he answers, "Some kind of instinct. Memory. What they used to do. This was an important place in their lives." This raises and complicates the horror of the living dead: not just that one will be torn to pieces and eaten alive—bad enough, surely—but that one will join the undead as an eternal mall-goer, never again able to conceive of anything higher or more interesting to do than wander about with a vacuous look of contentment, punctuated by longing, lustful stares at racks and displays full of useless, worthless stuff.

Peter will infer this eternal judgment of the zombies and themselves later in the film, as the human survivors again ponder the zombie hordes that are so eagerly and tenaciously trying to break in to their fortified mall, even though the humans have just finished slaughtering hundreds of them to secure it: "They don't know why, they just remember they want to be in here," to which Fran asks, "What the hell are they?" and Peter replies, "They're us, that's all . . . When there's no more room in hell, the dead will walk the earth." It is the most chilling line in a chilling movie, repeated in the remake in a cameo appearance by Ken Foree, who played Peter in

---

27. For a scholarly analysis of consumerism in the film, see Loudermilk, "Eating *dawn* in the dark." For a sociological application of the image of "living dead," but without reference to the film, see Ritzer, "Islands of the Living Dead."

the original. With this statement, Peter rightly judges both zombies and humans as damned to repeat their trivialities and mistakes for all eternity, never again with the possibility of learning from them or improving, because such education and improvement were so consistently spurned in life, and such trivial sinfulness was so enthusiastically embraced. Though people usually use the word "Dantean" to describe the horrible grotesquery and torture in a movie like *Dawn of the Dead*, it is really more applicable to a vision like this. For Dante's depiction of sin is that it is exactly like an addiction, as depicted here—one that is willingly embarked on in life, and hopelessly and eternally repeated in death: "I learned that to this place of punishment all those who sin in lust have been condemned, those who make reason slave to appetite."[28] When they had reason and could think of better things to do than go to the mall, the people who would become mall zombies did not. Instead, they enslaved and finally killed their reason with their mundane and trivial appetites, thereby dooming themselves to repeat their sinful actions forever, never able to correct or extricate themselves from their sinful mistake. If you "shop till you drop," you will drop very far indeed, and will be condemned to shop forever.[29]

Romero has increased the relevance and discomfort of his prophetic critique by showing how the live humans are no less obsessed with getting into and staying in the mall than are the zombies. The plot of the movie is consistently driven by the survivors' lust to acquire and possess, especially predominant in the male characters. Roger, Steve, and many of the bikers who attack their mall/fortress are killed for their mad, foolish lust for possessions, but all the characters succumb to it at one point or another. The bikers, comically portrayed as the least thoughtful among the characters, are even more obsessed with possessions and indiscriminate in acquiring them than our protagonists, killing and dying just to grab any old thing in sight.[30] Steve and Peter steal paper money and then

---

28. Dante, *Inferno*, 5.37–39.

29. The consumer motto is invoked similarly in Skal, *The Monster Show*, 376: "Ellis' world of blood-soaked designer labels recognizably upgrades the voracious mall zombies in *Dawn of the Dead*: they shop till they drop, eat your brains, then shop some more"

30. On the comparison of the bikers with our protagonists, see Wood, "Apocalypse Now," 96: "The motorcycle gang's mindless delight in violence and slaughter is anticipated in the development of Roger; all three groups are contaminated and motivated by consumer-greed (which the zombies simply carry to its logical conclusion by consuming people)"; and Waller, *Living and the Undead*, 317, who notes that "their looting of the

play poker with it, even though it's completely worthless now. Steve also epitomizes the attitude that possession is nine tenths of the law, and nine tenths of the value he puts on his life, apparently, when he snarls, "It's ours! We took it!" and madly sacrifices his life to die in his consumerist prison rather than give it up without a fight. Earlier, his only consolation to Fran when she was attacked and nearly killed by a zombie was to reassure her, "You should see all the great stuff we got . . . This place is terrific, it really is. It's perfect!" Roger, in his final, dying delirium, must be comforted by Peter that his sacrifice was worth it, but we know that this is simply and pathetically not so. When the four of them survey their "victory" over the undead for which Roger has sacrificed himself, Romero dresses them up in enormous, poofy fur coats, in what can only be described as the fashion choice of a pimp—gaudy, tasteless, flamboyant, androgynous, and utterly unnecessary in their climate-controlled fortress/prison.[31] Even Peter, who seems the most enlightened and thoughtful of the men, is in fact the first to utter a cry of delight at what they variously call their newfound "kingdom" and "gold mine": to Roger's objection that they are now cut off from Fran and Steve and trapped inside JC Penney's, Peter shouts, "Who the hell cares?! Let's go shopping!" From beginning to end, the film is full of men killing themselves and others to get and hold on to things that they do not really need, and which do not even make them happy. It is one of the saddest and most damning critiques of consumerism imaginable.

After Roger's death, the survivors' consumerist glee turns even more sour. As the saying goes, they no longer own their possessions; their possessions own them. The especially poignant aspect of this is how corrosive it is to their relationships, especially the romantic and sexual relation between Fran and Steve. The scene of Steve's marriage proposal is the most obvious example of this.[32] Although I strongly suspect that it is another ploy of our consumerist society to persuade men that they *have* to spend

---

mall is a parodic repetition of Fran, Stephen, Peter, and Roger's shopping spree."

31. The fur coats are also other corpses with which they surround themselves: cf. Waller, *Living and the Undead*, 311: "The mall—refuge or promised land or prison—belongs to the living. However, in making it safe and habitable, they have, figuratively at least, closed themselves in and surrounded themselves with corpses."

32. On the scene, see Wood, "Apocalypse Now," 96: "The pivotal scene is the parody of a romantic dinner, the white couple, in evening dress, cooked for and waited on by the black, with flowers and candlelight, the scene building to the man's offer and the woman's refusal of the rings that signify traditional union."

two months' salary on an engagement ring, it would also seem true that all of the romance and attraction is lost if one could just walk into a jewelry store and grab anything one wanted for free, as Steve has done with Fran's ring. Such a "gift" is not real, for it costs the giver nothing in a world where everything is simply lying around, worthless and unappreciated (even as it is ironically grabbed and pursued with such murderous zeal). Indeed, after their initial slaughter to take over the mall, our protagonists need make no effort for anything, and they settle into a smothering ennui, disinterested in everything, even sex. At one point, Steve is shown in his fancy bed and silk sheets, sullen and bored, and the camera pulls back to reveal Fran right next to him: they could be making love or cuddling or talking or even just playing checkers, but instead they are utterly miserable and alone together in their gilded prison.

Even Fran, although she seems ten times more perceptive and resistant to the mall's supposed charms than her male companions, is shown briefly succumbing to some kind of consumerist fantasy late in the movie. She sits at an enormous vanity mirror, made up with so much make-up that it is clownish and grotesque, not sexy or attractive. She tries to strike seductive or suggestive poses with a pearl handled pistol, like Bonnie in *Bonnie and Clyde* (1967), though it all seems quite unnecessary and absurd, for Fran is a very pretty woman, allowing for the clothes and hairstyles of the 70s, and this hideous posturing is clearly no improvement. Whatever the reasons for or content of her fantasy, it is already going badly enough, when the mall loudspeakers issue a call, "Attention shoppers!" The illusion of glamour and beauty is completely shattered by the loudspeakers' offer of a free bag of cheap candy with every purchase—when now every purchase is free. Following this wakeup, Fran seems more disgusted than ever, this time with herself as well.[33] She realizes the mall is hypnotizing them and making them as fake as it is, with its faux foliage in planter boxes, one of which now unceremoniously serves as a tomb for Roger; its hollow, toyland-like clock tower, chiming hours in a land where time

---

33. Cf. Waller, *Living and the Undead*, 314: "Striking 'provocative' poses with a six-gun, Fran resembles a painted mannequin or a poor imitation of a gangster's moll or a child costumed as an adult. Over the mall's loud-speakers, a voice calls all 'shoppers' to pay attention, and Fran looks up as if she realizes the extent to which she has become the willing, predictable 'shopper'—the prisoner who can no longer see the bars of her prison."

certainly does not matter anymore;[34] and its mannequins with painted tans and grins, in a world where there is no sun, and very little at which to smile. The mall is also making them as dead and numb as the other zombies that ravenously and impotently paw and slobber at its outside doors: they are trapped outside, and our three survivors are trapped inside.

As with biblical prophecy, however, the point of the movie is not simply to announce doom and judgment, but to issue a warning that its audience might actually act upon: "Hear the word of the Lord, O nations, and declare it in the coastlands far away; say, 'He who scattered Israel will gather him, and will keep him as a shepherd a flock.' . . . Indeed, I heard Ephraim pleading: 'You disciplined me, and I took the discipline; I was like a calf untrained. Bring me back, let me come back, for you are the Lord my God.'"[35] Right up until the death rattle or disembowelment that will make one permanently and irrevocably a zombie, one can make choices that matter. Fran takes responsibility for herself, not blaming the situation or others, when she confronts the men: "What have we done to ourselves?"[36] That question is really the fundamental one from a Christian perspective, much more so than the question of theodicy (i.e., "Why is God doing this to us?") that one usually expects in an apocalyptic scenario.

Land of the Dead (2005) returns to these themes of racism and consumerism with less humor and more action. The zombie hordes are not the real villains of this installment. That role is fulfilled by a power-hungry and power-mad capitalist, Kaufman, providing another pointed and memorable part of Romero's critique of current society. Kaufman seems to be a combination of capitalist robber baron, mad Roman emperor, and organized crime kingpin.[37] His name means "trader" or "merchant," as though that were the essence of his character. To have the new ruler of the

---

34. Waller observes this of the very end of the movie: "Ironically, the mall's clock chimes over and over, marking the hour for a crowd of shoppers who will never again worry about the passage of time" (Waller, *Living and the Undead*, 320).

35. Jer 31:10, 18, NRSV.

36. Cf. Waller, *Living and the Undead*, 314–15: "For unlike the automatistic zombies who still fill the parking lot and press against the entrances of the mall, the well-fed, safe, comfortable human beings inside this fortress have the freedom to choose."

37. Cf. S. Klawans, "Alien Nation," 44, where he calls Kaufman "an all-purpose realtor, corporate czar and crime boss." Russell, *Book of the Dead*, 190, makes the reference much more explicit and historically-contextualized: "Presenting Kaufman as a composite of George W. Bush and Defense Secretary Donald Rumsfeld, Romero makes his criticism of the regime more than transparent."

only remaining human society be named "merchant," shows how Romero believes that commerce is the highest form of power in the old, pre-zombie human society. In this chilling, cynical, but uncomfortably realistic view, it is not the military, government, or church that exercises real power, but the wealthy, who may use these other institutions as proxies or fronts for their selfish machinations. According to Romero, the White House, the Pentagon, and the Vatican do not run or exploit the world—Wall Street does.

Played by Dennis Hopper with more restraint than he often exercises, and therefore much more effectively, Kaufman is positively Satanic in the absurd and sadistic lengths to which he will go in order to perpetuate his reign, as the reviewer for the *New York Times* noted: "With this new movie, we jump straight to the ninth circle, where Satan is a guy in a suit and tie who feasts on the misery of others, much as the dead feast on the living."[38] Kaufman is one of the few, perhaps the only one of the characters in any of the films, to note how the zombie menace fundamentally changes all human interactions, and does so to his advantage: when informed that he's in "trouble," Kaufman quite correctly responds that, "In a world where the dead are returning to life, the word 'trouble' loses much of its meaning." Only the raiders in *Dawn of the Dead* would perhaps share Kaufman's preference for life in a world overrun by zombies, but the raiders were crude, disorganized, and comical amateurs compared to Kaufman. Again, *Land of the Dead* teases us with the idea that it is not the leather-clad, tattooed biker, or the big, scary black man who will do us harm, but the well-dressed, well-mannered, sinister, and well-organized banker and businessman who is the real threat to our well-being.

While others in the movie long to return to "normal" life, Kaufman sees how "good" life can be in a zombie-infested world, for it not only removes all restraints on him, it even lets him set up a hellish society based on his values of greed, envy, vice, and cruelty.[39] We see this when he explains his own version of "civic duty" at one point: according to him, he has a great and noble "responsibility" for his fellow citizens, because he "kept people off the streets by giving them games and vices." Like Milton's (1608–74) Satan more than Dante's, Kaufman believes that it is, "Better

38. Dargis, "Not Just Roaming, Zombies Rise Up."

39. Cf. Russell, *Book of the Dead*, 186: "What was threatened before in Romero's series has finally come to pass: the living are now more like monsters than the living dead."

to reign in Hell, than serve in Heav'n."[40] And while he's mixing in various classic depictions of Satan, Romero is, of course, not above the burlesque version of Goethe's (1749–1832) Mephistopheles, having Kaufman say, as probably only Hopper could pull it off, while picking his nose (!), "Zombies, man, creep me out!"

The fantasy of what Satan/Kaufman tempts us with is graphically shown in the advertisements and reality of Fiddler's Green, the safe tower in the middle of Kaufman's city. It is a place where "Life goes on!" as before, undisturbed by the miseries of others, or by the inevitable specter of (un)death. The ground floor of Fiddler's Green resembles a much more upscale mall than that depicted in the original *Dawn of the Dead*,[41] now made more horrible and wretched by its opulence, and by the fact that it is not just zombies and biker gangs that are being kept out, but sick and starving children. All attempts to dress the fantasy up as anything other than crass and cannibalistic consumption has finally been stripped away by the exigencies of a zombie-infested world. The inner sanctum of consumption and exclusion is not named something bellicose like The Citadel, or patriotic, like Freedom Tower: instead, it's got one of those generically happy-sounding names like the $1.5 million condos with 24-hour fitness centers, climate control, and security, cocooned in shining glass and steel towers and advertised in the back of in-flight magazines. It is an image of privileged irresponsibility in the face of suffering, like "fiddling while Rome burns."[42] Apparently the name even comes from an old Irish legend of where happy fishermen go when they die, a place where, "There's pubs and there's clubs and there's lassies there too. And the girls are all pretty and the beer is all free. And there's bottles of rum growing on every tree."[43] It is an adult version of Pleasure Island in *Pinocchio* or Neverland in *Peter Pan*, but it is no more mature, and no more real. The cut scene of a suicide (now available on the DVD version) makes the

---

40. Milton, *Paradise Lost*, 1.263.

41. Cf. Russell, *Book of the Dead*, 189: "With the apartments of Fiddler's Green a more luxurious take on the shopping mall enclave from *Dawn of the Dead*, it's obvious that Romero has lost none of his anti-consumerist fervour even when taking a major Hollywood studio's dollar."

42. The connection suggested by Russell, *Book of the Dead*, 189.

43. I was first alerted to this by the "Trivia" section for *Land of the Dead* on the Internet Movie Database site: http://www.imdb.com/title/tto418819/ (site visited November 14, 2005). The lyrics are from Conolly, "Brobdingnagian Bards" (see Bibliography).

fantastical and unsatisfying aspect of such an existence painfully clear: surrounded by comfort and ease, some people find their life so empty and meaningless that they kill themselves and become zombies, who at least have a lot more drive and ambition. And even if they don't avail themselves of suicide, zombie-hood is where they are all headed anyway, but before they get there, they have the added damnation of being the docile and cooperating thralls of Kaufman/Satan.

The reality of the hellish kingdom over which Kaufman rules is indelibly impressed on our imaginations by the view from his office, which is as Dantean and apocalyptic as anything else presented in the films. As far as the eye can see is a grey, blighted, lifeless urban moonscape that might as well be Hiroshima or Auschwitz, it is so dead and demoralizing, yet it represents the best view in Fiddler's Green, one for which Kaufman is eager to kill, protecting it and keeping it away from the "common" folk who dwell below, or from the hungry undead outside the walls. Twice as the zombies are attacking his kingdom, he cries out, "You have no right!" when, of course, Kaufman based his kingdom on ignoring others' rights and acting like a terrorist and a criminal. His evil reign is not based on any "right" other than "might makes right"—and if the zombie hordes now possess more might, than they are the rightful rulers.

Besides making a capitalist robber baron the villain, Romero increases the social criticism of this film with his choice of who leads the zombie army against Kaufman. The smartest zombie in this film, the one who thinks to launch a counterattack against the sadistic humans, and who thinks of various ways around the obstacles in getting there, is a black gas station attendant whose nametag reads "Big Daddy." One reviewer rightly noted that Big Daddy and Riley (the main human protagonist) are the only two sympathetic characters in the film, and even went as far as to say that Big Daddy is Riley's "zombie alter ego."[44] At the end of the movie, with Kaufman killed and his city in ruins, Big Daddy and Riley look at one another from a distance and seem to declare some truce—Big Daddy shambling off without further attacks, as the intelligent zombie Bub had done at the end of *Day of the Dead*. The films had begun with a black man lying dead at the hands of a white posse sent out to impose order on society; *Land of the Dead* ends with a black zombie bringing about the end of a corrupt, violent human society and then seemingly

44. Dargis, "Not Just Roaming, Zombies Rise Up."

ceasing his own rampage. If the former was a potent and uncomfortable indictment of 1960s America with its racism and pointless overseas wars in places like Vietnam, the new installment is a sobering implication of how it might end—with an army of those exploited rising up against the oppressors who have based their affluent and wasteful lifestyle on the toil and suffering of others.[45]

Modern Christians in the West often seem as smug as any caricature of the ancient Israelites to whom Amos prophesied. We too often assume our way of life will continue as it is now, maintaining our level of affluence and consumption indefinitely, even though such extravagance is at the expense of other people and the environment and will inevitably run out. Further, whether or not we espouse something as explicit as a "prosperity gospel," many seem to take it for granted that our material well-being is a good thing, ordained and approved by a God whom we have pleased through our behavior. Zombie movies stand as a stark, sobering, even terrifying counterbalance to such a vision of modern Christianity. They instead offer us Amos' bitter, disillusioned criticism of our wealth and skewed values, couched in the horrifying, monstrous terms of Ezekiel, and leading to the ultimate destruction and judgment of Revelation. The compatibility between zombie films and the biblical tradition seems to me irrefutable and compelling, and therefore their relevance to Christians— or, indeed, any religious or humanist person who seeks to expose the sinful, misguided excesses of the modern world—seems equally certain.

45. Cf. Degiglio-Bellemare, "*Land of the Dead*," 7: "Romero's new film offers a very important statement on the reality of 'lockdown America,' with its gated communities, its stark class divisions, and its racial demarcations."

Bibliography

Adorno, Theodor W. "Cultural Criticism and Society." *Can One Live after Auschwitz? A Philosophical Reader*, edited by Rolf Tiedemann, 146–62. Stanford, CA: Stanford University Press, 2003.

Anderson, Paul Thomas. *Magnolia*. New Line, 1999.

———. *Magnolia: The Shooting Script*. New York: Newmarket, 2000.

Aquinas. *The Pocket Aquinas*. Edited and translated by Vernon J. Bourke. New York: Washington Square, 1960.

———. *Summa Theologica*. Translated by the Fathers of the English Dominican Province, 1948. Reprint. Notre Dame, IN: Christian Classics, 1981.

Arendt, Hannah. *Eichmann in Jerusalem: A Report on the Banality of Evil*. London: Penguin, 1994.

Augustine. *Augustine: Later Works*. Edited by John Burnaby, translated by John Burnaby. Philadelphia: Westminster, 1980.

———. *Confessions*. Translated by Henry Chadwick. Oxford: Oxford University Press, 1998.

———. *On the Trinity*. Translated by Arthur West Haddan. From *Nicene and Post-Nicene Fathers*, First Series, Vol. 3, edited by Philip Schaff. Buffalo, NY: Christian Literature, 1887. Revised and edited for New Advent by Kevin Knight. No Pages. Online: http://www.newadvent.org/fathers/130101.htm.

———. *Soliloquies*. Translated by Kim Paffenroth and John E. Rotelle, O.S.A. New York: New City, 2000.

Babington, Charles. "Some GOP Legislators Hit Jarring Notes in Addressing Katrina." *Washington Post*. No Pages. Online: http://www.washingtonpost.com/wp-dyn/content/article/2005/09/09/AR2005090901930.html.

Balthasar, Hans Urs von. *Love Alone is Credible*. San Francisco: Ignatius, 2004.

———. *Theo-Drama: Theological Dramatic Theory, Volume I: Prolegomena*. Translated by Graham Harrison. San Francisco: Ignatius, 1988.

Beck, Donald R. *Star Trek 25th Anniversary Special*. Paramount Pictures, 1991.

Bennett, Compton. *King Solomon's Mines*. Warner Brothers, 2005.

Bennett, Jill and Rosanne Kennedy. *World Memory: Personal Trajectories in Global Time*. New York: Palgrave Macmillan, 2003.

Berry, Wendell. *Life is a Miracle: An Essay Against Modern Superstition*. New York: Counterpoint, 2001.

Bibliography

Blaisdell Tracy, Ann. *Patterns of Fear in the Gothic Novel, 1790–1830*. New York: Ayer, 1980.

Blake, Richard A. *Afterimage: The Indelible Catholic Imagination of Six American Filmmakers*. Chicago: Loyola, 2000.

Bole, Cliff. "Emergence." *Star Trek: The Next Generation*. Paramount Pictures, 1994.

———. "Hide and Q." *Star Trek: The Next Generation*. Paramount Pictures, 1987.

Bonhoeffer, Dietrich. *Creation and Fall: A Theological Exposition of Genesis 1–3*. Minneapolis, MN: Fortress, 1996.

Bordwell, David, et al. *The Classical Hollywood Cinema: Film Style and Mode of Production to 1960*. New York: Columbia University Press, 1985.

Britton, A. "The Devil, Probably: The Symbolism of Evil." In *American Nightmare: Essays on the Horror Film*, edited by R. Wood and R. Lippe, 34–42. Toronto: Festival of Festivals, 1979.

Carpenter, Humphrey. *Tolkien: A Biography*. New York: Ballantine, 1977.

Caruth, Cathy. *Unclaimed Experience: Trauma, Narrative and History*. Baltimore: Johns Hopkins University Press, 1995.

Celli, Carlo. *The Divine Comic: The Cinema of Roberto Benigni*. London: Scarcrow, 2001.

Chadwick, Henry. "Introduction." *Saint Augustine: Confessions*, translated by Henry Chadwick. Oxford, New York: Oxford University Press, 1998.

Chattaway, Peter. "Del Toro, *Pan's Labyrinth*, and *Narnia* Redux." *FilmChat*. No Pages. Online: http://filmchatblog.blogspot.com/2006/12/del-toro-pans-labyrinth-and-narnia.html.

Clines, David J. A. "The Image of God in Man." *Tyndale Bulletin* 19 (1968) 53–103.

Colman, Juliet Benita. *Ronald Colman: A Very Private Person*. London: Morrow, 1975.

Conolly, John. "Brobdingnagian Bards." No Pages. Online: http://www.thebards.net/music/lyrics/Fiddlers_Green.shtml.

Dante. *Inferno*. Translated by Mark Musa. New York: Penguin, 1984.

Dargis, M. "Not Just Roaming, Zombies Rise Up." *New York Times*. No Pages. Online: http://movies.nytimes.com/2005/06/24/movies/24rome.html.

Davis, Wade. *Passage of Darkness: The Ethnobiology of the Haitian Zombie*. Chapel Hill, NC: University of North Carolina Press, 1988.

———. *The Serpent and the Rainbow*. New York: Simon & Schuster, 1985.

Del Torro, Guillermo. "Pan's People." *The Guardian*. No Pages. Online: http://www.guardian.co.uk/film/2006/nov/17/2.

Dillard, R. H. W. "*Night of the Living Dead*: It's Not Like Just a Wind That's Passing Through." In *American Horrors: Essays on the Modern American Horror Film*, edited by G. A. Waller, 14–29. Urbana, IL: University of Illinois Press, 1988.

Donelson, Linda. "Appendix I: Karen Blixen's Medical History." *Out of Isak Dinesen: Karen Blixen's Untold Story*. Iowa City, Iowa: Coulsong List, 1998.

———. *Out of Isak Dinesen: Karen Blixen's Untold Story*. Iowa City, IA: Coulsong List, 1998.

Dunn, James D. G. *Jesus Remembered*. Christianity in the Making, vol. I. Grand Rapids: Eerdmans, 2003.

Edwards, Diane Tolomeo. "*Babette's Feast*, Sacramental Grace, and the Saga of Redemption." *Christianity and Literature* 42.3 (1993) 421–32.

Eldridge, Richard. "The Ends of Narrative." In *A Sense of the World: Essays on Fiction, Narrative, and Knowledge*, edited by John Gibson, Wolfgang Huemer and Luca Pocci, 138–50. London: Routledge, 2007.

Falcon, Richard. "*La Vie de Jesus/The Life of Jesus.*" *Sight and Sound* 8.9 (1998) 55.

Felman, Shoshana and Dori Laub. *Testimony: Crises of Witnessing in Literature, Psychoanalysis and History.* New York: Routledge, 1992.

Fitzpatrick, Tony. "Shock and Recall: Negative Emotion May Enhance Memory, Study Finds." No Pages. Online: http://news.wustl.edu/news/Pages/22439.aspx.

Fraser, J. "Watching Horror Movies." *Michigan Quarterly Review* 24.1 (1990) 39–54.

Grau, Marion. "Comment post on 'Creative Gaming.'" No Pages. Online:http://www.poptheology.com/2010/03/ben-x/, accessed December 20, 2010.

Grudem, Wayne. *Systematic Theology.* Grand Rapids: Zondervan, 1994.

Hall, Douglas John. *Imaging God.* Grand Rapids: Eerdmans, 1986.

Hansen, Miriam Bratu. "'Schindler's List' Is Not 'Shoah': The Second Commandment, Popular Modernism, and Public Memory." *Critical Inquiry* 22 (1996) 292–312.

———. "Schindler's List is Not Shoah: Second Commandment, Popular Modernism, and Public Memory." In *Spielberg's Holocaust: Critical Perspectives on* Schindler's List, edited by Yosefa Loshitzky, 77–103. Bloomington, IN: Indiana University Press, 1997.

Hart, David Bentley. *The Doors of the Sea: Where Was God in the Tsunami?* Grand Rapids: Eerdmans, 2005.

Hinduja, Sameer and Justin W. Patchin. "Cyberbullying Research Summary: Cyberbullying and Suicide." Online: http://www.cyberbullying.us/myspace_youth_research.pdf.

Hirsch, Joshua. *After Image: Film, Trauma, and the Holocaust.* Philadelphia: Temple University Press, 2004.

Hirschberg, Lynn. "His Way." *New York Times Magazine.* Pages 1–11. Online: http://www.nytimes.com/1999/12/19/magazine/his way.html.

Hughes, Darren. "Bruno Dumont's Bodies" *Senses of Cinema* 19 (2002). No Pages. Online: http://www.sensesofcinema.com/2002/feature articles/dumont_bodies.

Hutchings, P. *The Horror Film.* New York: Pearson Longman, 2004.

Insdorf, Annette. *Indelible Shadows: Film and the Holocaust.* 3rd ed. Cambridge: Cambridge University Press, 2003.

Jacobs, Alan. *Shaming the Devil: Essays in Truthtelling.* Grand Rapids: Eerdmans, 2004.

Johnston, Robert K. *Reframing Theology and Film: New Focus for an Emerging Discipline.* Grand Rapids: Baker Academic, 2007.

Jones, Gerald. "Violent Media is Good for Kids." No Pages. Online: http://motherjones.com/politics/2000/06/violent-media-good-kids-0.

Joost, Henry, and Ariel Schulman. *Catfish.* Universal Pictures, 2010.

Kaplan, E. Ann. *Trauma Culture: The Politics of Terror and Loss in Media and Literature.* Piscataway: Rutgers University Press, 2005.

Kaplan, E. Ann, and Ben Wang. "From Traumatic Paralysis to the Force Field of Modernity." In *Trauma and Cinema: Cross-Cultural Explorations*, edited by E. Kaplan, 1–22. Seattle: University of Washington Press, 2003.

Kelber, Werner H. "Narrative and Disclosure: Mechanisms of Concealing, Revealing, and Reveiling." *Semeia* 43 (1988) 1–20.

Kierkegaard, Søren. *The Point of View.* Edited and Translated by Howard V. Hong and Edna H. Hong. Princeton, NJ: Princeton University Press, 1998.

Kirk, Russell. "The Moral Imagination." *Literature and Belief* 1 (1981) 37–49.

———. "The Moral Imagination." In *Reclaiming a Patrimony: The Heritage Lectures*, 45–58. Washington, DC: The Heritage Foundation, 1982. Online: http://www.kirkcenter.org/index.php/detail/the-moral-imagination/.

Klawans, Stuart. "Alien Nation." *Nation* 281.4 (2005) 41–44.

———. "Urban and Other Anomies: *Chungking Express/Antonia's Line/Sonic Outlaws*." *The Nation* 262:9 (1996) 35–36.

Kline, Meredith. *Kingdom Prologue*. Hamilton, MA: Gordon-Conwell Theological Seminary, 1993.

Kolbe, Winrich. "Rightful Heir." *Star Trek: The Next Generation*. Paramount Pictures, 1993.

Lamarque, Peter, and Stein Haugon Olsen. *Truth, Fiction, and Literature: A Philosophical Perspective*. Oxford: Oxford University Press, 1997.

Lanier, Jaron. *You Are Not a Gadget: A Manifesto*. New York: Knoph, 2010.

Lewis, C. S. *The Collected Letters of C. S. Lewis, vol. 2, Books, Broadcasts, and the War, 1931–1949*. Edited by Walter Hooper. San Francisco: HarperCollins, 2004.

———. *The Collected Letters of C. S. Lewis, vol. 3, Narnia, Cambridge, and Joy, 1950–1963*. Edited by Walter Hooper. San Francisco: HarperCollins, 2007.

———. "De Descriptione Temporum." In *Selected Literary Essays*, 1–14. Cambridge: Cambridge University Press, 1969.

———. "It All Began With a Picture." In *Of Other Worlds: Essays and Stories*, 42. New York: Harcourt, 1964.

———. *Letters to an American Lady*. Grand Rapids: Eerdmans, 1967.

———. "On Myth." In *An Experiment in Criticism*, 40–49. Cambridge: Cambridge University Press, 1992.

———. "On Stories." In *Of Other Worlds: Essays and Stories*, 3–21. New York: Harcourt, 1966.

———. "On Stories." In *On Stories and Other Essays on Literature*, 3–21. San Diego: Harcourt, 1982.

———. "On Science Fiction." *Of Other Worlds: Essays and Stories*, 59–73. New York: Harcourt, 1966.

———. *A Preface to Paradise Lost*. Oxford: Oxford University Press, 1942.

———. "Sometimes Fairy Stories May Say Best What's to Be Said." *Of Other Worlds: Essays and Stories*, 35–38. New York: Harcourt, 1967.

———. *Surprised by Joy*. New York: Harcourt, 1955.

———. *They Stand Together: The Letters of C. S. Lewis to Arthur Greeves (1914–1963)*. New York: Macmillan, 1979.

———. "The Weight of Glory." In *The Weight of Glory and Other Addresses*, 24–45. San Francisco: HarperSanFrancisco, 2001.

Leys, Ruth. *Trauma: A Genealogy*. Chicago: University of Chicago Press, 2000.

Loudermilk, A. "Eating *Dawn* in the Dark: Zombie Desire and Commodified identity in George A. Romero's *Dawn of the Dead*." *Journal of Consumer Culture* 3.1 (2003) 83–108.

Lowenstein, Adam. *Shocking Representation: Historical Trauma, National Cinema, and the Modern Horror Film*. New York: Columbia University Press, 2005.

MacDonald, George. *Preface to Letters from Hell*. New York: Funk and Wagnalls, 1887.

Marcel, Gabriel. *The Mystery of Being, Volume II: Faith and Reality*. South Bend, IN: St. Augustine's, 2001.

Marsh, Clive. "Did You Say 'Grace'?: Eating in Community in *Babette's Feast*." In *Explorations in Theology and Film: Movies and Meaning*, edited by Clive Marsh and Gaye Ortiz, 207–18. Oxford: Blackwell, 1997.

Maslin, Janet. "Entangled Lives on the Cusp of the Millennium." *New York Times.* No Pages. Online: http://movies.nytimes.com/movie/review?res=940CE3DD1430F934 A25751C1A96F958260.

Meyer, Nicholas. *Star Trek VI: The Undiscovered Country.* Paramount Pictures, 1991.

———. "Nick Meyer On His Gene Roddenberry Regret." TrekMovie.com. No Pages. Online: http://www.youtube.com/watch?v=-3Z87KlOuD4.

Milbank, John. *Being Reconciled: Ontology and Pardon.* London: Routledge, 2003.

Miller, Neil. "An Interview with Zack Snyder, Director of 300. " Online: http://blogcritics. org/video/article/an-interview-with-zack-snyder-director/.

Milton, John. *Paradise Lost.* Edited by C. Ricks. New York: Signet, 1968.

Montoya, Angel F. Méndez. *The Theology of Food: Eating and the Eucharist.* Chicester, UK: Wiley-Blackwell, 2009.

Movies Central. "300 Full Production Notes." No Pages. Online: http://madeinatlantis. com/movies_central/2007/300_production_details.htm.

National Weather Service. No Pages. Online: http://www.hpc.ncep.noaa.gov/tropical/ rain/katrina2005.html.

Natov, Roni. "Harry Potter and the Extraordinariness of the Ordinary." *The Lion and the Unicorn* 25.2 (2001) 310–27.

Neuner, Josef, S.J., Karl Rahner, S.J., and Heinrich Roos, S.J., eds. *The Teaching of the Catholic Church as Contained In Her Documents.* Translated by Geoffrey Stevens. Staten Island, NY: Alba House, 1967.

Oliver, Simon, and John Milbank. *The Radical Orthodoxy Reader.* London: Routledge, 2009.

Overstreet, Jeffery. "Pan's Labyrinth." *Christianity Today* (2006). Online: http://www. christianitytoday.com/ct/movies/reviews/2006/panslabyrinth.html.

Paffenroth, Kim. *Gospel of the Living Dead: George Romero's Visions of Hell on Earth.* Waco, TX: Baylor University Press, 2006.

Percy, Walker. *Lost in the Cosmos.* New York: Picador, 1983.

Perry, Gerald. "*Life is Beautiful.*" No Pages. Online: http://geraldpeary.com/reviews/jkl/ life-is-beautiful.html.

Pickstock, Catherine. *After Writing: On the Liturgical Consummation of Philosophy.* Oxford: Blackwell, 1998.

Pilinovsky, Helen. "Spells of Enchantment: The Fairy Tale Cycle." Online: http://www. endicott-studio.com/rdrm/rrSpells.html, Accessed 11/23/10.

Pirie, David. *The Vampire Cinema.* New York: Crescent, 1977.

Plantinga, Carl. *Moving Viewers: American Film and the Spectator's Experience.* Berkeley: University of California Press, 2009.

Plantinga, Carl, and Greg M. Smith. *Passionate Views: Film, Cognition, and Emotion.* Baltimore, MD: The John Hopkins University Press, 1999.

Plato. *Complete Works.* Edited by John M. Cooper. Indianapolis: Hackett, 1997.

———. *The Great Dialogues of Plato.* Translated by W. H. D. Rouse. New York: Penguin, 1984.

———. *Republic. Complete Works.* Edited by John M Cooper. Indianapolis: Hackett, 1997.

Pope John Paul II. "Letter to Artists." No Pages. Online: http://www.vatican.va/holy_ father/john_paul_ii/letters/documents/hf_jp-ii_let_23041999_artists_en.html.

Regev, Eyal. *Sectarianism in Qumran: A Cross-Cultural Perspective.* Religion and Society Series 45. Berlin: de Gruyter, 2007.

Richards, H. *The Psalms: A New Translation.* London: Fontana, 1963.

Bibliography

Ricoeur, Paul. *Time and Narrative, Volume 1*. Translated by Kathleen McLaughlin and David Pellaur. Chicago: University of Chicago Press, 1984.

Ritzer, George. "Islands of the Living Dead: The Social Geography of McDonaldization." *American Behavioral Scientist* 47.2 (2003) 119–36.

Rose, Gillian. *Mourning Becomes the Law*. Cambridge: Cambridge University Press, 1996.

Rudder, Christian. "The Big Lies People Tell in Online Dating." No Pages. Online: http://blog.okcupid.com/index.php/the-biggest-lies-in-online-dating/.

Ruskin, John. "The Nature of Gothic." No Pages. Online: http://www47.homepage.villanova.edu/seth.koven/gothic.html.

Russell, Jamie. *Book of the Dead: The Complete History of Zombie Cinema*. Surrey, UK: FAB, 2005.

Ryken, Leland, et al. "Test motif." In *Dictionary of Biblical Imagery*, edited by Leland Ryken, James C. Wilhoit, and Tremper Longman III, 855–57. Downers Grover, IL: InterVarsity, 1998.

Schickel, Richard. "Cinema: Fascist Fable." No Pages. Online: http://www.time.com/time/magazine/article/0,9171,989504,00.html.

Schmidt, Steven. *Supergirl: The Last Daughter of Krypton*. Pendant Productions, 2008.

Schweitzer, Albert. *The Quest of the Historical Jesus*. London: SCM, 1906.

Scott, Ian W. *Paul's Way of Knowing: Story, Experience, and the Spirit*. Grand Rapids: Baker Academic, 2009.

Shafer, Ingrid. "The Catholic Imagination in Popular Film & Television." *Journal of Popular Film and Television* 19 (1991) 50–57.

Shakespeare, William. *Hamlet*. Edited by Ann Thompson and Neil Taylor. Arden Shakespeare, 3rd series. London: Thomson Learning, 2006.

Shepard, Sam, and Wim Wenders. *Paris, Texas*. Twentieth Century Fox, 2004.

Simpson, John. "Database." *Oxford English Dictionary*. Chief Editor John Simpson. No Pages. Online: http://www.oed.com/view/Entry/47411?redirectedFrom=database#eid.

Singer, Bryan. *Superman Returns*. Warner Brothers, 2006.

Skal, David J. *The Monster Show: A Cultural History of Horror, Revised Edition*. New York: Faber and Faber, 2001.

Skye, Obert. *Leven Thumps and the Whispered Secret*. New York: Aladdin, 2006.

Smith, James K. A. *Desiring the Kingdom: Worship, Worldview, and Cultural Formation*. Grand Rapids: Baker Academic, 2009.

———. *Thinking in Tongues: Pentecostal Contributions to Christian Philosophy*. Grand Rapids: Eerdmans, 2010.

Snyder, Zack, et al. *300*. Warner Brothers, 2007.

Spielberg, Steven, et al. *Poltergeist*. Metro-Goldwyn-Mayer, 1982.

Suchocki, Marjorie Hewitt. *The Fall to Violence: Original Sin in Relational Theology*. New York: Continuum, 1994.

Sweeney, Terrance. *God &*. Philadelphia: Winston, 1985.

Swinburne, Richard. *The Existence of God*. Oxford: Oxford University Press, 1992.

Syreeni, Kari. "In Memory of Jesus: Grief Work in the Gospels." *Biblical Interpretation* 12 (2004) 175–97.

Taylor, Mark C. *The Moment of Complexity: Emerging Network Culture*. Chicago: University of Chicago Press, 2001.

Thatcher, Tom. *Jesus, the Voice, and the Text: Beyond the Oral and Written Gospel*. Waco, TX: Baylor University Press, 2008.

Thurman, Judith. *Isak Dinesen: The Life of a Storyteller*. New York: St. Martin's, 1982.

Turkle, Sherry. *Alone Together: Why We Expect More From Technology and Less From Each Other*. New York: Basic, 2011.

Velde, Rudi te. *Aquinas on God: The Divine Science of the* Summa Theologiae. Aldershot, UK: Ashgate, 2006.

Velleman, J. David. "Narrative Explanation." Online: http://www.law.berkeley.edu/centers/kadish/Velleman%20NARRATIVE.pdf.

Viano, Maurizio. "*Life is Beautiful*: Reception, Allegory, and Holocaust Laughter." *Jewish Social Studies* 5.3 (1999) 47–66.

Vietti, Brandon. *Batman: Under the Red Hood*. Warner Brothers, 2010.

Waller, Gregory A. *The Living and the Undead: From Stoker's* Dracula *to Romero's* Dawn of the Dead. Urbana, IL: University of Illinois Press, 1986.

Walliss, John, and Lee Quinby. *Reel Revelations: Apocalypse and Film*. Sheffield, UK: Sheffield Academic Press, 2010.

Walsh, David. "Interview with Bruno Dumont, Director of *The Life of Jesus*." No Pages. Online: http://zakka.dk/euroscreenwriters/interviews/bruno_dumont.htm.

Wenders, Wim. "Artist of the Month: September 2008, Wim Wenders." No Pages. Online: http://imagejournal.org/page/artist-of-the-month/wim-wenders.

Whedon, Joss. *Serenity*. Shooting script. Online: http://www.scifiscripts.com/scripts/Serenity.pdf.

Wiemer, Robert. "Data's Day." *Star Trek: The Next Generation*. Paramount Pictures, 1991.

Wilson, John. "Excerpt: The Best Christian Writing 2004: An Interview with Wim Wenders." No Pages. Online: http://www.gracecathedral.org/enrichment/excerpts/exc_20031126.shtml).

Wood, Robin. "Apocalypse Now: Notes on the Living Dead." In *American Nightmare: Essays on the Horror Film*, edited by R. Wood and R. Lippe, 91–97. Toronto: Festival of Festivals, 1979.

Wright, Wendy. "*Babette's Feast*: A Religious Film." *The Journal of Religion and Film* 1.2 (1997). No Pages. Online: http://www.unomaha.edu/jrf/BabetteWW.htm.

Index

Made in the USA
Lexington, KY
5 February 2016